About the Author

Neil Atkinson is a versatile and accomplished author with multiple bestselling books spanning page turning thrillers, socially conscious novels, and transformative self-help guides. His diverse works include:

- *The Last Wild West* – A riveting account of life on remote Australian cattle stations, capturing the spirit of the land and the resilience of Aboriginal stockmen.
- *Along Came a Spider* – A courageous, real-life journey from childhood trauma to triumph, offering hope to survivors of abuse.
- *Mind Massage for Mad Times* and *Principles of Self-Healing* – Highly acclaimed natural health books blending wisdom and science to promote mental clarity and physical well-being.

Neil's passion for understanding human resilience is deeply rooted in his professional and academic journey. Holding a Doctorate in Naturopathic Medicine and Nutritional Biochemistry in Clinical Pathology, he has spent decades helping others find healing in body, mind, and spirit.

His latest book, *Job's Ladder*, is a profoundly moving true story that reflects Neil's compassionate understanding of life's darkest moments—and the extraordinary strength it takes to climb toward hope and faith once more.

When he's not writing, Neil can be found researching holistic health practices or listening to the stories of those who, like the characters in his books, refuse to give up on life, love, and faith.

Discover more at: www.readneilsbooks.com

Also By Neil Atkinson

The Last Wild West
Along Came a Spider
Mind Massage for Mad Times
Principles of Self-Healing
Wellness – Complete User Guide
Feminine Herbs Feminine Health
Job's Ladder

www.readneilsbooks.com

Job's Ladder

The true story of an extraordinary friendship

Neil H. Atkinson

First published 2025 by Neil H. Atkinson

Produced by Independent Ink
independentink.com.au

Copyright © Neil H. Atkinson 2025

The moral right of the author to be identified as the author of this work has been asserted.

All rights reserved. Except as permitted under the *Australian Copyright Act 1968*, no part of this publication may be reproduced, stored in a retrieval system, or transmitted in any form or by any means, electronic, mechanical, photocopying, recording or otherwise, without prior written permission from the publisher. All enquiries should be made to the author.

Cover design by Catucci Design
Edited by Brianna De Mann
Internal design by Independent Ink
Typeset in 12/17 pt Minion Pro by Post Pre-press Group, Brisbane

Cover image credits:
men in bench iStock-1178194378
cross on fire iStock-2080098416
church fire iStock-911053740

ISBN 978-1-7638647-0-2 (Paperback)
ISBN 978-1-7638647-1-9 (epub)
ISBN 978-1-7638647-2-6 (Kindle)

THIS BOOK IS DEDICATED WITH DEEPEST
GRATITUDE TO

My Beloved Daughter Tiffany, Nathan, Granddaughter Brianna and Family, and my Beloved son Anthony and family. Always Loved

Ms Lynette Winter for her determined inspiration, wisdom, spiritual insight and guidance that this book contained spiritual lessons of faith and belief in faith and was an essential read for believer and non-believer alike; that you are never alone, but always in company of good or evil and that we do not make mistakes, we make choices, good or bad

To Pastor Lyndon Weston, Pastor Michelle Weston and the Members of *Four Seasons Gospel Church*, Australia, deep gratitude for your spiritual love, guidance and support

To Jedele O'Shea for her expert reading, correction and tireless encouragement

Praise For *Job's Ladder*

I was very keen to read *Job's Ladder* as I love to read true stories. I always struggled in my faith as to how two strangers, believing in the same God, having different views, could ever get on. As I read this very profound book I couldn't put it down. Neil Atkinson has written and presented this book with tough theological questions I found myself asking. He has respected and been true to the people in real life, to whom this story relates.

This book shows unconditional love from one believer to another believer. To me this book shows how God's love abounds and can truly change people's lives no matter what race or belief. 'Pride before a fall' is true in all our lives. This lovely account of two men from different walks of life, has changed my way of thinking and viewing others. This is a must read, in my opinion, to any in whom would like to be challenged in their walk in life and as a believer.

But it's so, so much more than that. Even if you're not a believer it radiates a powerful message about the frailty of those in the community who claim themselves our "leaders" and how people fail and fall, blinded by their own importance, but in this case, a complete stranger, was there by some remarkable miracle, to catch the fall of a man who selfishly believed only he alone understood "truth", and stricken by misfortune, mostly of his own making, needed a Holocaust survivor to reveal the real truth of dignity through trials, hope in failure, and courage in defeat.

A remarkable read, a very powerful true story. Shalom.

JUDELE O'SHEA

Thank you for creating a masterclass book that teaches us to truly believe in a high power when all our hardships, loss, pain and sorrows against us are finally exposed through love faith, hope and unity. No matter how dark out lives there is always a light at the end of every tunnel. Through this wonderful wise, deep and beautiful book, the reader is guided to the light from a place of love, to overcome all obstacles life may bring no matter how dark moments and love and faith overcomes all things.

Two complete strangers, leaders in their own religious faiths, found a lifetime bonding of love and friendship through the horrors of their separate experiences and were divinely guided to meet, journey and find the same truth: God is real, the devil is real. In his experience, when he had to step up and face true evil for himself, family and friend, the Christian Pastor came face to face with evil and learnt the hard way the devil is very real with only one burning desire; kill, steal and destroy.

This is a book like a firewall in these last days' evil times, when believers and non-believers are swamped with media lies and doubts about the one true God, and that sometimes the Lord lets you go through the darkest times to find the light of His love and protection was always there.

Thank you Neil for giving me the opportunity to support you in your endeavours. May peace and blessing be upon you and your family God bless you!

ANH NGUYEN

UNSEEN REALM

"We don't get to accept life, but we get to accept the how," "We remember our past to inspire our future," "Life's lesson is only about forgiving yourself and never repeating it again," "God does not make evil, evil makes evil."

These statements in this book are extracted from difficult questions and hopeless challenges that life brings our way. And these have been expressed powerfully and effectively to the reader. Every human being will have their Job encounter, one that is relevant to their own life and not comparable to anyone else, but just as unique and purposeful.

The author has woven this story together in an identifiable way that makes it personal to everyone who reads it. Our world is discouraging dialogue between people, and here are two people from opposite ends of the religious spectrum, but have so much in common, which they discover through the expression of suffering, just as we were joined together with Christ through His suffering. Drawing from this I believe the author has addressed suffering, the most difficult subject in a powerful and relatable way. The words on the pages articulate God's love in a way that reveals how He uses suffering, that He did not create, as a tool to restore us that have lost hope along our life's journey, drawing us back to Him without violating or manipulating our free will.

"You made your ladder of faith and belief, my dear friend" Eli said. The image I was left with at the end of the story was Jesus waiting at the top of the ladder with His hand stretched out to help us take that last step of faith, like when Peter stepped out of the boat and was sinking in the water, His desire for us to draw from that measure of faith that He has given us, us exercising our free

will and not Him forcing us, but encouraging us to propel out of the smelly, dark, black, lifeless water of hopelessness into the path of light, as was described by Peter in verse 39 so mirrored Pastor Schembri's experience of being caught between two worlds. The author bringing us to the crescendo of this story with the battle between light and darkness over a man's soul, calling and destiny.

Inspired! Brilliant! A **MUST** read!

Pastor and Director *Unseen Realm*
Selwyn Van Wyk
selsurf@me.com www.unseenrealm.me

"Inspiring, riveting, challenging and brave. Neil Atkinson has written a very fine account using actual recorded notes of events spoken by the principles themselves, woven with inspired story telling based on fact of two different men from often opposing belief systems and dogma and their struggles to find common ground where life's brutal indifference and circumstances crushed faith in themselves and their religions. Their random meeting that could only be considered anything but coincidental but divinely inspired, made them realize we all fail, all fall short, but from the brutal madness of their experiences, the one thing they both wanted was to climb a ladder above their bruised lives into the loving arms of an always faithful, forgiving and loving Saviour. This book was an absolute pleasure to review and I wish the author every success. Essential reading."

Dr David Murray Sutcliffe
(PhD, Modern and Classical Theology)

An extraordinary and remarkable true story of two leaders of faith; one Christian, one Jewish, and how seemingly endless personal tragedies broke the Christian Pastor's life convincing him of divine torment like the story "Job" in the Bible. But how a complete stranger, a Rabbi, drawing on his experiences of surviving the Holocaust, saved the Pastors family, faith, and life.

This is a special testament how seemingly impossible circumstances of life's suffering and religious differences were overcome to discover a common humanity with a heart-warming testament to love, friendship and faith.

Neil H. Atkinson

Foreword

A celebration of an extraordinary friendship and forging of faith

This book has taken forty years to write.

This remarkable story is based on fact how seemingly endless personal tragedies broke a Christian Pastor's life convincing him of divine torment like the story "Job" in the Bible. But how a complete stranger, a Jewish Rabbi, drawing on his experiences of surviving the Holocaust, saved the Pastors sanity, family, faith, and life.

This is a special testament how seemingly impossible circumstances of life's suffering and faith differences were overcome to discover a common humanity forging a lifelong bond.

In an extraordinary twist, the Pastor connected the Rabbi with a fellow Holocaust survivor and beloved friend who had saved the Rabbi's life in the death camp, and who the Rabbi had been searching for over sixty years.

Certain sensitive topics require on the part of the writer an emotional and spiritual maturity to be able to identify and draw out the essential truths through the voices of the principals involved without excess interference or colouring of narrative by the writer, and in my case, also recorder. This is even more critically important and sensitive in subjects of faith and historical events such as the Jewish Shoah (Holocaust). It is such an event that there be no last witness, that remembrance not be a one-off, but an infinite, ever-evolving act, that dissolves the boundary that divides the past and the present, the dead and the living.

For these reasons the book sat in my "to do" archives all these decades with a whole folder of barely readable handwritten pages, many by the wife of the Pastor. I was just too immature in mind and spirit to author either subject in an honourably respectful manner.

What is true: the people, especially the two principals have since passed and any contact with relatives have long been lost. Their "events," have to the very best of my ability, been as faithfully recorded from my nearly 100 pages of hand written notes. I make no claim every single word is theirs, that's impossible, literary licence is necessary when writing a chronicle of other people's lives. But I have sincerely tried to weave their experiences through a narrative that is based on real people who shared, openly, completely and honestly, their lives without fear or favour.

What isn't true?

Although the people are absolutely true, likewise their experiences to the very best of recorded notes and recollections, to protect any possible link to surviving family members, using creative licence I have not included the years the events occurred or their location.

If researchers have nothing better to do they could probably locate where the church was burnt down. I'm sure newspaper archives will still have those records. How this bit of gravel would be of interest in shovelfuls of remarkable human suffering, endurance and ultimate victory is not for me to care. Further, I'm sure an old copy of the Pastor's book will still be available.

This story, after all, is a celebration of a remarkable friendship and a salute to human endurance and the struggle of the spirit to rise above life's often merciless hardships.

To begin ...

In the early eighties I returned to Melbourne after working in the Northern Territory among Aboriginal stockman on cattle stations. (*The Last Wild West* – Hybrid Publishing).

What monies I'd saved was vanishing after finding a broken down unit to rent in an even more broken part of Essendon, Victoria. Finding work was a priority so I searched the jobs available in *The Age* newspaper daily.

For some mysterious reason, an advertisement for *Sackville Suits* of Little Collins Street, pulled me like a magnet. I knew nothing about selling clothes, even less about suits, but my few rags were almost threadbare that I'd stuck in a backpack with most of the space taken up by notes and diaries that eventually became *The Last Wild West*.

I applied, and by some miracle I was put on for a few weeks trial. I happen to be the first "Gentile" that particular store had employed. We always laughed about that. They were wonderful to work for and to learn the tailoring tricks of the trade. It took me some time to learn the protocol and delicacies of measuring inside leg.

As it happened one day I was introduced to a gentleman by the name of Sackville. He was not only a CEO of *Sackville Suits* but also very interested in my background of working on the Territory cattle stations. My degree in clinical and therapeutic massage and Naturopathy seemed to attract him and he said he goes to a gym weekly for massage and would I be interested in some private sessions?

When he undressed to put on my robe, I saw a series of barely identifiable numbers tattooed on the inside of his left forearm. Apparently pleased with my work as clinical masseur, I soon had a number of, mostly older, clients. Many also had numbers tattoo on their forearms.

I worked only part time in suits, as I was also now studying for a Bachelor in Health Science plus private massage and Naturopathy.

The unit below mine had an absolutely treasure of a fiercely independent, very elderly lady Mrs Amsle. She also had a series of numbers tattooed but hers were on the outside of her right arm. Sadly she had a fall and I helped her until emergency services arrived. I told Mr Sackville about what happened and mentioned that Mrs Amsle was just lovely and, I wouldn't mind working with the elderly at some stage.

Before you could say *Sackville Suits* I was interviewed and put on as a "trainee nurse" at a large Jewish operated community permanent residential aged care and hospital, which is still in operation.

One evening I was looking through patient histories and was puzzled, considering the facility was principally run and operated for and by the Jewish community, to find a man, who was a Christian Pastor. I met the Pastor and his dearest best friend who was a Rabbi.

Over time I got to know them both very well. Even visits after hours or work were welcomed and a special trust developed, and so began filling in school exercise books with their talks.

I became their private nurse and masseur over time and have many photos that are private and will remain that way. But a story about a Jewish Rabbi and a Christian Pastor, two men from completely different faiths, through their common human struggles that bonded their humanness beyond vast religious differences, and to be part of that, was very humbling.

What struck me, all these decades later, was the absolute raw and brutal honesty that they opened about their lives and how, many times, their faith failed.

A few days before I left the hospital giving my farewells to the Rabbi and the Pastor, I recall saying "You know everything you've shared would make a wonderful book one day." I remember them looking at each other, sharing a smile saying, "Then why don't you write that very book one day."

This book is my homage to the astonishing intersection of their inspiring courage, endurance, faiths and friendship.

I have now quite a few decades behind me. And in that time I have met only a handful of human beings. I count these two beautiful souls among them.

The Author

Chapter 1

The man wearing a Jewish skull cap and carrying a book steps off a Melbourne tram and waits at the pedestrian island. He looks across the intersection to the opposite corner and his eyes cloud sadly. He sighs deeply with a small shake of his head. He'd read about the fire, but seeing the carnage was a shock.

Although the fire was four days ago, the smell of the seared and charred remains triggered memories that still torture him of another time long ago, when he witnessed scorched earth atrocities and heard the terrible screams of those being burnt alive in Ladontavick.

Some memories have a parallel life to those who own them, an existence time does not heal.

He crosses to the footpath when the lights change, and goes up several steps that led to a small park of sparse but welcoming grasses dotted with some native saplings.

He puts his book on the vandalised, paint-peeling and graffiti-covered wood bench seat, extending his arms along the top rail and crossing his legs. This seat has been his little perch of peace countless times.

The man was philosophical about this alcove of sanity overlooking the noisy, impatient intersection. Sometimes in your life, you seek mortification of the flesh by entering a desert, forest, mountain top, or a small patch of grass in an actual or symbolic way. You surmise that the impulse derives from disgust with the horrors of life. If there is a word for it, he felt certain the Germans have cobbled together a series of syllables to express the concept: *gemutlichschadenfreudegotterdamerung*. At any rate, it will be a word that acknowledges that humanity flourishes in unlikely circumstances. Like a flower on a dunghill, breeding in excrement and the remains of dead things.

He also knew too well something else: dead things and struggling in hell.

For several weeks the man had bought a book with him. A deeply disturbing book about another book. He was both appalled by what he'd read and intrigued, even fascinated, needing to know more about the author.

Before the fire, a magnificent building stood back from the road and on clear days when the sun reflected, it would shine and sparkle like a prism, almost shimmer, like a beacon calling the faithful. Now everything was burnt, finished, and over; nothing was left but puckered cinders and shanks of twisted metal as if agonised by the scorching heat.

They say we are made wise in life, the man in the skull cap ponders, not by the recollections of our past tragedies and pains so much, but by what lessons we can take into the future. Then why? Why for so many does life seem so unfair and just a long lesson in loss and brutality?

He recalls vividly the last words his father spoke to him before soldiers rounded up his whole family to be sent to death camps.

His father, a medical practitioner and Rabbi knowing his time was short, was desperate to leave something to his son to try and make sense of life's cruelty and madness: *"No matter how much good you try to do in this world Eli, evil can put the finger on you for no good reason at all. Life doesn't change because people don't change. Hate is easy for most people. But love must be learned, worked and it's hard. Always remember El Shaddai doesn't play favourites, He lets evil and good fall on saints and sinners. For us a mystery, for Him it's a plan."*

Eli remembers how his eyes became blurred with tears as his father held the sides of his face.

"Eli, Eli my beloved son. If you survive and wherever life takes you, listen to me and remember this: We have too many men of science and too few men of God. We have grasped the mystery of the atom and rejected the Ten Commandments. The world has achieved brilliance without wisdom, and power without conscience. Ours is a world of evil giants and ethical infants. We know more about war than we know about peace, more about killing than we know about living. Someday, I won't be here to see it, but someday my beloved son, after mastering winds, waves, tides, and gravity, we shall harness for God the energy of love, and for the second time in the history of the world, people will know creation. Eli, Eli. Hear me. Never. Never. Never let a single soul escape to damnation, Eli. Never let a soul in distress slip through the net. Always be there for them. If you do, one day El Shaddai will hold you to account and want to know why."

Eli lifts the book from the seat and turns to the back cover. A photo of a man wearing a very upmarket suit in his late sixties with perfect teeth and a shock of wavy, carefully coiffured silver hair poses smugly beside a large stained glass window. Such windows were once essential to the fabric of churches, illuminating the building and the people within, both literally and spiritually. Images and scenes leaded together into windows shed light on the central drama of spiritual salvation. They allowed the light of God into the church. Stained glass windows were never static. In the course of the day, they are animated by changing light, their patterns wandering across the floor, inviting parishioner thoughts to wander with them.

For this church, local gossip said, the bank of oversized windows was a deliberate ostentatious display of prosperity that garnered the building the name "Crystal Palace."

Although the congregation came from a broad mix of backgrounds, it was no secret the church favoured the well-heeled who would meet weekly to purge their capitalist souls with thick tithe's that kept the church pastor and family similarly well-pleasured.

Eli could see only tragic irony in all that vivid glass. Glass itself is one of the fruits of the art of fire. It is a fusion of the earth's rocks: a mixture of sand, soda, and lime melted at high temperatures. Now, only blackened molten, solidified globes and blobs scattered here and there glinting in the midday sun among the ash-black skeletal remains, isolated by multiple looped and twisted police and emergency service tapes.

Eli wondered what life or divine lessons could be taken from the destruction of a magnificent house of worship.

Eli's eyebrows pinch together in thought, and he tilts his head a little. Is this what happens when you mock God? No. That's too awful to contemplate. There must be a more pedestrian reason for all this. On the other hand, there's this book, and the church of the man who wrote it burns down? Strange. He needed to know more.

His contemplation was interrupted by a figure who emerged from the back of the blackened collapsed shell and wandered around in the scorched bowels of the building. He stoops to look at something here and there. Eli recognizes him from the author photo, but now a lonely, forsaken figure who occasionally shook his head as if uncomprehending.

Eli weighed if he should go over, it may be inappropriate, not the right time. But oddly, he felt drawn somehow, some mysterious and unsettling 'knowing' told him it was meant to be. Somehow the book, that man wandering in the ruins, and himself, have a strange connection. Well ... there was only one way to find out.

The man is unaware that he is being observed by Eli, who watches in silence, studying the sad, self-absorbed figure. Charred remains snap and shatter underfoot as the man crosses to a pile of water-soaked, distorted bible remnants giving mute testimony to the fire's ferocity. He picks one up and it crumbles to ashes in his hand. He stands dead still. He and his watcher remain absolutely still in a long, strange moment. Then suddenly, the man, imagining himself to be alone, throws back his head and lets out a strange and tormented, agonized animal cry of absolute grief and despair. It touches Eli deeply, he'd seen too many such tormented displays of futile horror and despair before. He sighs quietly, sadly.

The man takes another handful of the ash pile and fragments drop between his fingers. There are tears on his face, rage in his voice, and agony and tormented frustration in his heart.

'You didn't even save your own words ...' He shakes his head and wipes tears angrily with the back of one hand. Then he stares into the sky.

'Forty years since you called me to ministry ... I can't deal with this ... Why did this happen, God? Tell me ... what did I do wrong? Is this some kind of test? *Why-!*' He suddenly yells. 'I didn't raise anybody from the dead but I worked miracles, didn't I? I prophesied in your name, told people how they were screwing up their lives, helped them out of trouble, out of financial holes, saved their homes, fixed their finances, saved marriages … I've healed, made people well haven't I? In *your* name, set them free, cast out demons of drugs and booze. People were amazed, bringing souls to *you!* All for *you!* And *this* is my thanks!'

He looks around, sweeping an arm.

'I did everything for you but you did this to me! You've taken everything now – my wife, family, money, my health … now even my church. Our so-called "loving God."'

He turns looking around as if trying to comprehend. 'What are we to believe now? My generous parishioners built this – the crystal palace, *your* church – which *you* allowed to burn down!'

He's yelling; all the bottled-up grief and shock are now bubbling to the surface. 'My parishioners were well off? Is wealth a crime? Must we all be in rags and poverty, go door to door begging for crumbs while preaching God's abundance? "Treasures in Heaven!" Why not a few treasures on earth, is it a sin? Or was it my *book!* Was that it? You didn't want people to know the truth?'

He lets out a shuddering breath. 'My church is gone. I'm ruined. Where will my parishioners go? How will I and my family survive without my church? People will take their offerings and tithes elsewhere … but, but you will still expect me to believe in you! Have faith. *Faith!* Faith in what? Jacob, your prophet, had faith … He had a dream about a ladder between earth and heaven where angels went up and down. Well, there's another dream, *mine* – but it's a nightmare. *My ladder, the ladder I know … Job's ladder!* My ladder is only one way – it's where your angels with buckets of crap, pain, and misery, come down to dump over me. Am I just another Job for you to let the devil torment and play with? You ignore my prayers, my tears, and my suffering. It's like you don't care. Why are you blind to my needs and deaf to my prayers? Why are things so unfair? Why aren't you watching out for me? Why are you letting all this evil happen? Where is your protection? One disaster after another. *Why don't you hear me? What have I done to deserve this?*' His scream is strangled and weakening.

He's almost exhausted as his rage and frustration against the Heavens abruptly steers from the church destruction to pent-up, unconfessed feelings.

'I suppose you'll punish me even more for saying this if that's possible, not that anything's left, but … you always leave it to us, the Pastors, the Priests, the so-called vicars of heaven, to try to explain why God the *Father* ignores their suffering and pain. How many, their hearts breaking, have begged, screamed at me to tell them where God is when they needed him most … why doesn't He answer their prayers?'

'How many innocents have I seen suffer, without mercy, without compassion, without anything … where you were when they needed you … I can't lie to them anymore … *I won't lie to them anymore* it's all some divine plan. Why do you make people suffer so much and still claim to love them? Why is there so much agony in the world if you are our *loving* father? A father protects his children … but you are deaf and blind to an ocean of tears, pain, and suffering that would reach the heavens. And still … *Still* nothing changes. I've tried to serve you for forty years, why have you failed me? Why? What have I done to deserve all this?

Why are you punishing me? Why have you forsaken me? Even *Jesus, your-own-son,* called in fear and agony from the cross why had *you* forsaken him!'

He screams at the top of his lungs, expelling the last of exhausted strength. 'Why? Am I just another Job? Answer me God! *I want to know why – !*'

In a rage of tears, he grabs a handful of the ash and slings it skyward, as if into heaven's face. For a long time he staggers around on rubbery legs as if drunk: all his grief, pain, frustration, and anger to this moment transforms into almost an alcoholic stupor. As his shuddering chest slows and breathing becomes normal. He pushes the heels of both hands into his eyes.

'He never answers "why,"' Eli said. The man jumps and jerks his head around as Eli smiles reassuringly, carefully picking his way over to him.

'Millions of us getting murdered asked why. Perhaps it's one of those spiritual quandaries of the ages: If you pray to God for courage, does he give you courage or give you ways to be courageous? Perhaps the answer is in the question.'

Sullen, embarrassed and annoyed, the man turns away wiping a sleeve over his face.

Eli smiles kindly. 'Oh. Don't worry about tears, my friend. I and my people had shed oceans of them. There's no shame.'

Clearing his throat. 'I'm sorry Mr? I'm a little busy right now ... Are you a member of my congregation?'

'I'm a member of the congregation of God, but no, not of your church.'

The man pushes back his abundant silver hair off his face. Although with his hair swept back over his forehead, the narrow eyes and aquiline nose had the effect of making him look both distant and disdainful. But there were no mistaking the depths of his wounded spirit, the type with which Eli was only too familiar. 'Fine. Whatever.' The man sighs irritably. 'Look. I don't want to be rude – but this is –'

'I'm Eli Steinsaltz. Rabbi.'

'Rabbi? Well. What are you doing here Rabbi?'

'To see you. I just wish it was not under such sad circumstances.'

'See me? Why would a Rabbi want to see me?'

'I read. A lot. Put bookworms to shame,' Eli says warmly. 'I picked up a very interesting book. The more I read the more I wondered why Peter Schembri, a Pastor and more than forty year veteran would write a scathing, critical book attacking God's book.' Eli holds up the book. *The Bible. The World's Most Dangerous Book.* 'Intriguing title. As you can see I've added a stack of sticky notes on pages I hoped to talk about, but …' looking around sadly. 'It must have been very hard for you and your family. I am very sorry.'

'Thank you.' He takes a shuddering breath. 'I trust the read gave you something?'

'I found it … challenging.'

Peter pulls a cynical face. 'That's a nice way to put it.'

'Your book made me wonder more about the man than the writer.'

Eli studies Peter who seems as fragile as chipped China ready to fracture. He feels compassion for how exhausted and stressed the Pastor looks. He could excuse himself and walk away, but something tells him this is not the time, but it is time to offer support. As he felt on the park bench, for some mysterious, inexplicable reason, this meeting was no accident or coincidence – but meant to be.

'Look. I'm sure you have much to do, but, would you consider letting let me buy you a coffee perhaps?'

Peter looks around and his shoulders slump. He looks down, and when he looks up, he sighs wearily but seems to have made up his mind. 'Thank you. That'd be good right now.' He smiles appreciatively.

'Nothing I can do here. Besides, it might be interesting to hear what a Rabbi thinks of my book.' He looks around again. 'Let's try the park, where things still live.'

Chapter 2

LIKE BOOKENDS ON THE BENCH seat they sit at opposite ends stirring liquid with wooden spoons. 'Thanks for this. Been living on prayer and coffee for days.' Peter takes a sip, then sighs. 'I come here a lot to pray and think.'

'Oh? It's a wonder I haven't seen you. I do also.' Eli said. 'Good place to read.'

'After a while, you don't even hear or see the traffic. Amazing what you can adapt to.'

When he thinks enough time has passed, Peter steals a look at Eli, then away, embarrassed.

'About ... before. When I was ... "praying" let's call it.'

Eli smiles reassuringly. 'I'm sure God's heard it all before, Peter. Besides, only God's perfect, we can afford to be a little less.' Eli says kindly. Peter drops his head a little and nods appreciatively. Eli just looks at him with compassion. He gives Peter a moment and then asks, 'It's none of my business, but do you know how the fire started?'

It takes several moments before the reply as if considering what to say.

'They're looking at it.'

'Will you rebuild?' Eli says.

Peter remains silent. He then replies but doesn't answer the question, as if avoiding it.

'Time passes,' says a pensive Peter. 'How rarely do we stop to examine the path? What if we could stop to see the choices again, choose another path? Would I even be a Priest?' Peter sighs again. 'Over forty years in ministry and I still don't know how life works sometimes. No. Make that most times. It's ironic, isn't it, Rabbi, most times we do not know what we want and yet we are responsible for what we are.'

'*Eli.* Please. Well Peter, in my experience, two things I've tried to learn. Adonai asks no man whether he will accept life. That's not the choice. One must take it. The only choice we have is how. And every happening, I tend to believe, great or small, good or tragic, is a parable whereby Elohim speaks to us. The art of life is to understand the message. As a man of faith, you'd know that.'

Peter looks at Eli, a veil of corrosive doubt clouding his eyes suddenly growing melancholy. 'Do I?' He replies in a croak.

Peter shakes his head deeply troubled. When he speaks his words seem to Eli directed more at himself rather than the ruins. 'What a mess.'

Eli begins to suspect Peter is more fragile and problems go deeper than the fire. What Eli overheard in his "prayer" seems to confirm that.

'But this is the way life works, doesn't it? You work your guts out for years for something and in an instant, it's gone. Sometimes there's no villains. It is simply a messy situation that cannot be cleaned up. The foundations of our lives are far more fragile than we think. So we are severely shaken when life turns out to have a will of its own. In bygone eras, people used to be aware that disaster could strike at any time with arbitrary cruelty – that crops would fail or your family would succumb to the juggernaut of an epidemic. Tragedy was always terrible, but it could not be prevented. The modern aspect is our naive belief that everything is controllable. As a result, we are amazingly ill-equipped when the unexpected occurs.'

Eli studies this worn, angry, sad, and cynically bitter man compassionately. Peter seems to be thinking out loud, weighing his life and why it appears to have become such an unforgiving burden.

'But nothing much has changed, has it? Even Christ said in Mathew 10: *"I have not come to bring peace, but a sword. For I have come to set a man against his father, and a daughter against her mother, and a daughter-in-law against her mother-in-law, and one's foes will be members of one's own household."* What chance do we have? The Christian God, or Muslim God, or from the menagerie of deities that animates the Hindu faith. What are we? We are ants on the carcass of a dying world, spawned out of nothing, going busily nowhere. One of us dies, the others crawl over us to the pickings. Look at the world at this moment in time and count the dying and the dead, the blood sacrifices to faith. That's from my book.'

'Yes. I marked the page.' Eli holds the book up, opening to one of the pages he's tagged. *'The Bible: The world's "most" dangerous?'* Eli says it as a question with a furrowed brow.

'Hasn't done the world a lot of good has it?'

Eli tips his head, not agreeing. 'Oh, I don't know. Isn't "good" more of a personal perspective?'

'Perhaps,' Peter said. 'When I was in Pastoral College, I travelled extensively. I had a vision of becoming a biblical Anthropologist. In Asia, the Middle East, Africa … I saw the raw reality of life away from the pulpit, I saw the world there exploding into millions of hungry mouths. They could not eat their bibles. I had to ask myself … what kind of wisdom the church had to cope with this explosion. So I start writing, and I became a philosopher.'

Eli nods. 'And you … you have written many books?'

'Ten.'

'Oh, ten?' Eli smiles impressed. 'And how many published?'

'One. The rest were while a student. They came to the notice of the college fathers – and following examination by a special biblical council, I was accused of holding opinions dangerous to the faith. After feeding the starving I said who cares about theology except the theologians? We are necessary, but less important than we think. All the people want to know is whether or not there is a God, what is his relation with them, and why doesn't he appear to be there in their pain, and how they can get back to him when they stray. I was forbidden to teach or publish anything or be expelled, they said my works presented ambiguities and even grave errors … in philosophical and theological matters which offended doctrine. They were more interested in affirming my identity as dangerous to the faith without understanding my individuality. I had fallen into the error of all liberals; the belief that men are prepared to reform themselves, that good will attracts good will, that truth has a leavening virtue of its own. But each of us can walk only the path he sees at his own feet. Each of us is subject to the consequences of his own belief.'

Eli is puzzled. Something inexplicable about Peter. He suspects there's something deeper going on as if he's burdened by a lot of unresolved grief that extends beyond the immediate fire tragedy.

Eli knows such people; he recognizes the ache he sees in Peter as what he saw daily, almost hourly, from the death camps as the prisoners grew closer to the edge of abandonment of body and mind, leaving only one last entitlement: forever rest. He doesn't know how to help yet but wants to try.

'If you don't mind me saying, I'm confused. Isn't the whole idea of ministry to encourage people to read the Bible not frighten them? Isn't your book self-defeating, even self-destructive to your church and you as a Pastor?'

'What church?' He said bitterly. 'Yeah, I can't count the number of times I've been asked since it came out. One has to abandon altogether the search for security and reach out to the risk of living with both arms. You have to court doubt and darkness as the cost of knowing. I wanted to open discussion and minds. Often controversial but progressive ideas are unconventional Eli –'

'To teach about God by destroying His book?'

'Nobody is forced to agree,' he says like a sullen challenge. 'Is that what you think I'm doing, trying to destroy the Bible?'

'Although I'm a Jew, I've studied your Christianity a long time. I was curious to know its challenges and contradictions to our books. After all, your Old Testament has some similarities to our own holy books …' Eli waits to see what Peter will say.

Peter has a small, tired smile. 'I'm not going to die from your opinion, Eli.'

Eli smiles and nods. 'Alright. Let me put on a Christian hat for a moment. I found very little of your Christian faith, as I know it, in your book. There are some aspects of Hebrew faith and Christian faith very similar, faith in an omniscient and loving God. There was a very dark time in my life that faith alone kept me alive.'

'Go on.'

'I found it … speculative, dangerous … and full of …'

'Heresy,' Peter snaps.

'It … It challenges the *faith*. Even Hebrew faith. You claim the Israelites weren't slaves in Egypt?'

'They *weren't!*' Peter says. 'There's no evidence.'

Eli draws a breath letting the rising strain settle.

'For instance, your Jesus Christ speaks of the redemption of the soul. I find not one mention of the word "soul" in your writings.'

'But it's there, only under another name!'

'Why change a name if you're not afraid of it?'

'To express in modern terms … reality and truth more clearly.'

'Well, Peter, if you truly believe that … why did you remain a vicar?'

'I wanted to complete my work.'

'And what is your work, Peter?'

'To be the best Pastor I could and tell the truth about the Bible and gospels as I saw it.' Peter looks tense and defensive. 'Are you accusing me of dishonesty?'

Eli waves his hand dismissing his question. 'I'm not accusing you of anything. That is for you to answer. I'm just trying to understand. But are you sure you are honest with yourself?'

'I will face God in the judgement. I cannot afford to be otherwise.'

'How has it been received?'

'How has it been received?' He repeats, with raises his eyebrows, 'From brave and welcome biblical honesty to I will burn in hell forever. More than one will celebrate the loss of my church as divine judgement.'

'You know, Peter, for many people, belief is a place to crawl for safety. Of course, they will fear and accuse you. Your writings are a danger to their safety.'

'I'm not afraid of being accused, Eli. I'm only afraid of being silenced. You know, even God has not spoken His last word about His own creation. What about you? You haven't really told me what you think?'

'Oh. I hardly think my opinion matters in the big scheme of things, but as you have asked I will give it, wearing both a Hebrew and Christian hat if such a contradiction is even possible?'

Peter forces a small smile appreciating Eli's genuine effort to understand Peter's motives.

'Here's the first problem, Peter. It runs right through all your work. What are you? Philosopher? Theologian, poet, scientist? How are we to judge you?'

'Judge me as one man, trying to answer the questions of every man.'

'Which are?'

Peter sits back in his seat thoughtfully. 'Who am I? Why am I here? Where am I going? Is there any sense in beauty? In ugliness? In terror? In suffering? In the daily deaths … which make up the pattern of existence.'

'There speaks the poet.'

'Why only the poet? … Why not the theologian and the scientist? They breathe too. They die too.'

'Then you start me, Peter.'

'I've dug down through the crust of God's earth. There's a long record of life written there. A record full of wonders. Dinosaur or flying reptiles, giant moles. All gone. But the line is clear … traced by the creative finger of God. And it always points in the same direction, to us: The knowing man, the thinking man. And it points beyond us. To what? Either this world is a tragic trap … in which man lives without hope and dies without dignity … or it is like *Teilhard de Chardin* wrote many years ago … a great becoming … in which mankind is thrust towards a glorious completion in Christ. I believe in the plan of completion. I believe in the future union of the world with the Cosmic Christ.'

'Okay. Then let me walk in your country for a while, Peter. The dinosaur disappeared from history. Why?'

'We are not sure. The evidence points to the fact that he was a creature … adapted to a special environment. When the environment changed, he died out.'

'How?'

Peter shrugs. 'Sometimes by disease. Sometimes by violence. When creatures stronger than himself devoured him.'

'So the finger of God writes violence and destruction too?'

'Yes. They are part of the pattern of growth of evolution. Many land animals are prolific creatures. They would eat the lands bare. Stronger animals tear them down – so the balance of nature is preserved.'

'Right. Now we come to this. Talking about man … you called him a very special animal in your book. The animal who knows, and knows that he knows.'

'Exactly,' Peter says.

'In a museum in France is the skull of a prehistoric man. His skull is broken by a stone axe. He was obviously killed by one of his fellows. An act of violence, yes?'

'Yes.' Peter smiles as if he knows where the conversation is leading.

'An act of destruction, yes?' Eli asks. 'Committed by a thinking and knowing creature?'

'Yes.' Peter says smiling to himself.

'Is it the same act as the shooting of a man in a back alley in St. Kilda?'

'Essentially, yes. The same.'

'And that act, too, Peter, is a part of the design of God?'

Peter nods several times. 'The design includes it.'

'You did not answer "yes" to that question. Why?'

'Because dear Rabbi Eli Steinsaltz. I see where you are leading me.'

'Exactly. I suppose I am leading you to the problem of good or evil. Right or wrong in the religious sense. The killing of that Stone Age man by another man: Was it right or wrong do you think?'

Peter says nothing, just folds his arms. 'I don't know.'

Eli looks surprised. 'I beg your pardon. You don't know?'

'No, Eli, I don't. How can we know? It might have been an act imposed upon him … by the necessities of a time and place of which we know very little, almost nothing.'

Eli studies Peter for a moment. 'Imposed by the evolutionary plan?'

'Yes.'

'In other words, by God's plan?'

'Yes.'

'So God is the author of sin and evil. I can understand why some might think your book heresy, Peter.'

'No, it is not heresy. The reality is this: For certain primitive tribes … murder was a religious act. For us, it is a crime. The growth from one attitude to another is evidence of a divine plan. Even today, too many Christians justify mass murder under the name of war. Tomorrow, please God, they will outlaw war too, as a crime.'

The traffic roars around, lights sign to go and stop, pedestrians cross, trams trundle past, and people stand and gawk at the black shell that was a church. Two men who have just met sit on a park bench overlooking but indifferent to it all. They sit in silence, two men from vastly different lives and faiths only sharing the same God. For some reason he couldn't explain, Eli had such a burden in his chest that if he went away, something bad, terrible was going to happen to Peter. Eventually, Eli looked at him.

'What did you hope to achieve with your book, Peter?'

'To read the Bible like seeing the Sistine ceiling with hundreds of years of gunk removed. As with any translation, you can haggle over words, phrases, emphases, but versions available today is not the Bible of old, it has been smothered in solemnity and ambiguity since the sixteen century. I want to open eyes and challenge minds. Discovery consists of seeing what everyone has seen and thinking in a way nobody has thought. Pastors can't think? Challenge traditional thinking?' Peter said defensively. 'Reveal the truth. The real truth.'

'I see. But your book doesn't challenge … almost condemns … attacks. I only question the "why?"'

'Aren't Rabbis allowed to question or challenge your holy books, the Talmud?'

'We can but don't feel the need to do so,' Eli replied.

Peter's dark eyes flared. 'Maybe you're in the wrong faith Rabbi?' Peter said with a nasty challenge Eli ignores.

'Your book challenges the faith like no other I've read. The first night I read it as a matter of fact … I couldn't sleep. I saw a brilliant mind reaching out to the last frontiers of thought. A place where I wouldn't venture. It takes no prisoners, especially Christian ones. It would fit comfortably in any atheist's library.

But …' Eli looks at him, his brow creased. '… You're a *Pastor –*'

Eli, deeply troubled, leaves the question hanging between them.

Peter meets Eli's eyes briefly, then looks away across the intersection to the black and charred ruins. Eli keeps studying Peter thinking the remains of his church reflects Peter's inner torment and turmoil.

'There's something about you, Eli; I can't put my finger on it. You know, the scriptures often reveal more about a person than their own words, what people underline or call their favourite verses. Like a biblical bibliography, what speaks, touches and moves them. I will tell you the why of my book, but first, tell me the "why" of yours. What part of the Hebrew Bible says Eli?'

'It all says, Eli,' he says with a broad smile and laughing eyes. Even Peter forces a smile. Then, after a few moment's thought, 'All right, Gentile, I'll take you on,' Eli says with good humour.

'The books of Samuel talk to me more than any others. For me, the books of the Hebrew Bible constitute a world, not just an oeuvre. And in that world, the two books of Samuel have an extraordinary vigour and power. Samuel is the old prophet who foresees the greatness of David, and the two books of the Bible that take their name from him concentrate on how David comes to prominence, the subsequent jealousy of King Saul, the relationship of David and Jonathan and the days of David's greatness as King of Israel.'

'This is the point where, what you call the Old Testament, is at its most potently historical, and where the poetry comes like flint from stone out of the drama of men of power pushed up against each other in rage and sorrow and love.'

'It is arguably where the Hebrew Bible gets closest to Homer, the Greek poet, who, as you know, is the author of the Iliad and the Odyssey, two epic poems, the foundation of ancient Greek literature.'

Peter nods and stares at Eli intently as he continues, already impressed. 'Certainly you can feel the dark wings of tragedy in the portrait of Saul who becomes bent on David's destruction and – unwittingly – but with great bitterness of soul, on his own. It's there too in the greatest lament that David also utters in grief, first for the man he loved, Jonathan, and then for his dead son, the rebel Absalom. They are arguably the greatest things of their kind, outside of Shakespeare and the Greeks, and they have a piercing incomparable authority. No one who listens to David's "How are the mighty fallen" speech, in which he speaks of his love for Jonathan "passing the love of women", could doubt the authenticity of the emotion, this depth of feeling.'

'And the scene when David, as a king, learns of the death of his son Absalom, is extraordinary in the way it winds its way with all the promises of hope and then dashes the king who is now nothing but a father, as if from a tower. No wonder William Faulkner took *Absalom, Absalom* as the title of one of his greatest novels. For me you see Peter, it's a world, *The Books of Samuel* is like that. That's the kind of thing I teach. The story of David and Saul, of Jonathan and Bathsheba and Absalom, is a story where kings go forth but it is also a story of how the soul becomes darkened and how hearts break, whatever glory attends them. Written six to seven hundred BC, it is one of the oldest stories we have of the barbarism at the heart of civilization. It is also the tragic bedrock of the Hebrew civilization that has fathered our own.'

Peter shakes his head in admiration. 'The word is alive for you. Pity I can't say the same for many Christians.'

'Learning our Holy books is second nature to us, Peter. In Judaism, the age at which a boy begins to study the Torah varies depending on the community and the family but is typically around age three or four. The Torah is the central text of the Jewish religion and contains the laws and stories that are essential to our faith. Each of the four books is called the Yahwist, the Elohist, the Priestly Writers, and the Deuteronomist. Learning the Torah is a lifelong process, and beginning at a young age is seen as important to gain a thorough understanding of the text.'

'From about six or seven, Jewish boys were taught to recite Tanach aloud. I remember a time when there was only one book for children in the world: the Bible. My father was a Rabbi, so it was accepted that his son would be. My father Aaron was a doctor, philosopher, and one of the sweetest, gentlest souls I've ever known. Sarah, my beautiful mother, my father, and almost my whole family were lost during the Shoah. Only I and my sister, by the grace and mercy of God, managed to survive. It's hard for civilised minds to grasp, I know. It was a gut-wrenching daily fight to survive and to believe it would one day end was made all the more resonant and repulsive by the perfunctory, assembly-line efficiency with which prisoners were eliminated. The need to extinguish a whole people.'

'So you're a concentration camp survivor, Eli?'

'Our faith has different views of Heaven and Hell than Christians. But I came to believe in hell sent to a death camp. I would watch this black, sickly-smelling smoke billowing up to the sky from the cremation chimneys, carrying with it the ashes of human beings: an uncle, a daughter, a mother or father, or perhaps a brother, turned into smoke before our eyes, and we could do nothing. A guard told me it didn't matter because we weren't people – we were a pest to be eradicated, a Jewish plague, he said. The air we breathe, the food we eat, the very clothes we wear – when we were all turned into smoke and ash, this would allow space – *lebensraum* they called it – for Hitler-worshipping maniacs to feel uncluttered and unchallenged. By laying waste to a whole people, only in our deaths would we become "useful," he said, "to fertilise the ground to feed the Reich."'

'So you see, knowing the Tanach by heart became even more important … it gave us hope and sanity. They'd come for prayer – old, young, even children. I'd pray in Hebrew or languages I picked up. Many didn't understand a word – just the comfort. If you know you're waiting your turn to die in the gas chambers, can you think of anything more appropriate than last thoughts of loved ones and waiting arms of God? A Rabbi I met in the camp who became more than a friend but like another father to me, had amazing faith and said faith was the key to fit the door of hope, but there is no power anywhere that can turn it greater than faith and love. Somehow his faith told him the horror would end and we'd survive. After the war, many of us believed we could never love again, but our hope was to believe we could. As survivors, we would say we will never forget: We remember our past to inspire our future.'

Peter shakes his head. 'Hideous! But even today some say the Shoah didn't happen.'

Eli nods. 'But I also know some people eat gravy with a knife because the folk leaks.' Peter smiles. 'Every evil has a champion to defend it. Nothing in the world is more dangerous than sincere ignorance and conscientious stupidity.'

They are silent for a few moments and then Peter looks at Eli. 'Can I ask you something personal?'

'Of course.'

'You're obviously a very smart man so you must have an opinion. Doesn't it prove my point? Where was God then when you needed him the most? Why would a merciful God do that, allow that?'

Eli's eyes lowered and he stared without really seeing the grass. What is faith he thought, as a Rabbi he'd been asked countless times the same question; was he any closer to understanding God's mind?

'God didn't make anti-Semitism. God didn't make the Shoah.'

Peter shakes his head. He cocks an eyebrow like a challenge. 'You're sticking up for God who abandoned your whole people? Faith is one thing, *blind* faith another. Jews have been singled out, blamed and targeted around the world for centuries.'

'Another "why" question?' Eli sits back in his seat and sighs, pulling his thoughts together. 'There's no answer that suits everybody. In Jewish history it has been endlessly debated. I can give you my father's *opinion*, which is mine. Others are free to disagree.'

Peter settles back in the seat crossing his arms and legs.

'First some theological questions for you.'

'That is an old legal trick, Eli. Answer the question with a question.'

Eli shakes his head. 'Oh, I am not trying to trick you Peter, just understand what *you* believe.' Peter accepts this, nods and waits. 'Do you believe Jews are descended from the ancient Israelites, and "chosen," as found, for example, in the Book of Deuteronomy?'

'Leviticus, two-twenty six,' Peter adds, 'God said, *"You must be holy because I, the Lord am Holy. I have set you apart from all other people to be my very own,"* says it pretty plainly.'

Eli nods. 'And you also believe God is good?'

Peter stares into Eli's kindly deep-set hazel eyes for a moment. Considering his previous "prayer," Peter qualifies his answer. 'He *can* be good.'

'Satan, the devil is evil: kill, steal and destroy. You believe that?'

Peter looks across the busy road at the church ruins. 'Oh yes,' he sighs.

Eli watches him carefully and waits. Peter meets his eyes, wondering about Eli's silence but with eyes that invite Peter's revelation and understanding. A longer moment passes, then:

'You can't be serious?'

'Almost always,' Eli said.

'Because Jews are descended from the original Israelites who are considered God's own, the devil wants to destroy anything good of God, the Nazi Shoah was another in a long line of horrible pogroms and persecutions?' Peter asked.

'Satan blinds eyes and contaminates minds for believers and nonbelievers alike. *"You shall know them by their fruits."* Mathew seven. You know who owns their souls by antisemitism and hate. Look at it this way. Many Christians follow their faith religiously,' Eli said with a small smile, 'and you look forward to your Christ's second coming, correct? But it isn't to Toronto, Sydney, Paris, Berlin, London or New York, but Jerusalem. A big hint there.'

Peter nods thinking. 'Christians have also persecuted Jews.'

'We can't change the past. How Christians treat Jews *now* is what matters.'

They sit in silence. Peter looks over the intersection at the remains of his church, Eli leafs through a few pages. Peter's eyes flick down, noticing, he takes it as a cue.

'I was going to tell you why I wrote it wasn't I? The man behind the words as you put it.' Eli waits, looking at Peter and his roiling emotional burden and unhappiness. He sighs very deeply as if he can't pull in enough air.

'Let me ask you this first. Have you found Christ, Rabbi?'

Eli answers with an easy smile. 'Not as completely as you, Pastor.'

Peter becomes aware Eli is staring at him intently without blinking. Peter chews his lip a little as if building up. Moments pass and Peter sighs again. 'What if I told you ... and not even my wife knows. But, if I am totally honest, I haven't ... completely found him either. The dual substance of Christ – the yearning, so human, so superhuman, of man to attain to God, or more exactly, to return to God and identify with him – has always been a deep inscrutable mystery to me.' Peter looks at Eli. 'Does that shock you?'

'I am a survivor of the Shoah, Peter.' Eli sighs burdened. 'Little shocks me anymore.' Eli studies Peter for a long time, trying to understand. 'You gave your life to Christ without ever belonging to him?'

'Look around. Look at all the pain and destruction. For what? Why? What's the lesson the world's supposed to be learning if there is one? All I see is man builds and God destroys, right from the Tower of Babel to my church, and it's never stopped. How much destruction is enough?' His face clouds with bitterness. 'Sometimes I wonder, no, all the time, the last couple of years, you'll disagree I know, I've been giving serious thought to why we even need God. I can determine, as we all can, what is good and what is evil. I don't need some enigmatic cloud-based spirit father to tell me what the parameters of acceptable behaviours are. I can discern and determine that myself.'

'You're right. I strongly disagree with you Peter, and I'm

surprised you said that. What constitutes right and wrong is a straight line that leads directly back to God.'

Peter gives him a sideways look. 'So you're saying that we *must* need God to be moral?'

'Yes. If there's no God there's no reason to be moral. Are you going to sit there and tell me you don't believe that?'

Eli keeps his face impassive and puts a finger to his temple studying Peter as he waits for his reply. Peter looks as fragile as broken glass to Eli, who listens without judgment.

'I mean, society's morals have changed, and if faith is to survive it must change with it. What do heaven and hell really mean in today's world? Do you know the works of the fourteenth century mystic *Meister Eckhart?*'

'Not my favoured works,' Eli frowns, screwing up his mouth in distaste.

'One of *my* favourite writers,' Peter responds. 'Eckhart saw hell too. He said: *"The only thing that burns in hell is that part of you that won't let go of life: your memories, your attachments. They burn them all away. But they're not punishing you. They're freeing you from evil. So, if you're frightened of dying and … you're holding on, you'll see devils tearing your life away. But you've made your peace, then the devils are really angels, freeing you from the earth."'*

Eli sipped his coffee for a long time, occasionally stirring it, as if deep in thought. Eventually, he looks at Peter, but Eli's face is set in opposition.

'Not always right but I pride myself on being a pretty good judge of character. You're a sensitive, insightful, highly intelligent man. But, you can't seriously believe that? It's the perfect get-out-of-responsibility and judgment card – old dying Nazis would love it. Murder millions of innocent's, but make your peace and float away, demons who are actually angels, freeing you from earth without judgment. You seriously call that biblical and religious?'

Peter becomes increasingly irritated, almost offended. 'That's not what he meant. But that's the point dammit. It's that locked-in thinking again. You are not permitted to think outside the Bible box. Sometimes I think religion is like terrorism.'

Eli can't help but blink, jerk his head back, and arch his eyebrows.

'You *can't* be serious.'

Peter looks at him with a smug smile. 'Whatever the claims or complaints of the terrorists might be, Eli, religion is the prime factor.'

'Enlighten me.'

'Religion like terrorism, offers certainty – don't you agree? Religion like terrorism, asks people to sacrifice themselves for a cause greater than themselves. When traditional religion is abandoned, armies of religious martyrs form. Its place is taken by a new faith, be it nationalism, socialism or communism, the underlying intensity of a belief is still deeply religious in character.'

Eli looks away after focusing on Peter's eyes to see if he's serious. Another smug smile twists the corners of Peter's lips.

'I said I'd shock you. Ready to hit the road yet?'

Eli dismisses the jibe and replies calmly. 'If you believe all this, Peter, what, before Yahweh, have you been doing in the ministry all this time?'

He flares, offended. 'In God's name indeed! Waking up. The truth did set me free eventually. I wanted to serve God the best way I could.'

'Many people want to serve God – but in an advisory capacity only. Do your parishioners know your views?'

Peter contains himself, sits back in the seat, sighing glumly. 'Those who have read my book.'

'And they have stuck with you?'

'Some.' He sighs again. 'I know the church finances have taken a hit. A big serious hit.'

Eli finishes his coffee putting the cup on the ground. Eli sees Peter becoming increasingly agitated, so takes the opportunity to redirect his focus back to his book attempting to unravel Peter's obvious and increasing emotional turmoil that appear to go deeper than even tragedy of his church.

'Contrary to what they accuse me of I'm not tearing the Bible apart because it doesn't say what I think it should say,' he says exasperated and irritated, 'I'm actually trying to defend the Bible. So people can see its truth. It's *real* truth. The Bible is not being honest to countless millions who believe it. It's an incomplete book. Did you know that entire gospels that did not fit the traditional orthodox narrative were cut?'

Eli nods, 'Yes. Different scholars have suggested that.' Eli said cautiously. Peter's eyes roll in disdainful opposition, smirking at the non-committal answer.

'You Jews are so blessed. Over thousands of years, your five books of Moses, the Talmud, have been translated letter for letter, word for word. The Christian Bible, on the other hand, has been constantly twisted, distorted, and edited through countless translations until what's left is a patchwork almost unrecognisable from the original gospels. It gives false hope and false faith, betrays religious lives, cheats believers out of an honest gospel, and denies them the opportunity to understand God's message of deliverance, Christ's salvation.'

'Oh? How so?' Eli asks. He can see Peter is desperate to unload and Eli is drawn to know more about what drives this complex man.

'Alright. You asked for it. In the beginning, was the word right?' Peter enthusiastically begins as if drilling down into his core. Eli sees Peter like an overwound coiled spring; once freed, he's committed to what he believes is his epiphany of spiritual emancipation. But what Peter doesn't know is Eli's knowledge and experience with traumatised people. Something about Peter deeply troubles Eli, not only that he appears to have abandoned his faith, but in some deep way, has lost himself. Eli wants to know why.

'Few authorities would deny that the word was written by a writer who lived around 1000 BC. Most authorities I referenced also agree that what the Christians call Genesis, Exodus, and Numbers and what you Jews call the Five Books of Moses, were written nearly 3000 years ago, that an unknown author composed the work that has formed the spiritual consciousness of much of the world ever since. On the one hand, religious tradition ascribes the Pentateuch and the Old Testament authorship to Moses. On the other, scholars agree that it is a composite work consisting of texts by several different authors that were woven together around 400 BC by a master editor, known as the Redactor or "R." The oldest of these texts, and the most imaginative, are attributed to the author whom scholars call "J."'

''J's story begins with the creation, tells of Adam and Eve and the Garden of Eden, of Cain and Abel, of the Flood and Noah, of Sodom and Gomorrah, and has Moses leading the Israelites from bondage under Pharaoh. J provides many of the Bible's testimonies and scriptures, telling them with an energy and simplicity that makes them a delight to read. I argue Eli, that there's distinction from social and political decisions. I read the writings of J in that light – as critical scripture, closer to God, to Christ, and were singled out over the centuries and transformed by common assent into something else almost completely different. I argue Eli, would we even recognise Christ today from J's version if compared with modern gospels? Would he even be the same man in our sermons and churches?'

'There are minor and major augments as I'm sure you're aware, Eli, among scholars as to exactly what J contributed to Genesis, Exodus, and Numbers, but there is no argument about the existence and talent of the writer. Using the Phoenician Old Hebrew script, either marking a leather scroll with a dull knife or, more likely, writing in ink with a reed pen on papyrus, with the sheets glued together to make a scroll, J probably never made the stories into a composite unit. That was left to R in his editing job. How am going so far?'

'Go on,' Eli said thoughtfully.

'Now J's work can be separated from the writings of others by an analysis of style and attitude. And I'll tell you something else Eli, we're always hearing about archaeological digs that "prove" the Bible. I've been to Israel and Egypt multiple times to do just that. The trouble is, such digs can be a little like Rorschach blots – you can see almost anything in them. A case in point? I don't know if you're familiar with it – but a top group called the "city of scholars" excavated on the hilltop near the caves that concealed the Dead Sea Scrolls for 2000 years.'

Without segue or pause, Peter plunged on. 'The original team that sifted through the sand saw any amount of hard evidence that this was a monastery, wherein your scholarly Jews had copied out ancient texts before hiding them from the Romans in the caves. Later, a French team ridiculed this convenient interpretation, saying that all the evidence points to a place simply being a Roman fort. Another school of thought contends that this was a cool respite from the summer heat for a wealthy Jerusalem family. As they say, "the jury is still out."

'Then there's the uncomfortable reality,' Peter, on the boil, continues. 'That tips some off their little Biblical trolley, and perhaps the most significant disagreement between the Bible and history involves the epic tale of Moses leading your people out of bondage in Egypt. Do you realise that, despite the fact that the ancient Egyptians were prolific recorders of everything, with pharaohs leaving tons of hieroglyphs behind them detailing Egyptian life from the price of bread to astonishing records of celestial bodies, there is no evidence that this ever happened. Anywhere. In any archival Egyptology records. There are no such records outside the Bible for a spectacular event as the parting of the Red Sea. And what about Moses turning the Nile water into blood, raining frogs, a whole people covered in boils, and, of course, the big one – the death of Pharaoh's *son* and the deaths of firstborn *all-over-Egypt*? This was all so pedestrian that there's not a single letter, parchment, painting, hieroglyph, or cartouche anywhere that has ever been discovered recording these events. Nor is there any confirmation that the Egyptians held the Israelites "in bondage," let alone in slavery. What do you think of that, Eli? The Egyptians recorded their victories over their neighbours in both writing and wall paintings and carvings. But all the Egypt-shaking dramas with the Moses and the Israelites doesn't even rate some graffiti. How come?'

Eli waits patiently, his face set and inscrutable waiting for Peter's emotional spill to exhaust itself.

'For twenty years I researched. I haunted the archaeological libraries and universities in Egypt and Israel. The independent evidence just isn't there. There's plenty of suggestive data that many Jewish and Western biblical and archaeological scholars argue is evidence, but to me, remains inconclusive. I know I'm not the first sceptic who raised these questions and won't be the last. It's still my opinion but every author faces that. Nobody is forced to buy my book. You did and I'm grateful Eli.'

Eli curled the corners of his mouth with an accommodating smile.

'I know I've been going on but let me finish by saying this, what about all the dumped gospel books, now considered Gnostic texts by mainstream religions? Believers are robbed of the opportunity to truly embrace the faith message because they do not receive the full gospel, the full meaning, and the substance of faith. A library of Gnostic texts was discovered in the cliffs of Nag Hammadi, Egypt, in 1945. It is claimed, but not proven, that these extraordinary documents largely recount meetings between the risen Christ and his followers. The ideas in them are revolutionary and reveal some very contemporary ideas. In the Gospel of Thomas, for example, one of the discovered texts, it is claimed Christ says to his companions: *"If you bring forth what is within you, what you bring forth will save you. If you do not bring forth what is within you, what you do not bring forth will destroy you."* Still not saying anything, Eli?'

'I'm listening,' Eli took a deep breath and spoke calmly but flatly.

'In my opinion, when it was first published in 1611, the Bible was an elegant but flawed translation of Hebrew and Greek documents composed between 900 B.C. and A.D. 120. A clever man like you will know, Eli, that there is no manuscript of the Old Testament, that is, of the Hebrew Scriptures, written in Hebrew earlier than the ninth century B.C.'

Eli was staring at him intently.

'But we do know that these documents were first compiled and recognised as the Holy Scriptures by a convention of rabbis, as I'm sure you're aware, held at Jamina, or as it was called, Yavne, in Palestine, shortly before A.D. 100. Am I correct?'

Eli says nothing, his eyes narrow, face set, betraying little.

'Similarly, the composition of the Christian Bible – which documents to include and which to exclude that became the gnostic texts – was decided by a Catholic Church council held in Carthage in the late fourth century. Several books that were previously read in churches, including The *Shepherd of Hermas* and the marvellous *Gospel of Saint Thomas*, were discarded, presumably because they did not fit the church's narrative. My point is, what I argue in my book, only the selected books were translated and declared canonical and divinely inspired by, firstly, the authority of the Synod of Jamnia and, secondly, the Catholic Church, in a meeting in Carthage more than 300 years after the time of Christ. Wouldn't you call that a pretty large leap of faith?'

'To sum up, I suppose your ears are burning? However, fundamentalist Protestants derive their Bible's authority from Jews who rejected Jesus and Catholics who abominate, as the Scarlet Women mentioned in Revelation. And you're still not saying anything.'

Eli's continued silence begins to fluster Peter. Eli looks unfazed, listening attentively while studying Peter closely.

Peter begins to exhaust himself, his verbal propellant withering. His speech slows and he slumps slightly in his seat.

'In my opinion, some of the most important books of faith

were chopped or censored. For millennia, believers have been denied the full gospel. It's an anthology of Hebrew and Late Greek literature, edited and put forth by a council of Catholic bishops with their agenda; before that, it didn't exist. You're an intelligent man Eli, surely you can see my point? I don't know about your Talmud, I haven't read it. How much of it is the original and authentic word of God?'

Peter pauses. He gives Eli a brief glance before leaning back heavily in the seat.

'I'm certain you're aware … there were Hebrew Scriptures and their translations into Greek – the *Septuagint,* which was made in Alexandria between 250 B.C. and 100 B.C. There were also various codices, or Greek manuscripts, of various parts of the New Testament, such as the four gospels. Numerous other writings circulated among Christians, including the *Epistles of Saint Paul and Saint John,* the *Apocalypse or Revelation,* and such documents as the *Acts of John, the Didache,* the *Apostolic Constitutions,* and various Epistles of Clement, Ignatius, and Polycarp, which were all later excluded.'

'The facts speak for themselves, Eli. Why does one come to the opinion that the Bible, literally understood, is the truth, the whole truth, and nothing but the truth? Usually, one's "elders and betters" or an impressively large group of one's peers have this opinion. But this is to go along with the Bandar-log, or monkey tribe, in Rudyard Kipling's *Jungle Books,* who periodically get together and shout, "We all say so, so it must be true!" So … I wrote my book.'

The bookends sit in silence, the space taken up in talk now consumed by the roar of passing traffic. Eli's face is sage-like and impassive, not registering the congested din. He is, as the

Scriptures would say, pondering all these things in his heart. Peter, leaning forward with elbows on his thighs, keeps looking expectantly in Eli's direction. Peter is hungry for an opinion or any comment, but Eli seems to make him deliberately wait.

'You're a respectful listener, Eli. Is that a rabbinical thing or just you? I suppose I've given you a great deal to think about. My book does that,' he says with a thin, vain smile.

Eli remains thoughtful and silent. He sees Peter needs to talk and exhaust the pent-up passion. But Eli's considered silence begins to fluster Peter. Eli looks unfazed, listening, attentive, but studying Peter closely. Peter begins to exhaust himself, his verbal propellant withering. His speech slows and slumps in the seat a little. 'In my opinion, some of the most important books of faith were chopped or censored. For millennia believers have been denied the full gospel. Look at one of the most popular translations of the Bible today. In 1501 undertaken by a committee of 47 scholars and clergymen over the course of many years. For it to be accurately translated from original texts, they would've had to be proficient in Old Greek and even older Latin, Hebrew and Syriac to read the old testaments and the Pashto, and to a lesser degree Aramaic, Arabic Coptic and Phoenician.'

'And what about William Tyndale, as I'm sure a smart man like you would know, was the first to translate the Bible into English. Before his execution on trumped by charges of heresy and sedition, because he spoke out against the Catholic Church, Tyndale had translated the New Testament, the Pentateuch, and the historical books of the Old Testament including the Book of Jonah used in the creation of the Matthew Bible in 1522.'

'Of the Old Testament books, the Pentateuch, Book of Jonah, and a revised version of the Book of Genesis. Tyndale translated additional Old Testament books including Joshua, Judges, First and Second Samuel, First and Second Kings and First and Second Chronicles.'

'Like all great men and women who want to think outside the theological box, Tyndale's translations were condemned by Catholic authorities, his work banned and burned. They said he purposely mistranslated to promote heretical views, yet the whole world quotes his Bible references to this day: "Scapegoat," "Let there be light." "My brother's keeper." "Fight the good fight," "As you reap you sow," "Do unto others," "Sign of the times," "Flowing with milk and honey," "The spirit is willing but the flesh is weak," "Ye of little faith," "A prophet has no honour in his own country," "A law unto themselves," "Let my people go," even the word, "Passover," and literally hundreds of others all came from the pen of Tyndale not found in original texts.'

'Speaking of translations, look what they've done to them. Tyndale did an extraordinary, extraordinary job in translation. But look at two different versions of the Tower Of Babel among many. Tyndale's version is, from original documents, *"And all the world was one tongue and one language. And as they came from the east, they founde a playne in the lande of Synear, and there they dwelled. And they sayd one to another: come on, let us buyide ys a cyte and a toure, that toppe may reach unto heaven. And let us make us a name, for peradventure we shall be scattered abrode all the erth."*'

'Apart from scholars probably everybody is grateful they don't have to learn Old English to read their Bible. But content, meanings, context changed and drifted far from original writings and Gospel. For example, what eventually made its way into versions of King James, *"And the whole earth was of one language, and of one as they journeyed from the east, that they found a plain in the* land of Shinar; and they dwelt there. And they said one to other, Go to, let us make brick, and burn them. Thoroughly. And they had brick for stone, and slime had they for morter. And they said, Go to, let us build us a city and a tower, whose top may reach unto heaven; and let us make us a name, lest we be scattered abroad upon the face of the whole earth."'

'And what are people reading today, one of countless versions, "Now listen: all the earth uses one tongue, one and the same words. Watch: they journey from the east, arrive at a valley in the land of Summer." Peter said. "… Settle there. We can bring ourselves together," they said, "like stone on stone, use a brick for stone: bake it until hard. For mortar they heated bitumen. If we bring ourselves together," they said, "we can build a city and tower, its top touching the sky – to arrive to fame. Without a name we're unbound, scattered over the face of the earth."

'Do we have a duty to teach people the real word of God or confuse people with what is translated as the word of God?' Peter slumps, taking a deep breath, his feeble energy spent, he closes his eyes as if the lids of too heavy to keep open.

Eli waits in contemplative silence as if hooking together random thoughts.

'I am not qualified to say what is true or not. We agree you're not the first scholar to raise such questions. The way the world is going, I doubt you'll be the last.'

Eli lets it hang between them. Peter's face goes still, he's on a very tight, exhausted rein, and reads this as criticism. His posture becomes defensive.

'Peter … Allow me a question. Your Christian bible or our Hebrew books. If they didn't exist would the world be a better place?'

'I don't know,' Peter said tensely.

'What is more important to you, the mind of a believer or the spirit of their belief?'

'*Why* – can't the mind understand and the spirit believe?'

'And – for some reason, their mind could no longer understand could their spirit still believe?'

Peter is increasingly annoyed. 'I see where you're taking me and frankly … I'm disappointed. A man like you – with your history. So if the truth isn't important what do we believe? Truth in your Torah and Tanakh all that matters?'

Eli sustains his composure – with difficulty. The gloves are coming off. 'Did I say that? You're twisting what I said – now I'm disappointed. I never said truth wasn't important in the Christian Bible. What I am saying is it's proved its worth. For all its … so-called, flaws, failings, and faults, you're Bible, like our holy books has given solace, solitude, spirit, direction, hope, and happiness to countless billions for millennia. Do you think those wanting to feed their spirit or facing need, suffering, or support care in that context? Even with what is left according to *you*, are not scriptures still letters written by God's finger? Its power to influence human history for good for countless years has been profound. I ask again. What if the Bible or our Holy books didn't exist? Would the world be a better place? I am *not* saying scholastic proof is unimportant. No. Not at all. But I suppose the difference between us … you can judge, criticize and condemn your Bible in the luxury of peace and security.'

Eli looks across the intersection at the burnt out ruins. Memories press his heart and trouble his mind.

'Peter. I know you're Bible, our Holy books, in a time when prayer could have you shot at the whim of a guard. I know our Holy books when people desperately tore out pages to hide them being dragged out of their homes and sent to death camps. In the camps Christian and Jew risked their lives to huddle in a corner reading those few scrapes by candle while others watched. Prisoners who didn't speak a word of Hebrew would listen, it didn't matter – it was prayer. They risked their lives.'

Peter keeps staring in brooding silence.

'Do you know how I knew those shreds, those bits of books had the power of God in them? Evil hated it. Scrapes of Talmud were more powerful than all Nazi armies. Prayer, just a few fragments, gave light in the darkness, hope in despair. That is why when they were coming to power … they burnt all books by Jewish authors. But when you burn books, it isn't long before you burn people.'

Eli is quiet as an aching sadness grips him. Then pulls himself back.

'Hitler knew the power of the word. That's why he wrote his own book. *Mein Kampf, My Struggle* became almost a holy book to the Nazis.'

Peter is silent, thinking about what Eli said. He remains unconvinced. His mood has soured. He deflects Eli's words by refocusing on his own needs to avoid further arguments.

'Tragic, but all a long time ago. What's left of my church and life is *now*. You couldn't understand how it feels to lose something like a church you worked so hard to build.'

Eli shakes his head slowly, sadly. 'You're wrong Peter. I do understand. More than you realise. Would you mind if I shared a memory with you?'

'Of course not.'

'In that case Peter, I need to take you back to a darker and evil time.' Eli settles back in his seat, staring across the road at the ruins. For a long time, Eli has a faraway look, staring into the distance without seeing it. The pain deepens in his eyes and his face greys with tragic memories. It was a long time ago but bitter memories are like acid rain, once it falls it always leaves a scar.

In his memory, Eli goes back to another time and another place – the dark, dreadful days of the Jewish Shoah, the Holocaust and the Nazi scourge rounding up Jews all over parts of conquered Europe.

'Ladontavick in 1941 was my home,' Eli said, barely louder than a whisper. 'It was a long way from the capital Warsaw, deep in the Polish countryside. Very old, long way from the hustle and bustle, all farming and rural. My father was both Rabbi and doctor. We lived in Vienna, when the Rabbi passed my father volunteered to replace him.'

'One day, my father asked me to walk with him. I remember him bent over looking at the old cobblestones as we walked. I know it sounds odd, but he looked older somehow like he'd aged ten years just in the morning. For a long time, he said nothing. I can never remember a time when he looked so … worried, no, almost frightened. He didn't look up, and I started to become afraid for him. We walked, then he put his arm over my shoulders, pulling me in close.'

'We sat opposite the park, not so much unlike what we're doing now. I learnt the Torah on that seat, but no traffic, no noise.'

'He bent and put his head in his hands as if its weighed a ton, then sat back and looked up at the sky.'

'Word has come. Soon the Nazis will be here,' he said. 'Nothing will ever be the same, Eli. They are all over Poland. The whole country is on fire.'

'Nazis were targeting Jews,' Eli said, 'rounding them up. Stories spread like wildfire – stories of massacre after massacre – it was terrible.'

He said, 'We need to find Elohim more now than we have ever done. I learnt later the Nazis had a particular hatred for places of worship, especially synagogues, as their "God" was Hitler, a demon in human form – so my father's synagogue might be a special target for their evil. His hands were shaking. "I don't know how long we have," he said, "but I must say this to you." He said I had a calling on my life, to teach others what we know, what we will endure. "If you see one suffering, never turn your back," were his words, "always be there for them until they are strong enough again to walk alone. Eli … there is so much I wanted to teach you and your sister my beloved son, now we must count each minute by heartbeats. Listen to me, my son. No matter what happens you must carry on after me."'

'I didn't know what to say, but I started to panic. He must have seen that, so he said, "The machinery of evil beyond words will soon be here. Blind, merciless evil." I still remember to this day what he said to me. "Unlike the demon who sent them to destroy us," he said, "I don't want to be a dictator. That's not my business. I don't want to rule and conquer anyone. I should like to help everyone – if possible – Jew, Gentile, what's it matter? We all want to help one another. Human beings are like that. Demons are not. We must live by each other's happiness – not by each other's misery. We don't want to hate and despise one another. In this world, there is room for everyone. And the good earth is rich and can provide for everyone without greed. The way of life can be free and beautiful, but we have lost the way. Greed and evil has poisoned men's souls, has barricaded the world with hate, and has goose-stepped us into misery and bloodshed. We have developed speed, but we have shut ourselves in. Machinery that gives us abundance has left us in want facing cannons of death. Our knowledge has made us cynical. Our cleverness has made us hard and unkind. We think too much and feel too little. Are you hearing, Eli?"'

'To be honest, I was numb. Hearing but not comprehending, it was like a eulogy, and I remember feeling more sick by the moment.'

'More than the might of machinery,' he said, 'we need the power of humanity. More than cleverness we need kindness and gentleness. Without these qualities, life will be violent and all will be lost. The aeroplane and the radio have bought us closer together. The very nature of these inventions cries out for the goodness in men – cries out for universal brotherhood – for the unity of us all. If I were on the radio now my voice would reach millions throughout the world. But there are millions of despairing men, women, and little children who have only heard voices of hate – victims of a system that makes men hunt, torture and imprison innocent people for no other reason than that they are different with a different faith. To those who can hear me, perhaps through you, I say – do not despair. That is your message, Eli.'

'I could not answer him, couldn't speak, choking on my tears.'

'The misery,' he went on, 'that is now upon us is but a passing of greed – the bitterness of men who fear the way of human progress. The hate of men will pass and dictators will die, this Nazi darkness will one day be dust under our feet – and the power they took from the people will return to the people. And so long as men of hope live, liberty will never perish. If Elohim would grant me one blessing only, this one I'd ask above all then give up my life. That I would stand in front of those soon to arrive and say, Soldiers! Don't give yourselves to brutes – men who despise you – enslave you – tell you what to do – who to hate – what to think and what to feel. Who will drill you – treat you like cattle to the slaughter, use you as cannon fodder. Don't give yourselves to these unnatural men – machine men with machine minds and dead machine hearts. You are not machines! You are not cattle! You are men.'

'I remember my father stood then. Almost as if in the standing he was addressing, appealing to those coming in their trucks, that they could see him more clearly, hear him. In that moment, I could not remember ever loving him more.'

'You have the love of humanity in your hearts. You don't hate! Only the unloved hate – the unloved and the unnatural! I would say to them, Soldiers! Don't fight for slavery. Fight for liberty. In the 7th Chapter of Saint Luke, it is written: *"The Kingdom of God is within man."* Not one man nor a group of men, but in all men! In you! You the people have the power – they have the power to create the machine. The power to create happiness! You, the people, have the power to make this life free and beautiful, to make this life a wonderful adventure. Then – in the name of God and democracy – I beg you, let us have that power – let us all unite in the power of God's love. Let us fight for a new world – a life without fear – a decent world that will give men a chance to work – that will give youth a future and old age a security.'

'He was in tears, and me. I could hear but not see him …'

'By the promise of these things, brutes have risen to power. But they lie! They do not fulfil that promise. They never will! Dictators free themselves but they enslave the people. Now, let us fight to fulfil that promise! Let us fight to free the world – to do away with barriers of heart and mind – to do away with greed, with hate and intolerance. Let us fight for a world of reason, a world where science and progress will lead to all men's happiness. Let us fight for souls as well as minds. Soldiers! In the name of God and democracy, let us all unite to destroy the destroyers, the brutes, the dictators …'

'He finished from Samuel 2, *"Hannah's Prayer of Praise. My heart rejoices in the Lord! The Lord has made me strong. Now I have an answer for my enemies. I rejoice because you have rescued me. No one is holy like the Lord! There is no one besides you; there is no Rock like our God."*'

'Suddenly people were crying, hugging, clapping, we had no idea almost the whole village had come out and were there listening. You could feel the fear.'

For a long time Peter stared at Eli, full of compassion and admiration – perhaps for a courage he felt he no longer had.

'My father opened the Synagogue. It didn't matter, believers, non-believers, men, women, children, it was a place for comfort. Frightened people always seem to seek sanctuary in places of worship. My father wanted to save the Torah and other holy relics. He convinced people to put books, scrolls and stitch them inside the lining of their coats, or hide the menorah in their bags. He didn't think the Nazi's would search every suitcase. There must have been over a hundred people crammed inside. But when

Nazi's arrived ... nothing prepares you ... I saw the Devil in human form,' he said slowly.

'They went house to house, *"Aus Juden! Aus"* Out Jew out. Old, crippled or ill, they shot, right there in the street.' He stops. Shuts his eyes, and takes a breath.

'Soldiers rounded up any Jews they could find and loaded them onto trucks ... mothers screaming for children torn away, fathers begging for families. They ordered my father to get people out. People were jammed so tight inside you couldn't breathe. Suddenly we smelled petrol, there was a bright flash followed by an almighty explosion in the back of the Synagogue that shook our walls and shook my soul. Flames were suddenly everywhere. They had surrounded us with fire – we were trapped inside a literal hell-on-earth created by Nazi hands. No one knew what would happen next or if we'd even survive this day alive.'

He fell silent again, only looking moodily into the far distance, then shook his head, dropping his eyes.

'Screams. Panic. Everybody clawing, fighting over each other. I tried to stay near my father but was shoved on the floor. I'd no more than got on my feet when I was knocked down by people rushing for the door. I was crushed under their feet, smoke choked everybody. I really thought I would die right then. I could hear people screaming and telling each other they had to get out, the place was on fire. But every time I tried to get up, someone footed me right back down again.'

'It was my father who saved me. I saw this hand in front of me and I grabbed it like a drowning man grabs a life preserver. I grabbed and he hauled and up. I never let go of his hand, and he never let go of mine. I got to my feet, finally, just as the kitchen wall fell over. It made a noise a horrible noise like a puddle of petrol makes when you light it. I saw it go over in a big bundle of sparks, and I saw the people running to get out of its way as it fell. Some of them made it. Some didn't. More than one was buried underneath, and for just one second I saw somebodies hand underneath all those blazing coals, opening and closing. There was a girl, surely no more than ten or twelve, right in front of me, and the back of her dress went up. She was with a boy and I heard her screaming at him, begging him to help her. He took just about two swipes at it and then ran away with the others. She stood there screaming as her dress went up on her. I could do nothing.'

'It was like hell out where the kitchen had been. The flames were so bright you couldn't look at them. The heat was baking hot, you could feel your skin going shiny and blistering. He yelled at me that we had to get out, and starts to drag me along the wall. *"Come on!"*'

'Then a young man in our choir, Akiva Javorsky catches hold of him. He couldn't have been more than nineteen, and his eyes was as big as plates, but he kept his head better than we did. He saved our lives. "Not that way!" He yells. "This way!" And he pointed back toward the kitchen … toward the fire.'

'My father screamed at him "We can't!" Akiva yelled back, he had a big bull voice, but you could barely hear him over the thunder of the fire and the screaming people. "Die if you want to, but give me Eli we're getting out!"'

'My father still had me by the hand and he started to haul me toward the front again, although there were so many people around it by then you couldn't see it at all. I would have gone with him. I was so shocked, choking, eyes burning I didn't know where I was. All I knew was that I didn't want to be burnt alive. I saw Akiva grab my father by the hair of the head just as hard as he could, and when he turned back, Akiva slapped his face. I remember seeing my father's head bounce off the wall and thinking Akiva had gone crazy. Then he was shouting in my father's face: "You go that way and you going to die! They're jammed up against that door, Rabbi!"

"You don't know that!" my father screamed back at him, and then there was this loud BANG like a firecracker, only what it was, it was the heat exploding things in the kitchen. The fire was running along the beams overhead and cooking oil on the floor was catching alight.'

"I know it!" Akiva screams back. *"I know it!"*

'He grabbed my other hand, and for a minute there I felt like I was being pulled this way and that. Then Akiva pointed yelling, "Look! Look!" The smoke was like a blanket but we could just make out this huge pile of people jammed at the door. Akiva felt along the wall pulling me and I held my father's hand. He got us down to a window and grabbed a chair to bust it out, but before he could swing it, the heat blew it out for him. Akiva grabbed me by the back of my pants and pushed me up. "Climb!" he shouts. "Climb!" The sill was smoking and burning. My hands were blistered and bleeding but I pushed through and jumped down outside. My father was struggling, he was bigger and jammed in the window. Suddenly he was falling after Akiva pushed him through.'

'We turned back around, and it was like something from the worst nightmare you ever had. That window was just a yellow, blazing square of light. Flames were shooting up through that tin roof in a dozen places. We could hear people screaming inside.'

'My father was bleeding everywhere from broken glass in the

window, but he got me up on his shoulders. I saw two brown hands waving around in front of the fire at the window. I saw Akiva trying to get out. I reached through that window and grabbed him. When I took his weight my stomach went against the side of the building, and it was like leaning against a stove that's baking hot. Akiva's face came up and for a few seconds, I didn't think I was going to be able to get him. He couldn't breathe, his face black with ash and smoke, and he was close to passing out. His lips had cracked open. The back of his shirt was smouldering and catching alight.'

'And then I lost my grip and almost let go, I could smell the people burning inside. I prayed they were dead. I knew I couldn't take it anymore, my hair was smoking and my skin was raw so I gave one more great big pull, and out came Akiva on top of us and we all fell on the ground. He was on fire so we rolled him in the dirt.'

'We heard shooting. My father told me to stay with Akiva but I was too afraid I'd never see him again so went after him.' Eli stops, it's almost as if the horror is too monstrous and vivid for him to say it.

'They were shooting trying to stop people getting out, but even the Nazi's were driven back by flames. There was maybe forty or fifty people out there, some of them crying, some of them being sick, others screaming, many were laying all over the road unconscious from smoke. The door was in flames but shut. We heard people screaming on the other side, screaming to let them out, out for the love of God, they were burning up. It was the only door, to go in you pushed the door open. To go out you had to pull it.'

'Some people had gotten out and were yelling not push on the door. It must have been visions of hell as people pushed the door to open it from the outside those inside must have believed they were being trapped inside. The more panic inside the more they jammed up against the door, I can't even imagine the horror and hell of that inside. My father and I joined in pushing the door. Wasn't any way we could get that door open against the weight of all those behind. So there they were, trapped, and the fire raged.'

'Some escaped. I don't know how. I remember this women walking toward us, just walking totally covered in flames. Then she fell. I'll never forget it. We stood there, watching it end. It hadn't been five minutes all told, but it felt like forever. The last dozen or so that made it out were on fire. People grabbed them and started to roll them around on the ground, trying to put them out. There was a huge noise as the roof started to collapse – so we had to run. And all the screaming stopped … and I felt so helpless like I'd died inside.'

'My father grabbed my hand and I grabbed him back twice as hard. We stood there holding hands, crying. They were the real ghosts we saw, nothing but shimmers shaped like men and women in that fire, running, burning, some of them had their arms held out, like they expected someone to save them. The others just walked, but they didn't seem to get anywhere. Their clothes were blazing. Their faces were running. And one after another they just toppled over and you didn't see them anymore.'

'The Nazis shot the burned and hurt in a perverted act of mercy I thanked God for. Even though my hands and arms were all blistered and sliced up my father told me to hide my arms and pretend I wasn't hurt or they'd kill me. He pushed me onto a truck, and we tried to see our family but it was impossible. The commander starts shouting orders that didn't make much sense and which people couldn't hear or understand anyway and the trucks started pulling away. I looked back at the building, what was left of the door fell out and flames roared out where it had been.

'Hell was real that day … and the devil was real. I don't know. I'll probably never know. But looking at that wall of flame framed where the door had been, it sounds ridiculous I know but … I absolutely believe … as sure as I'm sitting here … I saw something I still can't explain … in those cruel flames, I saw it … and it saw me … like the devil's face.'

Chapter 3

For a long time both men sit in silence. Eli looked depleted and Peter was shocked and saddened. For a time the indifferent, rowdy domestic minutiae and its incessant noise dominates as traffic passes or stops, trams pick up or not, and pedestrians come or leave.

Eventually Peter uses thumb and forefinger to pinch the bridge of his nose. He clears his throat. 'Eli. I have no words for the agony of your experience. Probably like many, I really don't understand what happened in the Shoah.' Peter sits back in the seat, shakes his head with a small sigh.

'I don't doubt for one minute you saw the devils face that day.' Peter pauses, looks at Eli closely, 'But … doesn't it prove my point? The devils face. Where was God's?'

Eli smiles almost anticipating Peter would say something like that. 'God was there,' Eli said softly. 'Where evil abounds, grace abounds more.'

Peter rolls his eyes and almost snorts in opposition. Frustration and irritation colour his voice. 'Oh for Heaven's sake! *Enough*. After what you said do you understand how ridiculous that sounds?'

'You're upset Pastor because you know it's true,' Eli replied evenly.

'I'm *NOT!*' Tension pales his face as he grinds his teeth. 'I *was*. I have no idea what I am now!'

Peter throws away his coffee, the liquid spilling in an arc like a rooster's crest. He's on his feet, pointing and accusing.

'We've known each other what, five minutes and you're lecturing me! How in hell can I be trusted trusting God? I don't know *what* to believe anymore.'

Peter's hands start to shake as he fights to control his exhausted fury. Eli isn't responding the way Peter thinks he should. 'Look! Look across the road. That's how much His grace abounds. *I-lost-my-church!*' Spelling out the words for emphasis. 'I *trusted* God! The God I trusted asked me to sit down and yanked the chair away.'

Eli gives him a few moments for Peter to catch his breath. Peter pushes a shaky hand through his untidy mass of silver hair. Eli is apparently the calm but forceful centre of Peter's storm.

'Maybe it was time to find yourself. Your *true* self. Not church self or family self. The one Yahweh sees. It's a tough lesson, but sometimes trouble, even tragedy, is a time at which you most easily become acquainted with your *true* self, being especially free of friends and admirers then. Abraham Lincoln wrote when he felt he had nothing left at the height of the Civil War when even his Generals were doubting his decisions, "*I went to my knees before God with the overwhelming conviction there was nowhere else to go.*"'

Peter allows his pent-up hostility to explode through the surface.

'*To hell with that!* Don't give me that religious psychobabble shit.' The mask of piety fell from Peter with a thud. But all Eli sees is just a man coming apart at the seams. He's more convinced Peter's implosion is greater than the loss of his church.

Eli has had enough, and fires back. 'Give me an alternative if you know so much.' He has to pause and take a calming breath. 'Peter, you sound like a man who was once a man of faith but now has taken the easy way out with a massive chip on his shoulder against God. It seems to me like you wrote your book to "punish" Yahweh for some reason and all you did was hurt yourself and believers.'

Peter stares at him, open-mouthed, furious.

'The real question is why. You are or were a Christian, right? Isn't it time you worked out whether you're hanging on the cross or banging the nails after forty years?'

Peter is furious. *'How dare you say that to me!'* Peter's face is flushed, his hands shake. He went silent, and Eli could see the muscles roll back and forth against Peters jawbone. Eventually, he composes himself enough to speak in almost a croak. 'It's been – interesting meeting you Rabbi. I don't think we have anything more to say.'

To Peter's surprise, Eli sits back making a pose of being more comfortable in the seat.

'Oh, I think we have a lot more to say. I think you're in serious trouble and need some sort of help, Peter. I'm really worried what you might do. I've seen it in ministry, I saw it in the camps, and I'm seeing it now and I'm more convinced than ever our meeting was no accident. I want to help. I don't think losing your church is it. A tragedy, yes. But what the heck is the back story to all this? What's going on?'

'What do you mean, *what's going on?*'

'That's what I'd like to know, Peter: what *is* going on? Where did all this come from? After forty years as a Pastor, you abandon your faith in favour of a belly full of self-pity. I hardly know you, but I know you've got more chutzpah than that. Show me a man of God who says they've never lost hope and faith as part of their walk and I'll show you a liar. Nobody tosses away four decades of ministry on a whim, then writes a book demonising everything they loved and believed.'

'It's not a fucking crime!' Each word aches with frustration. Peter's hands go to his face. 'Are Rabbis so perfect? Sorry, we Gentiles aren't. Something is lost along the way, that's all. How could I teach belief when I have none?'

Peter falls broodingly silent, distressed. Eli is affected by his sadness. Peter looks away at his church ruins: perhaps an image of how he sees his life. Eventually, he closes his eyes, shakes his head. Suddenly, Peter's legs appear to lose all strength. He almost collapses back in the seat, leaning forward, elbows on his knees, hands covering his face. Eli hears a distressing choke.

'Where is God? Why is this happening?' he sobs.

Weeping openly and brokenly now. And Eli lets him cry, he slides closer and puts a comforting hand on his shuddering shoulder.

Observing Peter's inner collapse was like watching a man approaching a precipice and slowly leaning out until he loses his balance and destroys himself. Eli waits until Peters emotional exhaustion spends itself. 'You are not the first to ask, my friend …'

He slides back along the seat, runs a hand over his deeply lined forehead, bushy snowy eyebrows and sparse silvery hair. '… As the world becomes darker, you won't be the last. There is nothing special about me ... I have no answers. When you have no answers, you must live by example.'

Eli paused a moment but only heard Peters low sobbing. 'Where is God? Why is this happening, I heard almost the same words once. If you'll permit me, there was an example, a man. He didn't have an answer either, but he had something else. I'd like to share with you that day ...'

The roar of passing traffic seemed to suddenly fade from his hearing to be replaced by a mechanical, squeaky, whirring sound. But the worst, most heart wrenching sound, was the agonized, terrified cries of a child in fear and pain ...

ELI'S MIND GOES BACK TO the Sorbidor death camp in 1941 Poland. The sky hung low, dark, and menacing as if covered by a smoky evil shroud. There was like a dead hand in the sky Eli remembers, he could not take his eyes off it as if it was pointing a way to his final destination. It was clouds, just clouds shaped by wind to create the haunting spectre, an illusion of dark floating fingers, spread wide, ready to clutch up lives below.

He stood in a line of men and boys of all ages, their left arms were exposed to the elbow, jacket and coat sleeves pulled up. It was cold, exposed flesh froze. Pinned to his lapel was a tattered and yellowing Star of David, the stars tips curling. It looked old and tattered, and probably cut from the clothes of somebody who no longer stood in line. Behind Eli, a frail, grubby, sallow-faced elderly man with a long, scraggly beard, frightened eyes, hollow-cheeked pale lips, and a trembling voice whispered.

'Mark of the beast,' the old man whispered and nodded, agreeing with himself. Frightened eyes looking around. 'I heard them call it that.'

Eli only knew one "mark of the beast," from the book of Revelation: *"Let him who has understanding count the number of the beast, for it is the number of a man, and his number is 666." Revelation 13:18.*

'Prison camp number,' the old man muttered. 'No name,' he added, 'we are just a number.' Ahead of the line, grubby, white-coated attendants held a terrified, screaming, and struggling child of about 12. They were attempting to tattoo a series of numbers on his forearm.

Eli remembered the whirring of a battery operated hand tool holding the blunt needle that was dipped into ink with the needle punching up and down puncturing the skin.

The old man behind him was visibly shaking and the child's screaming tortured Eli's mind and broke his heart. He remembers catching his breath in panic and making his skin crawl, right before he witnessed an act of incomprehensible courage.

Standing nearby, a bored-looking officer's face suddenly sneered as his hand went to the cover of the holster he was wearing attached to his belt and flicked it up with his thumb so it flapped open to expose the menacing black handle of the pistol. The child's life hung by the slenderest thread.

Suddenly a man, with his balding head bowed, stepped out from near the front of the line and approached the officer.

Eli could hardly breathe as he saw the man stop near the officer, and the officer's sneer twisted into a look of confusion. The man's hand hovered for a moment above his gun, then dropped to his side. The officer looked him up and down with a menacing glare before speaking in a harsh and gruff voice, 'What do you think you are doing?'

The man kept his head bowed but Eli could hear clearly.

'My name is Rabbi Yulen Turovsky,' he said in German. Eli understood as German was often taught in Polish schools. 'I wish to help this child. Please allow me, I can take away some of his fear.' The child had already soiled himself and the muck ran down over his lace less shoes.

The officer continued to stare at Yulen for what felt like an eternity before finally turning away and motioning to the attendants. But what he said next chilled Eli to his soul.

'Very well, then. You may proceed. But be warned: if you fail to shut up the little Jew pig I shall have no mercy. I will shoot you both.' Eli saw many heads bow, or look away to avoid seeing the horror.

Yulen knelt down in front of the terrified boy who was shaking uncontrollably, speaking softly while gripping his arms in encouragement and assurance.

Yulen whispered softly. 'Are you a Jew?' Wide eyed and shaking, the boy nodded.

'Do you speak Yiddish?' He nodded again.

'It's ok. You are not alone. We will get through this together.' The child seemed to calm a little. Yulen stood, holding one of the child's hands. 'We will do this together. First you then me together.'

Eventually calming enough for Yulen to remove the child's jacket sleeve so that they could begin tattooing him with his identifying mark – which would serve as a reminder all his life that he had endured a living hell in this place. The child pulled a pained face, gritting his teeth, shaking but brave as Yulen stroked and caressed his head.

The needle pierced through skin and muscle alike over and over again until at last it was finished, leaving behind a permanent part of the horror forever etched onto this boy's arm – but also a symbol of hope that even in the darkest hours there is always something beautiful that we can cling on to; something that will carry us forward towards a better tomorrow, the love and support of another.

Yulen put his arm out, unflinching, head bowed but determined. His example, Eli felt, gave hope and courage to them all. When the bleeding tattoo was finished, his arm tightened around the young boy who now clung to him with growing hope in his eyes like a tiny light shining out from the darkness. He put a hand on the boy's shoulder and joined the others who had their numbers.

The procession of tortured souls slowly shuffled forward under Nazi guard; each person was forced to accept the number, and whatever fate to come.

As Eli watched these people bowed under the millstone of degradation and oppression, he felt an overwhelming sense of grim determination, when his time came, he'd stand like that Rabbi, no matter what it cost him personally.

The old man behind Eli stared into his twenty-year-old eyes, searching for something, anything, to make sense of the cruelty and madness, feeling abandoned and forgotten by the world.

Eli tries to form words, but his throat is parched; they've been travelling by train for days, jammed into stiflingly hot cattle trucks without food or water. Many died. He holds Eli's hand between his frail, pale trembling fingers, just to have a human touch.

'Where is God?' The frail old man said in a choked, haunted whisper. 'Why is this happening to us?'

Eli's heart rips, he has no answer. He was a Rabbi under the tutelage of his father and the synagogue elders. He knew the *Shema Yisrael*, the central affirmation of Judaism, so well. The prayer expresses belief in the singularity of God, that is, in God's oneness and incomparability. Where is the prayer now Eli asked himself, when it is needed? Why is he silent?

Now, in this terrible moment, he should say it. But to his shock and shame, no words seem to come. What is the mind of God? What is the truth? What is faith? Has his faith failed him? His mind reels, swamped with the horrible tragedy of it all. He recalls his father teaching him Deuteronomy 8:16: *"He did this to humble you and to test you for your own good."* Is *that* both the answer to where God is and the "why" of the happening? Perhaps the answer is there is no answer.

The old man holding Eli's hand is weeping now, openly and brokenly. And Eli lets him cry, as he did with Peter, not knowing what else to do without any answers, so, for whatever it was worth, put a comforting hand on his shuddering shoulder. Would he even have the courage to be courageous and follow Yulen's example – if he survived? But has God asked too much of them? Eli closes his eyes – as the line then shuffles forward. But he promises himself that, if he survives, he will never again let anyone feel abandoned.

Chapter 4

AGAIN THEY ARE LIKE BOOKENDS on the seat, stirring their takeaway drinks. Peter's book is open between them. His words have divided them in more ways than one.

'That's two coffees I owe you.'

Eli smiles, 'I'll put it on your tab.'

'You're an interesting man, Rabbi.' Peter said warmly. There was something implacable in the calm assuredness of Eli, Peter admires.

'Thank you. So are you, Pastor.' Peter throws a sharp look at Eli who is unfazed. 'Oh don't give me that look. You're still Pastor to me Peter, filled with crusader flame to change the Christian world.' Eli sips his coffee.

A blast of a vehicle horn pulls Peter's attention. 'Traffics getting awful. Do you think we're going to get some nasty little tumour from all that secondary exhaust fumes sitting here so long?' Eli says nothing and waits. 'Don't expect God to save you … never could figure out who He saves. Miracles by a roll of the dice?'

'If you have so many doubts, why did you join the Ministry? Following your Biblical namesake?'

'Nothing so grand and noble, Eli. As they say colloquially, "I was called." Peter made quotation marks with his fingers. 'Or believed I was. Now I wish I'd been deaf. My Christian walk as they call it, has been both spiritually rewarding and emotionally destroying trying to reach people that God and the devil are real, good and evil. To be honest, service to others was supposed to help my depression.'

Eli looks briefly at Peter, nodding. Eli suspected he wanted to unburden, share, that there was an ache and a fracture at the deepest core of Peter's life that was destroying his life, beyond the loss of his church. Eli took a breath, and a chance.

'Do you want to talk about it?'

For a few moments Eli thought Peter looked guarded and wary, ready to get up and leave, but a deep, long breathe seemed to settle Peter into his seat. He took a long drink and stared into his cup.

'I'm not good at confession. People usually come to me.' It was a lame, awkward little pause, but Eli smiled kindly.

'Well, what can I tell you? Last year, two, three … it goes way back, I guess. Chased by the black dog. Depression. Apparently, it's becoming more noticeable. A number of people have remarked on it, especially parishioners. Anyway, always prayed for miraculous healing … heaven doesn't seem to be taking requests. I lay hands on others to heal their depression while secretly taking handfuls of antidepressants. A demonstration of the ultimate hypocrisy.'

He looks down drawn and bitter, then rubs a hand over his forehead, pushing it through his thick, unruly white hair. He sighs again.

'Anyway, I can remember entertaining suicidal thoughts as a bible college student. At any rate, I've always found life demanding.

I'm an only child of lower-middle-class people. I was the glory of my parents. My son the doctor. I was always top of my class. Scholarship to Sydney Uni. The boy genius, the brilliant eccentric. I broke my parent's hearts dropping out to go to Bible College. They died … we never reconciled. God didn't fix that either,' he said sourly.

'Terrified of women, clumsy at sports. God, Eli, how the hell do I go about this?' He spreads his hand's palms up in a helpless, confused gesture.

'Are you married?'

'You could call it that. Do Rabbi's marry?' Peter said.

'Of course.'

'Divorce?'

'Sometimes.'

'My wife ran a beauty salon. She was already a budding believer. On fire for the Lord, but – we both liked lots of nice things. Maybe God didn't like that. Never understood why a minister's walk had to have their arse hanging out dirt poor cap-in-hand. If you don't have money how can you help others? Money isn't the crime, it's how you use it.' He sighs. 'Anyway. I denied her nothing.'

'Are you still together?' Eli asked.

Small head shake. 'I left her a dozen times. She left me a dozen times. We stayed together through a process of attrition. Obviously sadomasochistic dependency. We live together apart by my arrangement. We talk all the time but nothing is said. My home is hell. We've got two teenage brats who are almost atheists going to private college my parishioners pay for. They think I'm a banker created by God. They get what they want, do what they want. Last year they were arrested for pushing … drugs. I've prayed, elders in the church have prayed for our marriage, our children, and nothing ... has changed. Maybe I was born to be punished as an example to Christians of what not to do. I don't mean to be facile about this.' Indeed, he does not. He is horrified by the fact his eyes are wet and he is verging on tears. He turns away quickly.

'I blame myself for those two useless young people. I never exercised parental authority. I'm no good at that. Oh, God, I'm no good at this either. Eli, let's just forget the whole thing. I'm sorry I bothered you all this time. You're an amazing man Eli the Rabbi. But I'm sure you've got better things to do. Let's get together for some coffee sometime. I'll buy.' He tries to smile but it looks more like a grimace.

Peter's tone is peremptory, but Eli isn't ready for that, he isn't finished. Responding to Peter's inner turmoil is what matters.

'How serious are your suicidal speculations, Peter?'

'When God doesn't hear me to help me which is all the time, I amuse myself with different ways of killing myself that don't look like suicide. I wouldn't want to do my family out of the insurance not that they deserve it, or let down my church.'

Deeply troubled, Eli frowns unsure how to proceed, his deepest fears about Peter confirmed.

'You seem to have given considerable thought to the matter.'

Peter cuts to the air with his hand dismissing it.

'You ought to know a man who talks about it all the time never does it.'

Eli remains unconvinced. 'I don't know. I see a man who's exhausted, emotionally drained, riddled with guilt, and has been systematically stripping himself of his wife, children, friends, isolating himself from the world ... and finally his faith and God with this.' He holds up Peter's book. 'If you don't mind me asking, are you impotent?

'Intermittently,' Peter replies.

'What does that mean?'

'It means I haven't tried in so long, I don't know.' Again Peter makes a sweeping gesture with his hand like wiping down a blackboard. 'Let's just drop the whole thing, Eli. I feel humiliated and stupid. All I have to do is pull myself together and figure out what I'm going to do. I'm sorry I troubled you. Thank you for your patience and time. Your congregation, or whatever you call it, are very lucky to have you in their lives. Maybe if I'd had some of your qualities things might've turned out different.'

Peter stands and so does Eli. He mustn't let Peter walk away but doesn't know how to stop him. Eli is convinced Peter is right on the edge of self-destruction. However, Peter himself presents an indirect opportunity.

'In an hour it'll be mad here with the after-work rush. You can't hear yourself think. I love the waves, do you? Relaxing and hypnotic. The beach another favourite spot for a faith fugitives who needed to get away … I used to go down there all the time to pray, but as prayer doesn't work, now just sit and disappear for a while.'

'Beach sounds great. Mind if I join you?'

Peter pushes the chrome button at the crowded pedestrian crossing.

Smiling he glances at Eli. 'Are we the odd couple? We're getting a few looks. You in your kippah and me looking like some sort of priest.'

'Could be,' smiles Eli.

'I wonder how many times a Rabbi and an ex-pastor have sat on a park bench talking about.

God, faith, life, and the whole damn thing?'

'I doubt many,' Eli answers smiling.

'Reminds me of that a Rabbi and a Priest walk into a bar joke,' Peter says. 'You drink. Eli?'

'Socially. Ceremonially.'

'The Old Testament mentions wine about 140 times and beer, it's argued, "strong drink" about 20 times, from memory. Am I right?'

'For an "ex-pastor,"' Eli smirks, 'you know you're verses. In the middle of a song about God's gifts of creation, the poet praises God for wine. He says that the Lord causes plants to grow for people to cultivate, so *"that he may bring forth food from the earth and wine to gladden the heart of man."*

'Psalm 104:15, if I'm not mistaken?'

'Wine, yayin, and beer, Shekar, are commonly mentioned together as *"wine and strong drink."* I think that's Leviticus 10:9, and Deuteronomy, 29:5 if memory serves. The old Israelites were not averse to a drop or two,' Eli said. 'Melchizedek gifted Abram with wine, and Isaac drank wine before bestowing a blessing on Jacob, you'll recall in Genesis 14:18 and 27:25. When Isaac was weaned, Abraham threw a "feast," which in Hebrew is a mishteh, a word formed from shatah, "to drink."'

'Wine is included in gifts presented at the sanctuary,' Eli continues, 'The very fact that on-duty priests and Nazarites were to abstain from wine and beer is implicit proof that, in the regular course of life, drinking alcohol was the norm, not the exception … so there's nothing wrong with it – in *moderation*.'

'Ever been drunk, Eli?'

'No.' Shaking his head.

Peter cocks a dubious eyebrow. 'Not even when you were younger and a little more spiritually reckless and experimental? Come on.'

Eli pulls a face and shakes his head. "Well, I guess I'm the odd one out.'

'God Eli,' fixing him with a quizzically and disbelieving look. 'You sound too saintly to be true.'

'Saintly?' he laughs. 'Far from it according to my sister and friends without adding grog to my long list of lapses. My father never drank except ceremonially, and I guess I've just stuck to scripture. While I don't blame others, I remember Isaiah lambasts *"heroes at drinking wine."* Strong warnings are repeated by the prophets and sages against intoxication and its results, look at Proverbs, 20:1. Let's not forget several infamous episodes are connected with drunkenness: Noah's nakedness in Genesis 9, Lot's incest, Nabal's foolishness … David's scheming lies in 2 Samuel. What about you Peter?'

Who shrugs with a knowing smirk. 'Oh, I've tied a few on. I remember reading once a man isn't punished for his sins but *by* them. I wasn't overly fond of resisting temptation. Truth is my principal anguish and the source of all my joys and sorrows from my youth onward has been the incessant, merciless battle between the spirit and flesh.'

'But past is past, huh Peter?' Eli asks. It's a throwaway but really is a question, but the silence from Peter troubles him.

'A lot of churches and self-righteous priests and Pastors have a thing about it. They're wrapped up in piety so tight it's a wonder they can breathe. This moral indignation of better-than-thou. Moral indignation is jealousy with a halo. You can't judge somebody taking a drink. Things get too much sometimes. God is deaf and doesn't help, things don't change you know what I mean?' After a long pause. 'Who am I to judge?'

Looking at Peter, Eli suspects he's talking about himself. Eli is about to ask more, but the lights change and they join the impatient crush crossing the road.

They manoeuvre and jostle with the late afternoon crowd down the sidewalk past the shops until Peter abruptly stops near the gutter outside a clothing store next to a specialist wine shop. Eli hovers near him looking at the road and back to Peter.

'About two years ago,' Peter said. 'Right here.' Peter chews his lip a little, thinking. 'You believe in fate?'

'I'm sorry?'

'Fate. Fate, things you can't control, that make no sense, two hundred people die in a plane crash and one lives, that sort of thing. Some inexplicable order of things beyond your control, events, moments that happen without rhyme or reason. Things as they are that happen, you can't avoid or change it, like dominoes, sometimes events are dominoes. The first knocks over the second, the second knocks over the third, and there you are. Wouldn't it be great if we could make a better fate and luck?'

Looking surprised, Eli frowns. 'You can't make fate Peter. Then it's not fate it's voodoo. Besides, believing in luck and fate is occult and not scriptural,' Eli gently prods.

'Oh loosen up for God's sake, Eli,' responding sarcastically. 'A lot of scripture doesn't work today. Look. I've homosexual parishioners. Homosexuality is an abomination –'

'Leviticus, 18.22,' Eli said.

'Chapter and verse,' Peter replied. 'I'm required to think about killing them. I'm interested in selling my daughter into slavery as sanctioned in Exodus 21.7. What is a good price for her? She's lazy, untidy, got caught selling drugs but brilliant scholastically. While thinking about that can I ask another? My elders insist on working on the Sabbath. Exodus 35. 2 clearly says they should be put to death. I work also. Am I obligated to kill myself or is it ok to call the cops? Here's one that's really important to sports fans in Melbourne and is a big deal, including me. Touching the skin of a dead pig makes one unclean. Leviticus 11.7. If I promise to wear gloves can I kick around my old football marked "genuine pig skin bladder?" I have several farmers. Does my church really have to get together and stone my brothers for daring to plant different crops side by side? Can I stone my mother in a small family gathering for wearing garments made from different threads, or do I march into this clothing store and burn it down for the same reason? Think about those questions, will you? All of that's in the Hebrew bible am I right? And let's not forget, "Vengeance is mine." *"Dearly beloved, avenge not yourselves, but rather give place unto wrath: for it is written, Vengeance is mine."* Correct? Romans 12, I believe. According to the Bible revenge is the exclusive property of God Almighty. But if God admits to using revenge, and if God can only do good, does that mean revenge is good? Does that mean if we are made in God's image that revenge becomes not an act of hate but a holy crusade? A blessed thing?'

Eli smiles gently and thinks to himself, there's also another verse: *"Hear now this, O foolish people, and without understanding; which have eyes, and do see not; which have ears, and hear not."* Jeremiah 5:21 … but this is not the time and place for theological juggling or scriptural fencing. Hurting people hurt people and Peter looks so fragile if Eli flicked him with a fingernail like when testing fine glassware, he'd shatter.

Eli's mind goes back to the camps where he saw hundreds, perhaps thousands of tormented, haunted souls, feeling deserted by divine power, the only thing they had left was to retaliate by abandoning whatever "grain" of their faith they had. For many a sense of justice. But Eli still didn't know Peter's back story, only its consequences and collapse, what bought him to stand on the footpath near the gutter staring at the road between the rear and front of parked cars.

'As I said, dominoes. Two years ago, I'm not sure, but it seemed to start right about here. I've always tried to help, Eli, I hope you believe that … inside ministry and out, spiritually, financially … always available. My children accused, no, cursed me for spending more time with others than them, failed father. I don't know. Once I even had fantasies about quitting the church and doing missionary work somewhere – do some good for once … And what am I now? A walking encyclopaedia of dogma. A theological dictionary on two legs.'

Eli smiles warmly trying to encourage and lift the conversation.

'Each of us has his own cross.' Eli said for Peter's sake.

'Crosses have never looked very comfortable to me. Do you know what mine is? My cross, I mean. To be rich and content and fulfilled … and to know that I have deserved none of it. And that when I'm called to judgment … I must depend entirely on the mercy of God.'

'We are what we are, Peter. And God must take up the responsibility even for theologians, Jewish or Christian. Now, tell me … why did you decide against doing field ministry work?'

'Why?' Peter shook his head. 'Pray for food and healing miracles I don't believe in, give already struggling and starving people false hope of bread and fishes and a better tomorrow adding the weight of the Bible to their already breaking backs? That makes me a hypocrite, not a helper. Besides, Leanne said I was just a coward, running away, need is everywhere, all you have to do is step outside your front door. She was right. It's endless, isn't it? Always somebody or something in need. It never stops. You give so much one day you need help yourself. Was it ever like that for you Eli?'

'At times,' he said noncommittally.

'I *know* it's not scriptural, Ok' Peter said defiantly, 'but you hope, you know, hard labour down here earns you a few chips in the big game. You tuck them away, save them for a time when your ass is on the line, pull them out and God throws a few well-earned heavenly favours and indulgences in your direction. You can't blame Pastors for wanting a few things back. But … the game doesn't work that way does it?'

Eli doesn't answer but his expression says Peter answered his own question.

'You can't help but wonder where God is though can you? Life thrashes you until you're a husk …' He shakes his head and sighs. '… Got nothing left and just blow away. No resurrection for any of us. If only we could live again but know what we know now. Of all sad words of pen and tongue, the saddest are these: it might have been …' Peter hangs his head, and shakes it a little. 'You know what else? We believe at once in evil, we only believe in good upon reflection. Is that not sad?' Peter looks at him, a little shamefaced. He shrugs despondently. 'I'm rambling aren't I?'

'You're depressed,' Eli said kindly.

'I'm depressed.'

'What can I do?'

Peter looks at him and can't help but smile. 'You know, for somebody I've known five minutes you're being remarkably kind. Is that a Rabbi or Eli thing?'

Eli smiles warmly. 'Maybe a little of both perhaps?'

Peter smirks with a mischievous challenge. 'Being remarkably kind is a very *Christ* thing to be.'

Eli's smile increases a little. 'Jesus was Jewish. Maybe all Christians should become Jewish.'

Eli's small touch of levity almost forces Peter to grin. He clears his throat and continues. He sighs, almost sadly certainly deeply burdened and becomes instantly serious again as turns away and looks at the road again.

'Okay. It's hard to know where to begin there's been so much crap. But considering we're standing right where something big happened and I think it all started to go off the rails, I'll start here. What can I say? We got a call from the Ministry accountant wanting to meet without delay. Leanne was with me and we drove down to about here …'

THE IMMACULATE MERCEDES BENZ SWUNG left into the busy street moving slowly in dense traffic. Peter listened to one of his own sermons while Leanne, wearing a cream-coloured power suit, scanned a fashion magazine.

The car stops as Peter taps the brake, looking out the windscreen with a shocked look on his face.

'Will you look at that? Somebody. A person in the gutter?'

'My *God*, how disgusting.'

'Yes,' Peter replied abstracted, surprised at what he was seeing.

'Right outside the wine shop. Surprise. Surprise.' Leanne rolls her opal green eyes.

'Nobodies *doing* anything!' Peter was looking around, congested sidewalk filled with pedestrians.

She throws him a look. 'Why have you stopped?'

'Do you think I – ?' Peter indicates with his hand. 'You don't know he's drunk he could be hurt, Leanne.'

'Think again. Outside the wine shop! We're *late* already, Peter,' and carefully tossed blond hair off her Modigliani face.

Peter looks at her appealingly, then looks around. 'But what if somebody from church sees us? They'd expect me to –'

'Do church business. Of course it's sad, but ...' she cocks a meaningful eyebrow ... 'they wouldn't be expecting their Pastor to be with drunks in the street.'

Peter drops his eyes a moment admitting to himself Leanne's observation is probably true, but he still has to be *seen* to be compassionate. 'You don't *know* he is. Nobodies *doing* anything.'

'Don't *you* either. The Mayor comes to church, tell her.' The sharp blast of a car horn behind them. They turn to look back a little. Leanne glares at Peter indicating with her fingers: let's go!

'I just can't leave him in the gutter,' he says.

'What are you *doing?!*' As he opens the car door stepping out.

Peter guessed sixty. But it was hard to tell, he could have been half that. Peter couldn't see any blood. The head looks big, with cropped hair lolling off so that one cheek is pressed to the road among the throwaway plastics and other rubbish.

People bustle past, they laugh, chatter, and ignore.

Peter is standing above him; looking down; there's no sign of movement. The legs are twisted, which look like useless appendages. The jacket is some kind of bomber jacket, splayed open. The face is thick-featured, with strong seams from nose to mouth, and a mouth that hangs open. The eyes are closed. There is a sheen of sweaty grime on the skin of the face, a characteristic of thickening skin giving him that look of profound sordidness you always turn away from. No soap in this guy's life.

Peter looks around at the passing parade, at least get him onto the footpath. 'Hello! Please. Can you help?' People pass, nothing to see here.

He bends down, moves his hands towards him; Peter hasn't decided what to grab onto. He hears a long blast of a horn. I don't want to *drag* him; Peter thinks, you don't drag bodies through the gutter, do you? What to do? He reaches down and grips the sides of his jacket, the zip fitting across each of his palms, and starts to lift. He's incredibly heavy, Peter has to reposition his hands on the zip and heave. The flesh is willing but the flesh fades …

Peter mutters with strain. '*God!* Help me lift. Give me the strength of Sampson.'

He pulls on the jacket; the chest moves upward, the head still not leaving the ground. He pulls more, and the neck bends. Peter still hasn't let himself feel disgusted, or horrified, as he did in the car. He is being seen to be doing something, satisfying the inner and outer Pastor.

As Peter pulls the chest upwards, the arms flop down, and then the neck, and then there's an extra, very heavy weight as the head leaves the ground, hanging down loosely from the neck, weighing as much as a portable television.

'I hope you appreciate this!' Peter grunts. He's starting to pant a little. He takes a step toward the footpath, fighting against the weight, and moves him towards the pavement, the legs dragging, and Peter thinks: *he's dead Lord, too heavy, damn the Mayor, nobody helps … this is stupid … why do this? Why aren't you helping God?!'*

He's over the kerb, he's done that bit, still holding this

incredibly heavy thing. People are responding, starting to stop and briefly look, several stop quickly to film but lose interest, and Peter calls. 'Help me. *Please!*'

He grinds his teeth so he won't swear. He says out loud to himself, 'Nobody helped Christ ... Oh, that's right, one was forced to help carry the cross, no volunteers,' he says bitterly, grunting louder now with effort. 'I'm doing this for *you* God. Do something for me! You're supposed to *help* when your servants call! So *help* already!'

Peter's foot slips on a loose piece of pavement, and ... Peter pitches forward, can't help himself, still holding him and then not holding him, dropping him, keeping his balance, as people swing around Peter to avoid contact as he lurches forwards and sideways. The man's bottom smacks the pavement, and then the rest of him has half a meter to fall; the head hits first – *crack!* And Peter slumps, but there's a noise! There's definitely a noise.

'Damn!' Peter said. It's not the divine help he wanted, and he's angry.

But the man's not dead. At least he's now crumpled on the pavement. Air is coming out of his lungs in agonised, occasional hisses; something in his throat is flapping, gurgling.

Peter's back hurts, he straightens, gritting his teeth. He can almost feel his wife's glare scorching and burning holes in the back of his head. Ignoring the indifferent audience and their amused or judgemental staring, Peter decides to do what a Pastor does. He bends the knee beside the man in prayer.

A large Māori women appears, she has short, cropped pitch hair with a purple and green fringe, and traditional New Zealand Moko tattoos on her chin. Her big smile and perfect white teeth light up her face.

'Whatchadoin' bro? Heh, brother, no good prayin' for Gary. I've been watchin' ya from the shop.'

Peter stares disbelievingly as he stands. 'You've been *watching!*'

'Yeah! I served him not long ago. Called ambos but they'll like take forever bro, they're jacked off comin' now.'

'You know him?'

'Gary. Yeah. Sure. Well, as a customer, used to teach at some uni. Leave him, the stupid bastard. It's the drink. It's just the drink. Be in the gutter tomorrow. He's always in the gutter bro. Can't save 'em all.' She frowns staring at him intently. 'Heh! You're that fella in the glass church.'

'That's the media, it's not really that, we just love our stained glass windows.' But Peter is smiling proudly. 'Do you come to church?'

'Me!' she said automatically. 'Nah! Too rich for my blood. Look. You know best, but when he's pissed he's happy. See ya.' Throws the comment back over her shoulder as she returns to the wine shop.

Her words affect Peter, thinking out loud. *"Happy? Can't save them all."* Peter mutters to himself. 'Then who do we save God? How do you ever know? The Good Samaritan in Luke 10 tried to help *one*. There's not enough numbers for those in need today.' And he drops his eyes. Then he is interrupted by another women's voice, critical and harsh.

'What do you think you're doing?'

Peter turns and swallows guiltily. Leanne looks down at the man and back to Peter, shaking her head.

'Christ said you'll have the poor with you always, didn't He? Probably drunks too,' she adds. 'If God himself won't help them why should you? Peter. We're *late* for the accountant!'

'I'm just going to pray for him.'

She glares with narrowed eyes. 'Look around Peter. Seriously. What difference does prayer for one drunk make?' Her tone stopped just short of a sneer. 'Do what you want.' She tosses her hair and turns her shoulders.

'Just a *prayer*.' He said appealing.

'You pray and walk. I'll drive.' Her fierce glare leaves him in no doubt. 'Next time I'll bring my own car.' She appears to just ignore vehicles swinging past their car with a chorus of horn blasts.

Stung by her disregard and indifference, he calls annoyed, 'It's what I *do*, Leanne!'

Peter looks between his wife, who is storming back towards the driver's side, and the prone and gurgling Gary. Decision made, he digs out a card and pushes it into the pocket of the man's jacket.

'Bless you, Gary. Help will be here soon. You know, God helps too. Trust in him. Here's my card. Come to church. Bless you. I'll look forward to seeing you. We'll pray for you!'

Chapter 5

THE SUN WAS FADING LEAVING a saffron stain across the sky. The beach goers were packing up, strolling along or going in for a late dip. The inedible soothing sound of waves rolling in is in contrast to the emotional imbalance between the two "bookends," who have found another bench seat to occupy and continue their reflective journeys. Eli, arms crossed, seems at one with the relentless roll and spill of waves and the whitewash of foam soaking the sparkling sands. By contrast, Peter's melancholy gloom was almost palpable, and although he wanted to come to the beach to embrace majesty and peace, he is unhappily self-absorbed.

'They say heaven doesn't have spectacular sunsets and sunrises. It isn't so perfect after all.'

Eli chooses not to answer that.

'You did all you could for Gary,' Eli said.

'Did I, Eli? Did I really?' Peter's tone cynical and bitter. 'We're supposed to be led by the Lord helping the needy, not run like a rabbit when your wife barks. He died, just a few days later, tripped on the same gutter I pulled him up on and broke his neck. They found my business card in his coat. A card. My total spirit led contribution to that sad man's life.'

Eli sighs and nods as if anticipating hearing that.

'You can't blame yourself.'

'I do blame myself. For many things.'

'We all do things we're ashamed of. Carry guilt's. They say it's easier to forgive others a thousand times than forgive yourself once. Nobody's perfect Peter. We all fail. We all regret. All you can do is do and try and *believe* the doing is right.'

'See, that's what I'm talking about. What's it all about Eli? Ten years in Bible College and thirty years in ministry I still don't know. You pray and believe you're doing the right thing by helping, but there's just so much need and so much suffering. That Maori woman said you can't save them all. She was right. Not even Christ, the son of God could help everybody. Hate to admit it Lee was right, what difference does helping one man make? I gave him nothing. What good did I do?'

Eli shakes his head.

'You gave him back his humanity, Peter. You stopped. Who else did? You said somebody cared, that he was more than just another drunk in the gutter. That is the greatest gift of all.'

Eli took a deep breath and continued quietly. 'Can I give you an experience?'

'Sure.' Peter shrugs.

'You said, because I don't drink or get drunk I sound too "saintly." I remember something, that haunted me for years after, still grabs my guts sometimes. I was so full of shame and guilt I could hardly live with myself. Our hut was locked down. Somebody had done something and as punishment, they gave us a small piece of bread and potato. We had no idea how long our punishment would last. We tried to ration, live on tiny pieces. After a week we were going out our minds with hunger. Except for one man who was dying, I was trying to care for him. He went into a death coma. It was over. I stole. I stole a dying man's bread. I, a Rabbi, stole his bread ... I didn't tell the others ... That was a terrifying experience.'

'Oh for Heaven's sake Eli. Stop beating yourself up. Anybody would do it. You were starving to death!'

'They unlocked our hut the next day. I didn't eat it. I couldn't.' Eli stops, lowers his eyes, and shakes his head. 'In the death camp – there were thousands of people in need and suffering, starved and brutalized. I knew this school teacher and gave it to him. He fed it, crumb by crumb, to a man whose jaw had been broken by a guard. He fought to save that man. One man out of so, so many. The man with the broken jaw might have died anyway. But what the guard tried to destroy that act gave back: the man's humanity and the will to live.'

Unconvinced, Peter shakes his head sadly and stares at the sand.

'It isn't for us to always understand God's will,' Eli said. 'I don't think we can. It's enough for us to do, no matter how small. We never know how much good one small act of charity might do. Peter, you might not agree, it's just my opinion, but I believe every happening, great and small, good or tragic, is a parable whereby God speaks to us. The art of life is to get the message.'

The men fall into a silent impasse, each consumed in life's journey through their own worlds.

'But if I have only learnt one thing on this journey ... life isn't easy,' Eli continues. 'Things get confused ... What's choice, what's necessity? Because there's a constant conflict in every human heart between the rational and the irrational, between good and evil. The good does not always triumph. Sometimes the dark side overcomes what Abraham Lincoln called the better angels of our nature. Everybody has got a breaking point. You and I have.'

Sounds dare interrupt, caught on the breeze floating back of those enjoying the beach as shadows deepen. Dominating all is the emotionally embalming roll and spilling of insistent waves indifferent to moments and memories of men.

Then a very human sound intrudes commanding attention as Peter's stomach rumbles.

'That sounds like a trumpet call for eats.' Eli grins. 'There's a lovely Malaysian restaurant not far. They do a fantastic Mee goreng mamak that will knock your socks off. What do you say, Pastor Peter?'

Who can't help but smile at Eli's emphasis on "Pastor." 'Sounds good.' Peter looks at him and smiles, shaking his head a little, surprised.

'You know, we've only known each other half a day but I somehow feel I've known you a long time. Would you believe I've even found it easier to talk to a Jewish Rabbi than my fellow Pastors? You've been nonjudgmental and patient.'

Eli smiles warmly. Eli looks at Peter and studies him closely. He genuinely likes Peter, and couldn't ignore his vulnerability. Eli's gut instinct is that Peter is not only a lost soul in a sense, but might be floundering on the brink of self-destruction.

The encroaching dark seems to mirror Peter's emotions, looking withdrawn and deeply burdened, as if unable to push back against the depths of his pain and sadness. Suddenly Peter is talking, as if the words were tearing at him and desperate to escape.

'I'm ... ashamed about something ...'

Peter looks at Eli, then looks away and back again as if searching for courage. Eli keeps looking ahead in respectful silence. Eventually, Peter sighs, pushes a hand through his thick, untidy hair, rubs the hand across his forehead, and then seems to want to speak.

'There, um, huh, was ... this ... woman. A young girl really.'

Eli almost feels Peter submerge into deeper despondency so judges this is not the time to talk. Eli's eyes narrow a little in thought. Then he puts his hand on Peter's shoulder, giving it a firm, comforting and supportive squeeze.

'My friend. I'm sure you know Proverbs 18:21 says, "*The tongue has the power of life or death.*" It also needs feeding regularly.' Eli slaps Peter's shoulder. 'Come on. Mee goreng mamak awaits!'

THE ATMOSPHERE RICH WITH SPICY, pungent curries and meats as noisy diners sit in rattan chairs around the busy restaurant's food and drink-laden glass-topped tables.

Two men of faith who worship the same heavenly deity from vastly different beliefs yet embrace each other's sameness in life's relentless struggles sit in a corner table.

Peter pours them both glasses of iced tea.

'I'm a little confused.' Eli raises his eyebrow in response. 'I wouldn't think here will be serving kosher?'

A small smile tugs at Eli's mouth. Not wanting to labour the point, he moves on to explain.

'Oh, these days, it would be pretty rare to find a synagogue or community that would openly punish someone for eating non-kosher food or otherwise violating a law against God. There may be great consequences for these actions in the world to come, but who knows? My view is what happens if a Jewish family is in crisis or has lost their faith and will only meet you at MacDonald's. Do you cast them adrift because you don't like big macs? There are atheist Jews just like Gentiles. You dump them at the supermarket checkout when they want to talk about something anywhere but in a synagogue?'

'Do Rabbis give Grace?'

'Well, not "Grace." That's Christian. We give thanks. We have six possible blessings said before eating. *Birkat Hamazon*, the blessing after the meal, is also known colloquially as "benching," the English version of Yiddish bentshn: *to bless*. It's used following any meal where bread is eaten because bread is a meal.'

Peter smiles, 'Better not tear into the rolls yet.'

Eli smirks, 'Tear into what you want. The blessings before eating are all in the same format, just with a few words at the end indicating whether it's bread, non-bread grain, wine, or anything else. It's all derived from Deuteronomy 8 with three major parts and a fourth that is required by Rabbis: acknowledging G-d as the sustainer; thanking G-d for the land of Israel; asking G-d to rebuild Jerusalem; and the last part is basically acknowledging G-d's favour to us.'

Piles of noodles and other delights arrive at their table with the smiling waitress.

'Wow. Looks great.'

'Tastes better,' Eli said. 'Try all the sauces. Amazing.' Eli stops and looks at Peter. 'So? Do you want to give grace, Peter?'

'As I'm learning right now I think the Birkat Hamazon.'

'Ok. I'm sure Elohim won't be angry if I share with a Christian Pastor.' Eli winks.

'Ex-Pastor.' Peter adds.

'*Oh, Peter!*' Eli admonishes him with a "spare me" look in good humour. 'So let's do this before I collapse from hunger … *"Blessed art thou, O Lord our God, King of the universe, who feedest the whole world with thy goodness, with grace, with lovingkindness, and tender mercy; thou givest food to all flesh, for thy lovingkindness endureth forever. Through thy great goodness, food has never failed us; may it not fail us for ever and ever for thy great name's sake, since thou nourishes and sustainest all beings, doest good unto all, and providest food for all thy creatures whom thou hast created. Blessed art thou, O Lord, who givest food to all."*'

'Amen.'

'So-o-o, *ex-pastors* still say Amen?' smirks Eli.

'Reflex.' Peter replies as they enjoy their meal.

'Now I know you a little better you won't mind me asking. You feel on bottom of, what you called *"Job's ladder?"* I didn't read in our Holy Books there was a "Job's ladder?" You sneak in an extra chapter?'

Peter shrugs and sighs wearily. 'A one way ladder! When everything that's been dumped on me mercilessly without any rhyme or reason what else can I believe? Now even my church destroyed. If it isn't *God's will*, whose? What's the point of it all?'

'How're the noodles?'

'Wonderful!" replies Peter.'

'I've certainly thought about it in the death camps, believe me. Always the "why" questions. You Christians say even your Jesus on the cross said, *'Eloi, Eloi, lema sabachthani?'* "My God. My

God. Why has thou forsaken me?" My answer is I have no answer, my friend. In the end, we are still just human. Some say troubles like yours are a test. Perhaps, even like Job. Easy to have faith and trust in the dark when you know where you're going. To trust divine wisdom as your guide in the dark when you *don't* know where you're going is something else. I failed Yahweh many times. I'm no example.

Peter studied Eli a long time. 'I think you make a great example.' Eli smiles weakly and looks to be a little self-conscious. 'You'd *even* make a great Christian.'

Eli snorts a laugh, almost spraying his food, coughing a little, and wiping his mouth. An intense bond is building between the two. Eli then becomes serious and reflective.

'So many of us become smart too soon and wise too late because we can't comprehend that the soul may be the part of us that sees the light of real faith.'

'In those hideous death camps. Honestly. Did you ever lose faith?' Peter asks.

The question clutches Eli's heart. His shoulders slump a little as if weighed down by the painful memory.

'Honestly?' Eli said. 'Yes. Many times. And despair. Times it was easier to die.'

Peter frowns, searching Eli's face anxiously. 'But you found faith, denounced doubt?'

'I wish it was that simple. In the living I saw Yahweh and hope. In the cruelty and evil I saw the devil. It was a ceaseless struggle. My mind broke. I cursed and blamed everything including Yahweh. If I could do virtually nothing to help us why didn't He? Wasn't it enough trying to survive starvation, illness and beatings without a belief in what seemed futile faith? I came to realise

I wasn't a Job, Joseph or Jeremiah or had their courage or faith … I was just a failed man. Losing faith was liberating at first, I could blame everything on God and not care.'

Peter looks at him sideways resentfully, wondering to himself if Eli was judging and being critical without saying it out loud. He clamps his jaw with a hard expression.

'I was lost a long time, without knowing it. Without the faith, one is free I thought, and that is a pleasant feeling at first, dumping the religious burden. There are no questions of conscience, no inner constraints. It was only later that internal terror comes in addition to camp terror. I was free – but free in chaos, in an unexplainable world beyond the camp. I felt free of faith like in a desert, but lost in hope. There was nothing to believe in. I couldn't find me. Without faith there was no reason to want to survive. There was no hope in tomorrow.'

Eli leans back in his chair a few moments, as if pulling his thoughts together. 'When I lost it I had lots of time to wonder how I'd know it if I found it. I suppose I realized faith is not belief without proof, but trust without reservation. Faith sees the invisible, believes the incredible and receives the impossible.' He smiles warmly. 'Something like that. Anyway. If you can't accept anything on faith, your life will be dominated by doubt. Let me ask you a question. Considering you feel dumped on like Job, interested in astronomy or astrology?'

'What do you mean?' Peter frowns.

'As you know, God did eventually talk to Job reminding him how little he knew. *"Can you bind the cluster of the Pleiades or loose the belt of Orion? Can you bring Mazzaroth out in time for its season? Or can you guide the great bear and its cubs? Do you know the ordinances of the heavens?"* Are you capable of establishing *their dominion over the earth?"* For us Jews, Mazzaroth is interesting. Ironically, it is an ancient Hebrew name for the signs of the zodiac.'

Peter asks, surprised. 'Jews believe in *astrology?*'

'Not the esoteric junk of today. Mazzaroth's means circle of a belt of twelve constellations by which ancient peoples divided up the year into months, an arrangement that was known and used for thousands of years. Job obviously studied these constellations. But he could not answer God's questions about them. I guess what I'm trying to say is that everything has a reason – and things are not always as they may seem.'

'All this is some sort of divine message?' Peter said heavy with bitter sarcasm. 'If I'm expected to believe that crap God needs to write more plainly.'

In his chair, Eli remains silent allowing Peter time to process what was said. Peter remained motionless for a while until his eyes briefly blinked back to the table, but he avoided looking directly at Eli. Eli thought Peter appeared to be such a sympathetic, lost and broken man – a far cry from the energetic picture on the back of Peter's book.

'Sometimes … it's all too late.' Peter said eventually. Eli waits, he can see Peter struggling with some inner turmoil. Peter continues, almost to himself, '… to put things right, make things right.'

'With the women?' Eli takes a guess.

Peter meets his eyes briefly, then ashamed, looks down.

'More a girl,' Peter corrects, 'and a women, that had almost the same sounding names.'

Eli remains silent while attempting to convey encouragement in his face. Peter looks so broken and burden, and ashamed. He can't look Eli in the eye. 'Something happened between me and those two women about a year ago that makes my skin crawl to this day. Something I can't forgive myself for.' Now Peter looks up, 'Was my church Gods punishment?' It wasn't really a question, Peter thinking out loud. Peters shame and grief just radiates off him.

'God doesn't do that,' Eli replied firmly. 'Are you seriously suggesting God is *vindictive*?'

Peter snaps. 'Your Torah is full of God being vengeful, *Rabbi*!'

Eli fires back. 'And full of forgiveness, *Pastor*. Because if He wasn't there wouldn't be anybody around who didn't look like they just escaped Sodom and Gomorrah!'

'Alright. Alright!' He said fed up, and too tired to argue. Peter sighs, cupping his chin in one hand, rubbing it across his several days' beard stubble. So much a contrast to the dynamic, scrubbed and rubbed author portrait on the book back cover. He keeps staring at the table. Eli takes a big breathe and exhales loudly as if releasing tension.

'Remember this morning in the park I asked how serious are your suicidal thoughts? You blew it off, saying people who talk about it never do it.'

'That why you're spending so much time with me? You're worried over nothing?'

Eli wasn't convinced there was "nothing." 'I like you, Peter. I'd like to get to know you. Despite our faiths, I think we have a lot in common. As a man, I think you're a good man. You sincerely believed you were doing the best you could. But I'll never agree with your book. What you wrote isn't faith or even philosophy. It's not even atheism. What you're teaching is anti-theism. It's not enough that you don't believe, you need all of the others not to believe also.'

Peter squints challenging, his shoulders push forward aggressively. He doesn't like his own words holding up mirrors. 'Oh really! Hypocrisy writ large, *Rabbi*. Jew going on about the Christian Bible? *You* Jews didn't and mostly still don't even *believe* Jesus Christ was and is the *Messiah!*'

Eli's face is tight as his fury is stoked. 'Do *you*? Our holy books are – similar – to your Old Testament, you attack them also! You want to get down to the nitty-gritty hypocrisy, welcome to the stage, Peter. Spotlights all on you. You've been teaching and preaching about your Christian Jesus for years, but lying to your family, friends, and congregation at the same time. What did you say this morning? Something like, "I haven't completely found him either. The dual substance of Christ – the yearning, so human and yet so superhuman, of man to attain to God, or more precisely, to return to God and identify with him – has always been a deep and inscrutable mystery to me."'

Peter's jaw sets angrily with his own words in his face. 'You'd make one helluva prosecutor you know that!'

Eli throws down the gauntlet. He spoke in a quiet, precise voice.

'Listen to me carefully. *Really* listen. I have run out of mathematics to count the number of good men and women I've lost in my life. Through the Shoah. After the Shoah. Just because life broke them. In the end, too many looked like you.'

Peter just stares sullen and distant. Eli tries to pick his words carefully. His tone is softer, but almost urgent.

'We all fail my friend,' using the words deliberately. 'I have. We all have. We'll do so again. I am sure you've said something similar to so many who came to you in need. That it's never about failing. It's about forgiving yourself and never repeating it again.' There is a tense pause. The moment is strained.

'But that's the tricky part,' Eli continued. 'That's why talk is so cheap. Forgiving yourself is fine for those who don't have to do it. Believe me I know *personally* there are few things worse than locked in a guilt prison with the jailer your conscience. Peter. Please listen carefully. No matter how your feeling, nothing, I repeat nothing, is worth losing your life, your sanity or your faith over. It just isn't.'

'I appreciate what you're saying,' Peter said glumly. 'I do. But what about everything that's happened. I can't just ignore that. If it isn't God's punishment what is it? My health is at risk. My children are on drugs. My marriage a disaster. I'm bankrupt. About to lose my home. My church is ashes. So you tell me Eli, if it isn't God's judgement of Job what is it?'

Peter stops, almost out of breath. For a time he buries his face in his hands. Eli shakes his head sadly. Eli just didn't know how to pull so many threads together. Eli understood clearly why Peter felt, "like Job" and created his own "ladder" in some desperate pleading to climb out of the pain and loss. Peter's exhausted mind and broken spirit trying to make sense of circumstances, some of his own making, not all, that not only appeared to ridicule his beliefs, but hopes. Eli remembers the comment Peter made while sitting at the park earlier today: "How can I be trusted trusting God." Peter felt betrayed and abandoned by belief that had carried him more than half his life.

Again Peter rubs a hand across his face. Eli sees Peter's eyes red and glassy. It takes him some time to find something in himself to continue. Eli cups his chin in his fingers, his face encouragement and care.

'One good thing. All the bank owns now are ashes.' The bitterness of those words spills from him as his face clenches as a fist and lips pressed so hard together they are like two pale scars.

Eli felt something grip his stomach and twist. He dreads to think Peter is responsible for the fire but now he can't shake it. On top of everything else that would be a criminal act. The dreadful apprehension came over Eli, he could feel it like an ache in his chest, the sense that something bad was going to happen, the *dread*.

'What do you need from me my friend?'

Peter heard the question. For a moment Peter could not answer. He closed his eyes as if he just wanted to slip beneath the imagined waves and disappear. He felt frozen, underwater, as if he were moving in such extreme slow motion that it would take whole minutes for his lips to form words.

Peter felt damned and he knew it ... Yes, it was circular, he was damned because he knew he was damned and therefore *acted* damned and therefore *became* damned ... So there was some justice for his church. Even if he had the strength, Peter avoided staring into pleading and frustrated eyes of Eli.

But the real reason Peter couldn't hold Eli's eyes, was that eyes are the vision of the soul. And even now, Pastor Peter knew he was still lying, holding back the last dark secret of shame, he couldn't face about himself.

For some moments, Eli said nothing, just continued to stare at the man opposite. Every instinct Eli possessed told him he had to discover the hidden agony that was tearing apart Peter's physical and mental health. And it wasn't about finances, his book, or church.

'How did your family take the bad news about your church account?'

Peter shakes his head wearily and sighs. 'They declared war.'

Chapter 6

DOMINATING PASTOR SCHREMBRI'S LOUNGE ROOM was a long richly polished table. At one end, a very sombre Peter sits with his elbows on the table and clasped hands supporting his chin as if praying. A large, opened leather-bound Bible beside him doesn't appear to be comforting. The 17-year-old girl, at the other end, with a mock blond "mullet," vivid purple school jacket with crest, and a purple and white striped tie pulled down and twisted off centre, looks at Leanne with a hand gesture: *"What?"*

Leanne mixes a drink dropping ice into a crystal tumbler followed by a big shot of liquid. She drinks then leans against a wall, and drinks again. Her arms were crossed over her chest, her ankles crossed as if she was gathering and holding her mood, which was like her beverage, dark.

Peter glanced at the huge, antique Bible open on the table besides him. He was quite reluctant to approach the issues. But the longer he stalled, the more restless and impatient the kids became. The girl looked at her mother again, pulling a face, *"Well? We--ll!"*

Leanne finishes her glass and crosses to the bar to refill. She makes a 'show' of sighing.

'I have squash Peter!'

'Can't squash wait just for tonight?' He says stressed. 'It's *our* family, *our* church we're talking about. Aren't our futures more important than your game right now?'

'But it won't be resolved tonight will it?' Taking a seat at the table beside the girl dismissing Peters mounting anxiety.

'Mum! My *soccer!*' groaned the teenage boy sitting opposite his sister wearing the same coloured jacket and tie.

'Like. Driving lesson. *Hello!*' the girl pulling a face as if the world will collapse any moment.

'Mum-mmmy'! She said with an exaggerated play on the word. 'He's not going to sermon us again?'

'Kill me now!' the boy groaned.

'Your father needs to say something.'

'Oh wow. This is so uncool.' The kid's heads are now slumped back on their seats, eyes rolling in exaggerated distress.

Peter eventually cleared his throat, lowered his chin at the same time raising his eyes toward them. 'Things happen, um, plans, ah, change. Change is forced upon us and sometimes we don't understand why. Happens to everybody, including Christian families. Being a Christian doesn't protect you from *life*. Light and dark, good and evil. The devil sets out to destroy all that's good.'

The kids look at each other blankly, then simultaneously, stare puzzled at their mother: *"What's he on about?"*

Leanne finishes her second glass. Announcing her roiling impatience with a deliberate slap of her glass on the table. However, the good trooper Peter preaches on …

'Sometimes …' another throat clearing. '… When things go wrong or don't appear to be working out, especially our plans, we just have to trust and believe God has better plans for us.

We'll throw our burdens upon the Lord, and He'll make a way when there is no way. A light to our troubles and all truth shall be revealed.'

He stops, looking at his family at the opposite end of the table. 'If we all tighten our belts and pull together ... a family guided by the Lord. Christian families have a special calling to be an example to others, especially in tough times where sacrifices have to be made without grumbling or complaining, standing together against Satan's kill, steal and destroy. Ah, huh, sacrifices *do* have to be made.'

Even to himself, his voice came out feeble, with a pleading quality for understanding and support. He searched their faces, all needy and appealing, looking for a glimmer they would pull together. But Leanne didn't give him the complicit nod he was angling for; her lips pressed into a tight, resentful line. He opened his mouth to speak again but she cut him off.

'Oh for God's *sake* Peter!' Leanne snapped. 'We've all got stuff to do tonight!'

He shook his head and wriggled back into his chair. At that moment the kids looked at their mother, each other, and back to Peter and they knew that this wasn't going to be welcome news.

Peter took a deep breath. 'We, ah, saw our church accountant today. Unfortunately things are going to change, we, ah ...' He desperately wanted to pick his way slowly and looked at his children appealingly. 'If it wasn't going to affect you directly I wouldn't say anything.'

Leanne snaps. 'Your fathers broke. Church is broke. Bank owns church. Bank owns house.'

Peter stares critically at her for usurping how he wanted to discuss this. Leanne's fixed accusing stare lets him know dropping the lead balloon was deliberate. Whatever pantomime the kids indulged a few moments before the news was like a bucket of ice water in their faces.

Their eyes do a circuit from looking at each other to their mother, finally, Peter who isn't looking at anybody except his folded hands.

'Wow!' The girl said. 'No way.' Her face was animated and wide-eyed.

'Heh! That's so whacked.' Said the boy looking at his sister confused, who shrugs, not following, equally lost.

'So … What happens now?' She asked. 'We're going to be cool aren't we Mum?' But Leanne's glare is drilling into Peter.

'Your fathers about to tell you how *he's* going to fix things. Tell them what genius plan *you*, bank and church board came up with.' Her voice had the bite of a blunt drill in metal and Peter winces inwardly.

Peter didn't say anything. Just sat there frowning as though his brain was shuddering between the different hideous scenarios that could have led to this outcome.

'Bottom line Mary and Jacob … the church cannot … cannot carry certain things any longer. Our house has been living way, way beyond its means. The church board and bank made it very clear there needs to be significant belt-tightening and changes.'

Peter then went on and tried to explain their family had been spending more than the church earned for some time. It wasn't complicated, aggressive or blaming. No finger pointing or fault finding. Every word uttered had a word of prayer between them – he needed them, needed them to understand, to be a family. He was encouraged when Mary appeared to spring to the families defence.

Mary met the eyes of her brother who pinched his eyebrows at her. She then looked at Peter. 'Screw them. Screw the bank. Screw the board. It's still your church.'

'I pray it was the Lord's will to be that simple, Mary. The *bank's* church.'

'You don't tell them, I will.' Leanne ordered. She stared at him, her eyes hooded and disdainful.

'After much prayer and talks with the bank and church board, as tough as it is, and I know it will be tough at the start, your mother and I decided …'

If looks were a scythe, Peter's head would be decorating the table as her eyes slice down the table to his. He immediately backtracks. He again clears his throat.

'College fees is a big one. I've spoken to the Aden College Dean. Unfortunately … next year you may have to transfer to state school. Many are absolutely top academic performers,' he said quickly, trying to sandbag enough holes before the inevitable protest wave. 'With extremely highly credited teachers and curricula.'

But no verbal sparring, just deafening silence as three pairs of eyes bore into him. He felt like he was facing family inquisition.

'I wish I'd had the opportunity to deal with it earlier and it hadn't blown up in our faces. But it is what it is. I'm very sorry about that. I know if we pull together as a family we'll get through this okay? I need you on my side to sort out what to do next.'

Mary cocks her head at her mother. No adolescent hysterics of the end of the world. Just the silent message between siblings as they, first, look at each other, then at Peter. From supportive moments ago, Mary now flexes her claws.

'Mummy. Peters unwell. Call somebody.'

Peter expected resistance but not like this. Perhaps if he explains in a practised way by using the familiar messages he knows best.

'Believe me, I have the whole family's best interests at heart. If there were other choices I'd make them? I remember this story. Anyway, the workman did not know what was growing on the mountain …'

'Mummy,' Mary said mockingly, 'he *is* going to sermon us again. Isn't that abuse?'

'Like kill me. *Again! Now.*' Jacob rolled his eyes.

Leanne shot them both a warning and sipped her drink. Mary shrugged. A promise to be quiet. Jacob rolls his eyes.

Patiently he repeats, 'They did not know what was growing on the mountain. They just knew they had to get rid of it before construction could start. They tried to hack at it, but it was too thick. They tried explosives, but each time the dust cleared, the stuff was still there. They even tried burning it off with laser beams, but they could not get through to the roots, which were very, very deep. So they decided to use a poison bomb. Safely inside their protective shelters, they watched on their monitors as the bomb exploded over the mountain. The shroud of deadly gas descended, and the changing colours on a computer image showed the stuff quickly dying until it had all gone. They breathed a sigh of relief, but, as they set out, someone noticed on a monitor that the stuff was reappearing and growing back. Strangely, the stuff did not grow beyond where it had been before. It just grew back to where it was before and then stopped.'

Peter pauses, taking a breath to calm himself. 'It just so happened the boss was a Christian.'

Jacob rolls his eyes again. *'Here we go.'*

'Like. Wow.' Mary said, shaking her head.

'So he prayed and wanted to know what they should do. While waiting for an answer, they dropped another poison bomb, but the same thing happened. They tried again and again. But, however dead the stuff appeared to be, it kept coming back. This is ridiculous, said the boss. Get the dozers. So they razed the mountain until it was no more. The complex of buildings and spaceports that were to occupy the mountain were redesigned for flat ground and quickly built. Two days after the opening ceremony, cracks began appearing in the floors and walls. The stuff had returned. It did not tear the building apart or upset the foundations. It just grew a bit and then stopped. The team returned and inspected the stuff. Well, what do we do now? Someone asked the boss. He shrugged. But God had answered his prayer. So he said ...' And Peter stops.

'What?' Mary said rolling her eyes and screwing up her face with exaggerated indifference.

'We learn to live with it.'

Kids stare at each other, followed by a contemptuous slow clap. Peter shoots a look at Leanne for support. She just stares back.

Peter drops his eyes and sighs, his fingers steepled like an 'A' frame.

Leanne clicked her tongue in irritation. 'What's wrong with you Peter? Look at your hands. Even your fingers think they're in church. This is our *dining room* in case you haven't noticed! Why can't you just talk to Mary and Jacob as their father and me as my husband for once like a *normal* family?'

'I'm sorry. For everything. I really am. Everything is my fault okay? That what you want to hear? I cannot tell you how serious things are. As head of our family,' Peter doesn't miss the deliberately mocking eye roll from his wife. 'And the church, I accept responsibility. If the board had kept me informed and done their job ...' Spreading his hands in a helpless, confessional gesture, then chopped the air with his hand cutting off the thought.

'Nonetheless. Nonetheless, it is what it is. We've all had a part to play to get in this mess and we're all going to need to pull together to get out.'

'Oh wow. I'm so over this already. You're not dumped in a crap state school.' Mary said.

'You're screwing us over because we got busted. This is payback!' snapped Jacob.

Peter fought himself to sound even-handed. 'Getting arrested didn't help! You have no idea how much I was forced to borrow from the church to keep you out of jail. My dear God, you got off with a warning and no conviction. Special Counsel was over a thousand dollars a day.'

'Aren't your children worth it, Peter?'

Peter ignored the sarcastic comment. 'That's *not* the point, Leanne! Look at how much I had to "donate" to Aden College just so they could finish this year. They were going to expel you on the spot! You two have no idea.'

'Why don't you just lecture us *again now*, and we can get it over with!' Mary sneered, tossing her mane that wasn't there, her clipped-back hair made witchy by the gesture.

Peter studies his children for a moment, and they returned his look with their heads cocked back in that defiant adolescent give-us-all-you-got set. He felt like he could evaporate from the seat at that moment and they wouldn't notice. They would look at the lingering, smoking mist and give it no thought; so long as the comforts were maintained, the world would turn. A mix of despair and outrage deflates into the realities of dysfunctional family life. The bluebird of happiness had long since flown the coup. Sadly, Peter knew that it had been that way for a long time. Where was God? Peter thought. So many prayers for so long. Where was the divine help? Some still small voice that whispered guidance, support and direction – heaven was silent. Again. Peter could see Mary talking, but the part of his brain that deals with listening seemed to have derailed; he stared without really hearing her.

Mary was imitating his voice, frowning theatrically: *"You know Mary and Jacob, I'm very concerned about your soooo ba-a-d behaviour. Associating with bottom feeders, selling drugs* – She looks across the table with mock innocence cocking her eyebrow at her brother, and pretends to whisper, *'Anybody who doesn't do the crystal palace is a bottom feeder.'*

Jacob snorts trying to hold back laughing out loud, as Mary mockingly continues. *'I'm a public figure, Gods fan club pres of the community and that's spelled m-e-d-i-a.'*

Peter takes the barbs. 'You can be as sarcastic and as clever as you think you are Mary and Jacob, but I *am* a public figure and churches stand or fall on their reputations in the community not only what they preach.' He takes a breath, trying to gain some control. He wipes a hand across his face calming himself. 'But the church board has forgiven me. I've assured them it'll never happen again on my watch.'

There is a moment when his family just stare as if weighing if he's serious. 'We're busted,' Mary said, 'and the church forgives *you*. Wow. Just wow! How uncool. Are you going to lock us in our rooms?'

Leanne stands and goes to the heavily laden, richly carved bar, to refill her glass. 'That's enough both of you.'

Mary's face flushes and eyes suddenly glisten with an uprush of angry tears. 'Mum! We're not going to some crummy state school. We're not. No way!'

Keeping his voice conciliatory was taking every ounce of his slipping self-control. 'Drugs! *Drugs* in a Christian family. I'm still unable to wrap my head around why you'd both do such a thing. Illegal drugs are demonic. They are of the devil don't you understand? The killer and destroyer of lives.'

'Oh get over yourself,' Mary said furious. She appeared right at the verge of tears. 'You gonna say you never did anything uncool growing up or were you already born "Saint Peter?"'

Peter snapped. 'You broke the law. And God's law. Doing drugs –'

'We didn't *do* drugs.' Jacob said defiantly.

'Do. Selling, my sweet Lord does it matter? It isn't how Christians behave. And you were both raised as Christians, in a Christian house. Now you're acting like you don't even believe in God!'

'God! I'm-so-*over*-God.' She almost spells it out, her face and throat flushed in defiance.

Her comment brings Peter up short. It's hard to hear. He focused on his daughter and son, and they returned his look with their heads defiantly cocked back. Peter slowly fizzles, and turned his head to Leanne, looking for support, but the cupboard was bare. Then he dropped his eyes and sighed, passion turning to husk.

There was nothing he could say or do; there was nothing anybody could do. They were "lost" in his opinion – he couldn't even "save" his own family. Peter looked deflated like he'd been for a moment a balloon of bravado that somebody had just stuck with a pin. Now he was just weary and exhausted as if he didn't see why he had to go through this.

'Get yourselves ready. We're leaving in five minutes,' Leanne said. Mary and Jacob stand.

'Why wouldn't you tell the police who gave you the drugs?'

Mary laughed, dismissing the question. 'We don't know.' The siblings met each other's eyes and something passed between them. 'Who cares? Somebody as school just had them. It's no big deal. Besides, why would I tell you that? So you can drive round and have a word. Give them a scripture? Cast out demons? Go around and preach to them? Wooo … bet they're shaking in their boots.' Mary looks at him. She made a sad, pretend face. 'Poor, Peter,' she said. 'You don't get it at all do you?'

Peter sinks in his chair even further watching Mary and Jacob leave. His anger collided with his despair at their disrespect, their rudeness. He could order them back to apologise but nothing good would come from insisting on more confrontation now. How had we become this family? Leanne pulls out a chair closer to Peter and sits. She drinks and then swirls the liquid around in the glass as if feeling the same spin of agitation and emotions.

But Peter is hardly focused consumed by his own emotional grief. 'They never call me Dad,' he said. Leanne studied her husband, then looks away, and for a moment almost felt sorry for him – clearly the leading pastor didn't have the faintest idea how to deal with his troubled children.

'And a man's foes shall be they of his own household,' Peter mutters. 'Matthew 10:36. Thanks for your support, Leanne.'

'I was letting you be head of the family.' They stare at each other. Peter is first to look away. 'Sometimes I think they do it deliberately,' Leanne adds.

'What?'

'Misbehave. Just to get your attention. You either ignore them or sermon them. But it's been a long time since you've fathered them. When was the last time you took Jacob to soccer? Mary's having trouble with her driving. Did you know that? You even remember how to work our BBQ? Or maybe they're just rebelling against this monastery we're forced to live in?'

'You're blaming me for our children getting mixed up in drugs? It's a wonder they're not in jail or something. To be let off with a warning is a miracle by the grace of God and a small fortune in legal fees.'

"Let he who is without sin cast the first stone." John 8 if I don't miss my guess.'

'They broke the law!'

"Judge not," Mathew 7 if memory serves, *"lest you be judged."*

Peter stares at her knowing Leanne will checkmate him with scripture whatever he says. She reads his face and silence. 'Yes... I still remember most of them. While we're at it let's throw in Mathew 18:22, *"forgive seventy times seven."* They made a mistake. What do you want from them? Maybe we buy a lamb as a guilt offering, or is that a sheep and sacrifice it on the front lawn? Oh, that's right, we're poor now, better just pinch a couple of pigeons from somewhere. What's the cost of a "peace offering" these days? Can we still afford that? I mean we're expected to do so many weird ancient Jewish festivals and holidays in this house why not? I mean, *why not?*'

Peter saw Leanne's face flushed with alcohol and anger. Peter made one last attempt to move his anger and offence from rampaging to rational. 'Why are you doing this?'

'Because you're such a *damn* hypocrite. You pray all the time to a "father" in Heaven but I don't think you know how to be one. You've turned our house into your own little monastery. Other normal families go from one month to the next. Not ours. You expect us to go through prayer and fasting welcoming each month like it's some sort of so-called new spiritual baptism or something. Let's not forget there's weekly communion, special meals for Passover, and the delivery of the Israelites from Egypt you claim didn't happen but we're still expected to celebrate it. *We're – not – Jews!*' Spelling it out for emphasis.

Peter is stung. He could slam his clenched fist on the table but doesn't. His throat was tight as he forced the words out past the indignation lodging there.

'It's not about being Jew or Gentile. But celebrating the foundations of the Lord because He came not to destroy the Law but to fulfil. It's about celebrating special and biblical historical events and festivals.'

'Really!' Leanne's anger is boiling. 'How many Jews in turn will celebrate Easter and Christmas for us?'

Leanne throws back her drink. Peter focuses on controlling his breathing and squeezing his clasped hands together until the knuckles are white.

'You know what you do Peter? You teach God hate.' It was like she slapped him. He was stunned and all he could do is stare, shocked and wide-eyed. 'And I have another news flash for you Peter. They are *not* getting yanked out of Aden College and dumped in any state school this close to finishing higher years.'

Peter looked at her, his face full of uncertainty and confusion. He's trying to please the church, the bank, and his family – and after all the pie is divided, nothing is left for himself but an overwhelming sense of helplessness. Leanne reads his uncertainty and deliberately sets out to remind him of his "duty."

'Our best friends are in your congregation and their kids go to Aden. They also happen to be the church's biggest financial backers by the way.'

She leaves the sentence hanging with a cocked eyebrow but the message is clear. Peter's mouth pinches in angry frustration. He pushes a shaking hand through his hair, dropping his chin to his chest. His voice cracked. 'Oh, God.'

'Are you listening, Peter?' Her voice had a tone of threatening calm. 'You're a prosperity pastor. So make prosperity. Think of something.'

Peter's eyes dropped, looking lost. He gave a tiny shake of his head but did not really answer, just rubbing a weary hand over his chin.

'Remind God that you've worked hard enough for him.'

He met her eyes and held up his hands, a gesture of helpless failure. Leanne shook her head as if astonished at Peters' incompetence.

'Isn't that the way the prosperity ministry works? What you've been preaching for twenty years? Give fifty dollars to God's work, and he will double, even triple, your donation in gratitude. Or are you saying now that it's all been a lie?'

His face flushed angrily. 'God does bless. It's not a lie. But He's not an ATM. It's the law of Godly abundance – it's a spiritual thing. It doesn't have anything to do with people.'

'Isn't God supposed to supply all our needs?'

'Needs. *Needs!*' his strain erupts: 'Not what –' He stops, biting his lip, forcing himself not to say the word "greedy" '– people *want*!' Leanne smirks, she knows he stopped himself to avoid throwing fuel on their already bitter argument. He looks at her, tension turning his lips to two pale scars. 'There's nothing in the Bible about overdrawn credit cards maxing out eye-watering Aden College fees, private golf lessons, endless salon, and, and heavens knows what.'

'You married me, not God. What did you just lecture us: "Learn to live with it?" I think you're not hearing me. We're your show ponies. Peter, how God has showered you with abundance for being faithful! I heard somebody once say good friends are God's apology for inventing marriage. My good friends are in squash, golf, or the salon. I'm not giving them up. You work to save your parishioners' souls from eternal damnation; why shouldn't tithes be a bit extra for the privilege? Make your sermon *tomorrow* about that.'

Peter just sits in brooding silence.

'Peter!'

Silence.

'Understand!'

'I understand,' Peter said, his voice precise in barely repressed anger.

She stares at him like a challenge until it becomes too uncomfortable for him to ignore. He flicks his eyes up at her and then back to his clasped hands. 'All I've ever, ever wanted was just to teach the truth.'

'Truth is a luxury only available to those who are not involved in its consequences. One way or the other you always pay.'

'You have no faith!'

'Faith is great. Faith should always sustain and support you – but as your standard bearer, not this families pall bearer.'

She looks at him for a moment. He looked so truly lost and

worried that Leanne even felt a pang of sorrow, for him – felt even *tender* for him. It was amazing she could still feel that way, she thought, considering everything that's happened, he was still her husband and father to their children. That part was hard to be angry with. He falls broodingly silent. She seems affected by his sadness. She keeps looking at him then crosses to the drink counter and takes a whiskey glass and a crystal decanter. She puts them on the table near him and fills a glass. He looks at the glass and decanter, then furrows his brow at her.

'That won't help –'

'Helps me!' She said flippantly as she started to leave.

'Leanne.' She stops and looks back with a *"what now?"* irritated frown. 'You have to go I know. Does the family have just a few minutes? Something important to share. Very personal.'

'Our family has had enough *"sharing"* for one evening, don't you think? Talk later Ok?'

Peter looks down, crestfallen. 'Ok.' He closes his eyes and sighs. He said it wearily and impassively as if he'd accepted the absurd and cruel lessons this particular doom had to teach.

Somewhere, the sound of a door closing. Then a vehicle starts and leaves. He sighs … staring into the room without seeing it. He blinks then his rheumy eyes slowly scan the dining room. The antiques, paintings, polished wood and rich leather furniture, everything the flesh would desire.

'All these nice things Leanne. Well they're all on the chopping block too. My wonderful congregation giveth and the bank taketh away. And you know something else Leanne, Mary and Jacob … just to top it all off … I have prostate cancer. All a bit of a shock really. Start treatment next week. I'm so glad I have a family to share with.'

Suddenly his eyes blur with an uprush of tears that cascade down his face.

'I cannot, cannot deal with all this, God.' He looks to the ceiling. His voice was almost a croak. 'Is this some kind of test? Am I really just another Job? I'm supposed to be your Vicar, teaching your love, grace, forgiveness and mercy. Especially mercy. Now cancer. It's never ending. When is it enough? When? My death? Well that won't be long. One way or the other.'

Peter puts his fingers under the thick leather of the big Bible on the table and closes it. It was for him, his spiritual "full stop." He reaches for the glass, raises it like a toast, his voice breaks.

'To Job. Shalom.'

IN THE MALAYSIAN RESTAURANT, ELI is watching Peter sympathetically, his hands on the table. Peter is sitting back in his chair, shoulders slumped, leaning forward, fiddling with a napkin abstractly.

'I was still sitting at the table when they arrived back. She was wrong about one thing, having a few drinks didn't help and all. All I could think about was tomorrow's sermon and how to ask the church to give more. They walked in and just ignored me. I asked Mary how the driving lesson went and all she said was "awful." Then Jacob about soccer. "Okay," and they disappeared into their rooms. Before I even asked Leanne said she was tired and talk tomorrow. Well "tomorrow" meant I'd be behind the pulpit telling the congregation how things could be "all things bright and beautiful" if the coffers were full. I don't mean to sound facile about it, I was just so pissed off with everything. I thought my cancer might kill me and no money might do the same to the church. How ironic. Maybe we can die together.'

Eli watches Peter intently, saddened by his crises of faith and life. He remembers the words of Rabbi Yulen Turovsky, giving in the death camp to a dying man, *Viduy*, "Confession." Viduy is supposed to remind the dying what really matters is our relationship with G-d and with our fellow man, and not material possessions or accomplishments. Eli recalls Yulen stopping the Viuy, looking at Eli and saying, "The dying is easy. It is the living that defeats us."

'I felt so lonely,' Peter continued. 'I had "things," soon to be taken away,' he said bitterly. 'What I didn't have was love. Suddenly, for some reason, John Lennon's, 1967 *"All you need is Love,"* sprung suddenly to mind. And also suddenly I had the theme of my sermon. Remind the congregation that giving a bit extra and helping save the church is an act of love. The Lord will approve of and bless them for it. It all sounded cynical and hypocritical even when I said the words. The necessary, *"business of salvation."* Peter sighs loudly in despair. 'The rich man asked Christ how he could find salvation. Christ told him to give up all he owned and follow him.'

Peter goes silent, burdened. 'What a hypocrite I was. I was no vicar. So I drowned my conscience in the rest of the bottle ... but at least now I had my sermon: *"Love is all you need."*

'Now comes the difficult part.' Peter pauses. Suddenly there is a pain in his eyes, he looks up briefly at Eli, then away quickly as if embarrassed. Eli just waits, the good listener. This is Peter's moment to unload, Eli had encouraged that. Peter is quiet, reflective, and shakes his head as if he still can't accept what occurred himself. He sighs, nods to himself.

'Two things happened. Both to do with women. I had the sermon worked out, but what I didn't know Eli … What I'll never forget, what I can't forgive in myself … was how much that love would break my heart. The first of my shame.'

'That sunday morning the sky was cloudless, dynamic,' Peter said as if seeing it all again, 'everything I could hope for to take advantage of those massive, highly ornate church windows. I can still see a kaleidoscope of colours washing over the altar. Rays from the morning sun shafted through the stained-glass domes embedded high in the walls, creating a glorious spectacle that filled every corner and crevice with light.'

'The sight was awe-inspiring; one that seemed to be straight out of a dream. It illuminated the sacred space with its vibrant hues and reminded all who watched of something greater than themselves – something eternal beyond this temporal world. It was like the promise of eternity to come in this beautiful moment, like a spiritual dazzle.'

Eli could almost feel the tearing at Peter's soul as he spoke. Whatever Eli would hear, he knew this experience of Peters had almost broken him.

'I was one-third of the way through my sermon,' Peter continued. 'I thought it was going well … I sensed the congregation was receptive to the message, perhaps I'd been just tired and over-stressed last night, and the wine didn't help. Anyway ...' Peter stopped, sighing, 'I started to really thank God that there was light at the end of the tunnel when something out of the ordinary caught my eye. It was a face that seemed to be cut from a different cloth than the rest: a small oval face with skin like caramelized sugar and eyes as deep and mysterious as my stained glass windows. She sat four rows from the front, tucked beside an elderly couple diligently taking notes on every word I spoke.'

He stops, almost seeing the face again opposite instead of Eli. 'I couldn't remember seeing her before, certainly, I would never have forgotten that, so sweet face, and those big, searching and embracing eyes looking up at me. But then I noticed her lips moving in silent prayer and realized that she was one of us–just another person searching for spiritual guidance in these uncertain times.'

'The congregation was listening intently, as usual, their eyes darting back and forth between me and their notebooks or following scripture in their Bibles as if expecting some profound insight at any moment. They were eager to hear what I had to say, but also ready to judge or accept each word; relying on me to lead them down a path both spiritually and rewarding, while in turn that path rewarded the church with good offerings.' Peter looks up and shrugs a little as if to say, *that's the way it is.*

'Anyway, before entering the church that morning, I had prayed for strength and guidance; strength to say what was right, and guidance in choosing the right words so that none of them would feel cheated out of their hard-earned offerings when pressed to give even more into church coffers.'

'And now as I looked out over this attentive crowd, humbled by their presence yet fearful my message of need would be misunderstood as selfish, just for a moment, Eli, just for a moment her face and beautiful gaze almost made me stumble over my message, and wondered why God had put this strange girl in my path – and especially why she had such an effect on me. For a moment I felt quite disarmed by her, especially her eyes, eyes that seemed somehow to be reaching out, wanting something, something more from me than just scripture.'

Peter looks at Eli who nods encouragingly. 'As I continued speaking – nervously glancing towards her every now and then hoping for some kind of sign–she leaned forward ever so slightly and met my gaze with a gentle smile; reassuring me without saying a word that God's gift of compassion is greater than all our understanding.'

'I mean, countless pubescent young girls had attended church over the decades and I never saw them as anything but worshippers on their own spiritual journeys, whether they came or went. Leanne, and sometimes by the miracle of threats, my children attended, so anything beyond embracing just scripture wasn't even the remotest consideration. Nor should it be for a man of God. Such temptations are traps for others, and my job is only to teach the Word.'

'From the pulpit, as the sun rose higher it peered through the stained-glass windows casting colourful hues of light that shone upon the congregation they were not even aware.'

'It was all so spiritually uplifting for the congregation, Eli, except for me. This service had begun oddly, I reflected, and I didn't know why. I was well over feeling nervous after taking countless services. They were my sheep, and you don't fleece them in the spirit or pocket. But ... today was different. Nervous panic had started to flood through me, I remember, bringing with it its own doubts and uncertainties, was it the fight with the family yesterday, because Leanne or the kids had hardly said two words to me since? So many things loaded up; health, money, marriage, future, past. Everywhere I turned there was something else. Poor Gary was still haunting me. Should I have stayed and done more, was I neglectful, and did my neglect lead to his accident and death? Only God can answer that but knowing that did nothing to rest my conscience.'

Eli watched Peter pause briefly, thinking, recalling the day. 'I was ridiculous,' he continued. 'It was like these cold fingers gripped my stomach muscles tightly, and I started to feel sweat spring on my body; just a light sheen on my face and from the palms of my hands, but it was there. The pulpit area had strong lighting and I was far enough back and removed from the congregation that they wouldn't see anything.'

'Panic? With all my experience? After years of countless sermons, I had preached? Panic! Seriously? Ridiculous.'

'I tried to, no that's wrong, I really fought to brush my fears aside but failed. I remember clearly. Had I chosen the right subject? The word I had chosen was love. Did these people really want to hear about love? On its surface, it should have been an easy enough task for an experienced preacher like myself, after all, I'd preached about love many times before. Yet there was something about this particular subject that filled me with dread and anxiety like never before. Had they heard 1st Corinthians, 13 so often that Paul's words no longer held any meaning for these people?'

'Was it presumptuous of me to speak to them of the real meaning of love, of what it meant and how easily it could be killed? Did I have any right to talk of love when the whole service will end on asking for money? And my family. Am I a hypocrite?

Did I have any right to talk about love? My own family is hardly an example of spiritual or physical love.'

Peter pauses and looks up into Eli's face. 'I hope I'm making sense?'

'You're doing fine,' Eli replied with an encouraging smile. 'Take your time.'

Peter sighed again, loudly this time as if the more he spoke, the greater the tormenting burden of memory. 'Where is love under my roof? What do I do? See a priest about a priest's marital failure? Then sermon my own congregation on the importance of love to a happy and stable marriage to bring up children? I cannot recall being so conflicted. I was expected to give a sermon, but what did the congregation expect from it. How many would be still sitting there if they knew the truth?'

It was a rhetorical question, but Eli felt deeply for Peters increasing sadness.

'What did Lee say about truth, truth is fine for those who don't have to live with its consequences.' He stops, looking past Eli into the distance without really seeing. 'I can still remember that day like yesterday. I was so distracted somehow. Focused on my own problems instead of giving my congregation spiritual tools to unburden their own. I glanced out at the congregation before me, taking in their expectant faces as they waited for me to continue. So many negative thoughts came. What if they've heard it all before? What if my words no longer hold any meaning for these people?'

'I could feel a heavy weight pressing down on me as I searched desperately for something inspiring and meaningful to say – something that would truly capture their attention, leave a lasting impression in their hearts and minds. I tried valiantly not to panic as thoughts raced through my mind like runaway horses; yet still, a feeling of uncertainty lingered over me like a dark cloud threatening rain at any moment. This odd, strange fear mixed with doubt till I could feel it like an ache in my chest, the sense that something bad was going to happen, some *dread* I couldn't see.'

'And then there was that girl. I kept flicking a glance at her, but I didn't really want to … as I went on; 'Love is something precious,' I said, and then waiting, one of those meaningful pauses, as they say, for the words to impress themselves on the minds behind the faces. 'It is precious to the one who receives it and to the one who gives it. It should never be rejected because if you reject any love that is offered to you, something within the giver dies. Forever.'

'I remember how intent they were … those faces; oh, so intent. Peering over the shoulders of those in front of them. Faces. All kinds: inquiring, expectant, critical, weary, old, young, blank, troubled, challenging …' Eli observed Peter has his hands gripped tightly together on the table as if afraid if he opened them some part of him would escape.

'But … all I could think … was the face of the girl, with her soul shining out through her eyes.' Peter said, almost as an ashamed whisper. 'A few more words from Paul's letter to the people at Corinth, and then waited while they mulled the words over in their minds and extracted from them whatever they so desired – comfort, hope, inspiration, guidance – whatever.'

'Then … it came back, the panic, I was so stressed I thought my skin was shrinking and didn't understand why. Take it easy. Take your time with the words; give them time to apply their own interpretation of love to the message I was giving. At every point, I knew that I had every face in the congregation waiting for my next words. 'I have your complete attention!' I thought exultantly.

'I have their complete attention!' and a singing was in my ears as though all the angels in Heaven were raising their voices and praising me. At least ... that's what I wanted to think.'

'I remember then ... looking up, to the high wood ceiling beams, those windows of stained glass between them filled with a kaleidoscope of colour as the sun saturated them, shafts of light. It was amazing, like I could feel the Spirit of God working strongly within me, despite all the distractions that seemed to be happening. And the feeling was wonderfully exhilarating. How could I fail in this stained-glass rainbow of a temple with such a powerful force supporting me? It was like the light coming through the windows made me immune, Satan couldn't touch me.'

For the first time Peter looks into Eli's eyes, then at his hands again. 'God! How wrong I was. It was actually a trap. What do they say Eli, pride comes before the fall? Anyway. I paused again praying they'd savour the words, my eyes roving the rows of faces, confident, at least more confident, I had chosen my subject well: *"Love is all you need,"* according to Lennon, I said. The apostle Paul thought so also in his letter to the Corinth church located in Greece.'

'The words came clearly to mind and flowed smoothly as I told them of the message of love inherent in all that Paul wrote. 'If you love someone, you will be loyal to him, no matter what the cost. You will always believe in him, always expect the best from him, and always stand your ground in defending him.' Then I quoted verse 7 in full: *"Love is patient, love is kind. It does not envy, it does not boast, it is not proud. It is not rude, it is not self-seeking, it is not easily angered, it keeps no account of wrongs. Love takes no pleasure in evil, but rejoices in the truth. It bears all things, believes all things, hopes all things, endures all things."*

'I ... at first, I really didn't *look,* more glance, slide over the intent, pixie face peering at me from the fourth row, but … something kept drawing my eyes back. Something I could not define. Something irresistible. I remember I had to take a deep breath to continue, but again I paused. And this time it was not a deliberately planned pause. I just could not help it because I had looked fully into the face of the girl.'

'Oh God,' Peter shook his head, taking a breath. 'Then all these thoughts came; did she come regularly? I don't know; I can't recall seeing her; she might have; did she usually sit there or further back? There are nearly 200 people; I can't remember them all, but for some reason, I think I would remember her. My lips had gone dry for some reason. I had to run my tongue over them quickly, and I saw several faces frown. I could feel my own heart pound. My God! What's wrong with me, I kept thinking. And then I was speaking again, but I was only half aware of what I was saying because I kept my eyes on my notes but …' Eli saw Peter stop and swallow awkwardly. 'God Eli, all I could think of was the intent face of the girl with her soul shining out through her eyes.'

'My voice seemed to falter as I glanced at her again, staring at me with those beautiful, adoring cobalt eyes. They seemed to pierce into my very soul, Eli. She seemed to be expecting something special, and I couldn't help but feel a little intrigued. Could she sense the power of love in my words? Was that why her eyes were so desperately searching mine? Again, I asked God what was happening to me. I was a Pastor, councillor, pillar of the community, *I'm* the one; people came to *me* when they lived in the shadow cast by their lost hope. I gave them light; besides, I'm married. Countless young girls have come and gone over the years. I have to pull myself together … I said to myself thank God Leanne doesn't know what I'm struggling with, or she'd divorce me and take everything, including my church ...'

Peter eventually looks up from his hands, looking appealing, even desperate. 'I suppose all this is starting to sound a bit grubby?'

Eli shakes his head, 'I don't judge Peter. I told you that.'

Peter searchers Eli's face to see if he is lying, but nothing says he is. He sighs and continues. 'But ... at first, if I were totally honest ... I was flattered that a young girl – maybe 17 or 18, would take such an interest in my sermon, should be so deeply absorbed in the words I spoke. Was it the way I presented the sermon? Was it the theme I had chosen? Or was it that she received some comforting message from the text? I was half way through my service now, but felt – distracted. Where was I? Had I spoken those words or had I been leading up to them? What had I meant by that one word when I prepared my notes? I felt confused, lost, and even as I spoke I was wondering what had happened to me? Why had the face of this particular girl so affected me?'

'Then I knew. It came to me. I had known all the time, but before it had only been a vague thought. Now it had crystallised in my mind and I stopped in mid-sentence and again the faces frowned: *She's in love with me!* I told myself.'

'My mind was awhirl as I had these thoughts. I fought to look out across the many faces focused on mine. How can there be two hundred faces but the only face I saw was hers?'

'I could hear the words echoing in my mind, and it was as though someone was shouting them out aloud, so loud that everyone in the congregation could hear, 'The girl is in love with me!' And there would be that horrid, cringingly awful moment when the congregation would all turn to look and crane their necks pointing and leaning their heads together that the girl was in love with me. Once again, you understand, for another brief moment, I was flattered; flattered by the love of a girl for a middle-aged pastor. Then reason took over, and conflicting emotions fought for supremacy inside me. But this is absurd! I am a pastor, an aging pastor, and by some miracle, still married! How could a girl so young, who looks almost the same age as my daughter, love a man like me? I was mistaken. I had misread the look in her eyes. I must *surely* be deceiving myself!'

'I remember … lifting my eyes from my notes and stole another look at the girl's face. And then I was sure. I was convinced that she had fallen deeply in love with me. I was conflicted Eli, the scripture just seemed to keep coming at me, not wanting to end. I forced my eyes on the notes, although I didn't need them. I was trying to focus and talk to the whole congregation and not just those needing eyes reaching up to me. "*If I speak in the tongues of men and of angels, but have not love, I am only a ringing gong or a clanging cymbal. If I have the gift of prophecy and can fathom all mysteries and all knowledge, and if I have absolute faith so as to move mountains, but have not love, I am nothing. If I give all I possess to the poor and exult in the surrender of my body, but have not love, I gain nothing.*"'

'I stopped. I felt almost, I don't know, out of breath, but the words kept coming … And love is,' I said, hurrying on desperately, "*Love is very patient and kind.*" Because I had spoken them so often, the words still came, but I was not fully aware of what I was saying. I looked over the watching faces, and again they met those of the girl. Met and held them. Locked there like some invisible wave-lengths along which flowed the love that the girl felt for me, flowing from her to me and each knowing of this love.'

'The power of the love that was in her gaze made me want

to look away, yet I stayed there, Eli, transfixed by her stare. I felt my heart skip a beat as I began to acknowledge the fact that she had more than just "feelings" for me. It was a feeling that both terrified and exhilarated me at once; I could feel warmth flooding through my veins like molten lava. I hadn't felt that with Leanne for such a long, long time, but, Oh God, God, no, no, I'm going to hell! Matthew 5:27 *"You shall not commit adultery, but I tell you that everyone who gazes at a woman to lust after her has already committed adultery with her in his heart."* Especially if the woman looks a bit older than my own daughter!'

'So I prayed: *Oh God no*, I prayed silently, my eyes closed. Oh God, don't let this happen. Please, God, take this knowledge from me and do something to dim that adoring light in her eyes. Please, God, speak to me and guide me! But, but God remained silent as usual, and I was left confused and unsure of myself. I again prayed for some revelation that did not come.'

'Oh God, I asked myself, and Him, why, why did you make me choose this subject? Why did God, who knows everything, allow me to speak about love when I had so many other subjects on which I could have preached? Is this *another* test? But not even Job had *this* temptation!'

'Love. Love in all its forms,' and every time I spoke *that* word, I believed a fresh flame was kindled in the girl's eyes. Why? Why, God, didn't you warn me, I prayed. Why did you bring this girl here today? What are you doing to me? Why did you allow her to offer her heart to me through her shining eyes? What are you saying to me? Let me *see* what you're saying.'

'Then I got angry … with God. So angry. Questions. Questions. I have so many questions, I told God. One day I'll write a book, I threatened, about your book, full of questions I've always had.

About prayers never answered. Scripture never read. But I had to finish the sermon, so went back to it quoting scripture and said, there are three things that remain, "*faith, hope, and love – and the greatest of these is love.*" Amen. I started with great expectations and ended so glad it was over. There was only one way to break this: talk church business. The hard, unemotional, pointy end of business reality, nuts and bolts that kept the ministry going. After all the sweet charity and boundless adoration of songs, sermons, prayers and worship, faith is a business like any other; it just comes with heavenly ever-after promises.'

Peter shook his head. 'I don't mean to be fascial about this … I'm too tired to pretend.'

'Do you want more tea or coffee, Peter?'

'No, I – No. I'd rather get this over with.' Peter took some moments to gather his thoughts. Eli could see the pain in his face.

'Before I dismiss you, I said, the Lord spoke to me about receiving and extra offering. I'm not asking what you don't want to do – I'm going to ask so the Lord's heart doesn't break any more. I'm going to say it again, ask you all to help me so the Lords heart doesn't break any more. And why is the Lords heart breaking? And He said from His heart to mine, that He is feeling cheated by some in our church. Malachi 3 says, "*Will a mere mortal rob God? Yet you rob me. But you ask, how are we robbing you? In tithes and offerings. Bring the whole tithe into the storehouse, that there may be food in my house. Test me in this, says the LORD Almighty, and see if I will not throw open the floodgates of heaven and pour out so much blessing that there will not be room enough to store it.*"'

'This glorious church is not mine, I remember saying, I'm only the administrator; it belongs to *you*, this congregation of God's children. I wasn't going to ask for an extra love offering but here's the word of God so we must obey that and have to ask this. I wasn't going to do it but God insists on this not me. I want you to help me God said, for His sake, not mine. So his cathedral, his edifice, his church remains safe – because there are many demons who don't want God's word taught, lives healed, souls saved, who want to bring down this very building, God's kingdom, and it's your tithes, your donations, keeping it safe from the Devils destruction. So God weeps and worries about how this, His building, will stay open, keep His glorious sun beams shining through those magnificent windows. So I said to God, I will obey you, but I ask a boon Lord, a love favour. I know my congregation, I know they'll freely give if you will do something for them; so I asked the Lord for every dollar given to my ministry give them a soul into the Kingdom that comes in, would be a soul saved for the kingdom of God.'

'Then ... I talked about Second Corinthians 9 as you know Eli says, *"Each must give as has decided in his heart, not reluctantly or under compulsion, for God loves a cheerful giver."* So I said I really believe this – if everybody here dug deep for God's glory he would reward you with more abundance you've ever known because God and you built this "Crystal Palace" to His glory through his devoted sons and daughters, the last thing you need is God upset by a lack of giving for the scales of eternal life of eternal donations is weighed by many things. In the generous hearts you don't want to be found lacking on the day of judgement because we don't know when that will be, a year, a month, day or minute. So to be sure your name is written in the book of life in heaven by giving freely here on earth – your offerings are given as investments on earth because God sees you as a cheerful giver, and in heaven, when good and bad is weighed on the scales of judgement, that giving will have those scales swing big time toward God's reward as a good and faithful servant.'

'These investments will reap future benefits and blessings in return, I told them. Then I said I know 99.99% of people are not bad people because I know they are all here in this church. The more you give to me the more I give back to you, the more God gives to all. And when tribulations and trials come, you can say, you see God, I've been faithful to sow and to give unselfishly and obeyed your word, I have got my receipt from my sowing and I have a need and I'm cashing in that receipt. It's always been about you Lord, to do your work Lord, to put a financial shield around this your house of pray and worship.

Make your vow today, now, and then obey the Lord and so that seed and watch what God will do for you and with you, your family, your work, every part of your lives watch that seed burst forth in glorious abundance. Then you can tell us all about your miracle, because remember His promises from Malachi 3 –'

"Test me in this," Eli said, *"says the LORD Almighty, and see if I will not throw open the floodgates of heaven and pour out so much blessing that there will not be room enough to store it."*

'Yes that's right,' Peter said. 'But thinking it wasn't enough to just quote the Bible, I added a bit extra and said, you all can sleep well at night saying in your prayers, do not weep or worry about how this, your building will stay open Lord, my giving will keep your glorious sun beams shining through overhead through those magnificent windows. I and my family have given joyfully Lord, now shower us with your miracles and blessings, because I know for every dollar I give, that is the meaning of true love as Paul wrote, for not only is a soul is saved into the Kingdom, but you sure up your heavenly receipts for judgement and watch Gods storehouse of miracles burst out with abundance in your lives in every way. Amen.'

'While I was speaking, Eli, not really listening to what I was saying ... in fact I was praying, that when I finished, when I looked up, that girl had lost interest and had stopped looking at me. I closed my eyes, but not before I had again seen the soul of the girl reaching out through her eyes, reaching out lovingly toward me. Toward me, a man of God, towards me, at my age, from a stunning young girl. My mind was awhirl as I had these thoughts; I knew the sermon was coming to an end. I fought to look out across the many faces focused on mine. How can there be two hundred faces but the only face I saw was hers?'

'I looked down closing my eyes, thinking what a fool I am, I am wrong. I am imagining something that does not exist, I am just a terribly unhappy man. Soon I will open my eyes, and she will be looking elsewhere, talking to some companion – the pastor forgotten. I prayed. With every fibre of my being, I prayed that this would be so when I opened my eyes.'

'But it was not so. The girl had not moved. Illogically, I wondered if she had even blinked.'

'My heart raced, God, Eli, my stomach churned with conflicting emotions. It was the kind of feeling that only comes at the crossroads of life, when decisions must be made, and our very beliefs about ourselves are challenged. I had been struggling to take control of my life for a long time now, as I sought to find a way out from under my oppressive, sterile marriage. My wife had become increasingly controlling over the years, her tongue like a lash that seemed never to rest; so it was no surprise that I was sometimes tempted for something different. I was just looking for a female companion, a friend, nothing serious, at least that's what I convinced myself. But when this young girl looked at me with such obvious adoration in her eyes, it threw all my assumptions into disarray.'

Eli watches compassionately as Peter drops his head into his hands, covering his face, as if trying to block out the memories. Eventually he looks up, sighs and leans back in his seat as if exhausted.

'But that's not all. Not the worst of it. I couldn't control my imagination. It was like I was in two minds, one in the church … the other, I don't know. I started to doubt what was real. I *believed* there she stood before me in church on Sunday morning, her gaze unwavering while the congregation sang its hymns. She was fragile in appearance yet glowed with an inner strength which belied her delicate form; stillness exuded from her being like a silent promise of love and understanding. Despite having heard too many stories of other pastors who'd succumbed to temptation and professional and domestic disasters that followed – I felt deeply drawn towards her innocence for what could have been no more than a brief moment in time.'

'I don't know how else to explain it … the air around us thickened with expectation somehow, as we locked eyes across the pews; it seemed our collective breath had been held in anticipation of whatever might happen next in this unexpected encounter between pastor and parishioner. But then reality struck like a bell toll announcing the end of day's respite: I am married! Married to a woman who would undoubtedly never understand or accept such feelings if they ever became known beyond these four walls! As quickly as it had come upon me this strange sensation dissipated leaving only confusion in its wake.'

'I tried desperately to order my thoughts but found myself increasingly torn by contrasting emotions: one part longing for something infinitely precious yet completely impossible; another part feeling lost within its confines – an older man surrounded by youth yet unable or unwilling to let go of his past life. The time suspended between these two conflicting states seemed both infinite and fleeting as I eventually broke off our gaze and returned to reality: I was wrong! There would be no escape here today after all.'

'I pronounced the Benediction … left the pulpit and moved down the stairs into her aisle and walked slowly towards the girl, not wanting to seem too eager or desperate, but before I could reach her row of seats, the moment had passed, and all around us people started moving again; standing up, moving into the aisles, toward the front door. As if they had never noticed what had transpired between us.'

'My final words had been almost whispered in reverence for this mysterious girl and her precious gaze. I was tempted to allow, for a few moments, the temptation as she slowly rose from her seat into the aisle, and started walking towards me. The congregation around us was now quietly filing out of the church. What exactly had been accomplished there today has yet to be seen, but I wanted to believe they all felt that it would indeed have an impact on their lives somehow. But all cares and concerns faded away when the girl came closer, tenderly placing one hand on my arm as if asking me to remain where I was. To wait for her … and spoke in a low voice that was only meant for me: "You spoke of love tonight with such depth and emotion … I can feel its power radiating from your words still. It is almost like you are saying something real yet unspoken between us?"'

'But then something happened that gave me hope: an almost imperceptible gesture of fondness from her side before she left – a gentle brush of fingers against mine. In those fleeting seconds, everything changed for me; suddenly, it seemed like all my doubts were gone and what remained was pure certainty: this girl loves me!'

'My heart raced as she held my gaze steadily until finally breaking away and turning towards the door with a certain graceful ease about her movements that left me wanting more time with her – more conversation, perhaps? But she was gone just as quickly as she had come, and suddenly, I found myself alone once again in my beloved church, wondering if perhaps our paths could ever cross again ..?'

'My heart felt heavy as I watched her walk out and disappear into the crowd.'

'For days afterwards, I could not stop thinking about our moment together. Every day brought with it a new realization until one night when I finally accepted what had been true from the beginning: that beautiful young girl was madly in love with me …'

'You know the worst of it Eli? All of that was in my head, imagination. I was still standing behind the pulpit, my place of office, my authority, and this going on. I screamed at myself *'Stop It!* That's enough! Where's all this coming from? All through the Bible men have been tempted and failed. Sampson and Delilah, David and Bathsheba, Solomon had so many wives and concubines … But why it is happening to *me? Why* doesn't my faith protect me? Why is God failing me again? Failing to protect me? These imaginings, impossible things with her!'

'But that … wasn't the worst I'm ashamed to say. Then came God's judgement for my guilt, punishment for the failed vicar. I closed the service, going down the aisle toward the front door,

I … I walked passed where she was sitting, not looking and took my place at the door. All the asking God what I should do when she comes up – open my eyes to see the truth, I prayed; how to kill this love, her adoration with understanding on either side and without hurt.'

'Then the faces were moving out. More animated now and joined to bodies. Talking together so that a constant buzz hung over the shuffling queue moving down the aisle and through the double doorway, shaking hands with me, as they passed words of appreciation and thanks for my message – promises of extra tithes. I gave my thanks, words that reached my ears while my smile remained fixed and my eyes sought the girl from the fourth row.'

'And then I saw her leave her place, alone, and move up the aisle toward me, a large bible in one hand and in the other a white envelope. She was carefully making her way just touching the top of each row of seats with her eyes fixed on me. The love is still deeply ingrained in their shining depths; reaching out to me and begging for a smile, a response, even a recognition of her love. Anything that she could take home with her and hug to herself through the coming week and treasure in her heart and renew next Sunday and …'

'Oh God, no. Not that! I could not allow the girl to go away with that in her heart. My mind racing to think what best to do and say. It all came up with a jerk that made me jump as an older woman looked at me curiously as she took my hand to shake and felt it tremble.'

'Then she was standing beside the older lady. She reached out to shake my hand – to feel the warm response that she was sure would flow from me to her. In her eyes, it was plain. Because her heart and love was in her eyes.'

'Take it! A voice shouted in my mind. *Do it!* Take her hand. Smile at her. Can't you see that a world of happiness lives in the touch of your hand? That's what I told myself. Take her hand – that's all you have to do!'

Peter stopped. He looked into Eli's eyes and Eli could see such pain such pain in Peters face.

'But I did not take her hand.'

'I glanced briefly at the girl and ignored her hand, she was left standing there with her hand outstretched and the love still shining in her eyes because it had not yet had time to die. Now feeling hurt and foolish and wishes the ground would open up and swallow her. She must have wished she could step into a deep hole – into oblivion. And my rejection of her hand did that.'

'My gaze was drawn to the older woman's face, but I was not looking at her. I was watching the girl while my heart twisted.'

'I saw her lower her hand slowly and turn away, her head held high, ready to defy the world. I saw her eyes half-closed, but not before I had seen the sad, disillusioned look that had wiped away the shining adoration moments before. Saw how she fought to hold back the tears, hold them back until she could be alone.'

'That was a wonderful service today Pastor,' the older women said. She was wearing a hat that must have come from her closet in the 1950's, and her face a little too thick with makeup to hide the many creases and wrinkles. '*Love. Love*, so important to our lives, the very heart of our Lord. I was so moved.'

'I did what was expected … smiled my gratitude but the eyes of my heart if not in my head were focused on the girl. And then she said something I'll never forget, I'll never forgive …' 'Oh, I'm sorry,' the women said. 'Have you met Melanie, Pastor? My niece.'

'I felt my breath catch and my throat tighten as my eyes looked between the girl and the woman. Melanie's eyes stared into mine in pools of devotion and love that I felt I could just jump in and sink to the bottom in them. But now all I could still see was the confused, hurt look of a child who had been in love but now felt that life in my love was a lie. I don't know, it was like my mind had been moving in slow motion behind the words that suddenly caught up.'

'Your niece?' I heard myself say from somewhere.

'Do you really believe the Lord Jesus will heal if we always pray and give thanks, Pastor?'

'Oh yes. A hundred times so. Isaiah 53:5 says: *"But He was wounded for our transgressions, He was bruised for our iniquities; The chastisement for our peace was upon Him, And by His stripes, we are healed."* The ultimate plan of God is not only divine healing but divine health. God smiles his blessings, especially on those who give generously.'

'The woman, I could feel her grief and sadness, she looked at her niece whose eyes had not shifted from my face. 'We can't give much. I'm on a windows pension … and Melanie is receiving disability. She lost her sight after an accident when she was just ten.'

Eli saw Peter drop his eyes to his clutched hands held like prayer on the table. He shakes his head.

'For a moment, Eli, I felt my knees give and my heart stop, I stared into those beautiful, adoring eyes. What had I missed? Again I felt that disorientated swimming in my stomach, the tug of fear … shock, humiliation. The glow in her face, the radiation of love that blazed through her eyes was for God, not for me. Through my voice, my message, she saw *Him*.'

'She's –'

'Yes, she's blind.'

'Oh, God.' I thought I heard myself say from somewhere. *Oh my dear God Jesus, oh no Jesus,* I kept repeating over and over in my head.'

'You'd never know would you, she's just wonderful.' The women shook her head tiredly. 'All our family has prayed for God to be merciful and heal her for so long. But he doesn't seem to hear us.'

'The man with all the words had no words. None. I was drowning in shock and shame. The same hand, a moment ago I had deliberately ignored, the hand that was reaching out to me for comfort, touch, love and care was extended again holding the envelope.'

'It isn't much,' the woman said awkwardly, 'but it's all she has. She wants to give something to the church so God might hear us.'

'I was imploding, almost feeling ill and light-headed. 'No!' I said too loud, too quickly and saw that beautiful forehead frown. 'Please. Don't, Jesus, he *does* hear you, he does, it's not about the – God doesn't heal by the size of your donation.'

'But you said –' said the women looking confused, even alarmed.

'It's got nothing to do –' I remember I had to stop and take a breath, like a shudder, then I made this excuse, this … 'You keep your precious gift, Melanie. It's what God would want! I'm going to pray for you. Everybody will pray for you. You keep it. I promise you God is already listening. Keep praying, Melanie, don't stop. He's a God of mercy and miracles!'

'Melanie stood still as if thinking a moment. But I couldn't look at her face and lowered my eyes. Then the hand holding the envelope went to her side. I had refused her again. First her hand of sharing. And now her offering. I felt ill, sick, as if stomach acid of shame rise into my throat.'

'Nan.' She said. 'I'll wait outside.'

'Of course dear.' I watched Melanie carefully feel her way, touch the door, and stop. Then from where it had been hidden under the bible, she removed a collapsible white cane. She flipped it out and it seemed to lock, then she carefully but confidently manipulated the two stone steps, and as if she could somehow sense where the path edge was, stepped onto the grass. She was almost immediately surrounded by people wanting to talk and thankfully blocking her from my view.'

The women watched her a moment then said, 'She's a miracle. She sees God through blind eyes. It's amazing what she can do. It's like she can see the truth behind what people say.'

"Can see the truth behind what people say." 'I could feel the blood drain from my face, I felt so weak I could go to my knees. 'I've always believed its God's gift to her to make up for her eyes,' the lady said. 'I think she sees in a sense more about spirit and faith than we do with eyes. Do you think that's possible Pastor?'

'I didn't know what to say. There was no scripture, no fancy references, and no sage wisdoms ... just a beautiful Godly soul and her blind, God loving and believing niece.'

'It's just amazing really,' the women continued. 'Sometimes I might say or do something that isn't, well quite right. And she says, "Now Nan, that isn't truth is it?" You know we're both on the pension. I'm her sole carer while her parents work out their divorce. So sad. Oh well ...' She sighed deeply. 'Do you know something strange? For weeks she's been saving to give you a donation. She said God told her, actually spoke to her about what your sermon would be today.'

'I was staring at the women without really seeing her face.'

'Pastor?'

'Yes, I think I croaked.'

'In the Bible it says God searches the heart. I know it sounds strange, but I think Melanie does too. She searches and sees the real heart of people beyond what they say with eyes that can't see. I call that a real miracle.' 'A *real* miracle, Eli.' Peter was still a moment, then restarted himself.

'Anyway … on the lawn it was as if Melanie somehow knew we were talking about her because she did something I'll never forget, she turned her head in our direction and "looked" at me, *looked* somehow, with the same adoration and love, but within that look, almost a forgiveness. I almost broke and cried right there and then, but the stepped forward. "God bless you and your family Pastor. Perhaps we'll see you next week," she said.'

'Yes. I'll look forward to seeing you. The moment I said "seeing" I felt my soul rip … Perhaps guilt does that.'

'God bless you. Especially you Melanie.' Peter shakes his head shamefully, 'Too late then. How pathetic. I don't know if she heard me as the woman crossed the footpath onto the lawn and hooked her arm around her niece and they went down the path.'

'Other church members were still leaving and filing past, but when the last of the congregation had gone I … I just stood there and leant my head on the old oak door that the shining coloured stained glass window inserts.'

'I prayed. Prayed for the biggest hole in the world to open under my feet so I could disappear forever and be swallowed up right then. God didn't let me escape … *of course*. So I just tried to block everything out by closing my eyes hard, Eli. And failed. *Again*. You simply cannot ignore anything like that. Then I went back down the aisle. I stopped where she had been sitting. What was I expecting: her to materialise and me say sorry? Sorry you're blind – or my blindness?'

'The sun must have gone beneath a dark cloud hovering over the church because all the colours in the windows had gone.'

'All of the stained glass windows that usually glowed with bright colours were now muted, crepuscular and dull; as if all life had been drained from them by some unseen force. Even worse was what I found at the altar; instead of being lit up with vibrant light from above, it was shrouded in darkness and gloom as if God Himself had turned away from this place.'

'I remember trying to catch my breath, like I couldn't breathe, I don't remember going down the alter and looking up at the crucifix with Christ still hanging off it ... I went to my knees, looking up at the half-naked figure hanging there, and the anguish within his heart was mirrored in his eyes. Then I closed my eyes, clasped my hands under my chin, and prayed.'

'Please. Father, from the depths of my heart, please, let her hate me and not Thee. God strike me blind. Give her my eyes, I beg you. What have I done to her? God, what have I done?'

'He didn't answer ... as usual. But somebody else did. 'What have you done?' Leanne attacked, her voice was like the scythe of doom, slicing through the atmosphere. 'And who is *"her."*'

'I didn't know what to say. There was no way I was going to confess all that, besides, it was none of her business. All I could think of was, 'The Lord tested me today – and found me wanting.'

'She was having none of that. 'He tests us every day and finds us wanting.' It wasn't the answer she wanted and the tilt of her head and narrowed eyes said so. 'Especially the weak and tempted.' The look on her face told me that she thought the worst, and she wanted answers.'

'I took a deep breath and braced myself for impact. I looked away at something just to avoid her accusing stare as my mind searched desperately for an answer that would satisfy her without revealing too much. 'She was a young lady with special needs I missed.' It wasn't a complete lie, but enough to try to avoid an argument. But Leanne folded her arms not buying it. The best form of defence is distraction. Looking at the ceiling and dull stained glass windows –'

'Is it cloudy outside now?'

'I didn't notice,' she said. 'I understood that to mean she didn't care. I forced a smile I hoped would be convincing and encouraging. Then tried to remind her where we were. You're in *our* church.'

'She ignored that and just reminded me of my duty, to accommodate those, to her, that mattered more. 'Jim and Peggy's Lim's daughter's birthday in an hour remember?' 'I had forgotten and she read that.' 'Well you better start remembering. Lim's are one of your biggest backers.'

'Money. Yeah. Debt. Is it *always* going to be this way? God, I remember thinking, I so hate hearing that all the time.'

She seemed to read my mind. 'Get used to it,' she said. 'This mess won't go away any time soon.' 'I was again the subject of blame and really pissed off. So right there, in our stain glass windowed God-fearing chapel, we had a fight that anybody could hear. Right after my sermon on love. I can't remember the exact words but it went something like … *You* wanted this church Leanne. *Don't make out you didn't.*'

'I wanted what made *you* happy,' she threw at me, 'And I'd support that. Isn't that's what a good wife is supposed to do according to Ephesians 5: *Wives, understand and support your husbands in ways that show your support for Christ?* You ever think to ask *Him* what *He* wanted, before you drowned us in debt for this glass tower of Babel.' Her eyes sliced from the crucifix with obvious adoration back to me with challenge, rejection and defiance. 'Did you build for *Him* or *you*?'

'That's *bullshit!* I prayed every hour it was His will be done. You're so insulting and rude Leanne, you sound like you wouldn't care if we lost the church? It's not just us! It's the congregation. It's their families. What they've sacrificed to help build it. I believed it's what our family and Gods family wanted.'

'Sacrificed? Really? What about family? No wonder your kids are going off the rails. They have everything they want except one thing. You have no idea what our family wants. No wonder we want to enjoy the payoffs. You're always here. *This* is your life and your tomb. "*This!*" *as* she threw her arms around. "*Is* your family."

'I remember thinking I was being railroaded into a corner and hated it – and right then, God forgive me, I hated her!'

'It's my job. What I do. You married a Pastor. A Vicar of Christ who –'

'Who *lies!*' I was stunned. Shocked into angry silence. I was blinking, processing her words. 'I was in the kitchen. You can't believe half the stuff you were telling them? Or do you *have* to believe it because of this glass albatross?'

'I cracked Eli, right then. Lost all control, I yelled at her, I was ropeable. We've had fights before but not like this. 'Listen to me! It's *your* church too. Or don't you want it anymore? Look at you! You're not exactly in sackcloth and ashes. How much did those jeans cost? Don't tell me you and the kids didn't get everything out of the churches success! We lose the church they won't be going to the money black hole of a college any more I can tell you that!'

'Don't threaten us, Peter.' 'We looked right into each other's eyes a moment and neither of us looked away. But her fierce glare left me in no doubt the "discussion" is over. And I thought at that moment, so was our marriage, or deathly close to it.'

'Leanne turned abruptly going up the aisle between chairs to the door. I felt sorry, but it was too late. I didn't want to fight, but didn't want to be blamed either. She stopped at the same doors a few minutes ago where I had rejected and broken that poor, blind girls heart. We just glared at each other, I don't know how long, so much to say and nothing to say. I had just run out of words, hope, redemption and everything else.

Then she said, 'It's a wonder the word didn't stick in your throat and choke you.'

'What word?' I asked.

'Love.'

'Then she left. And I was alone. My church empty. Like I felt. All the light had gone. I stood there, trying to pull it together, I couldn't see any way out or through. Problem was Eli, horrible as it sounds, us going at each other in our church, if it'd ended there … I could've sort of managed somehow. But it didn't. Things got worse, much worse.'

Chapter 7

The crowd in the restaurant was thinning as hours had passed.

Eli poured Peter a coffee from a unique, bamboo covered pot. He remarked that the Malaysian coffee, what they call kopi, required some getting used to because of its robust flavour and scent. They avoid each other's eyes, words already said, words best left unspoken passing between them, others that must be said. Prevarication of awkward spoon stirring, the irrelevant fudge of Peter commenting, the awkward subterfuge of sighs and inner conflicts. The business of silence with so much more to say.

'Sorry I'm loading all this on you. Don't know why I am. Your look says you're pretty disgusted.'

'Eli nods several times. Then smiles reassuringly. 'I don't judge, Peter,' he said. 'You've been doing a good enough job on yourself. Ripping your guts up for how long now? If you were a mongrel of a man you wouldn't care. Because you do care, says a lot. We all fail. Because there's a conflict in every human heart between good and evil. And good does not always triumph. Sometimes, the dark side overcomes what Abraham Lincoln called the better angels of our nature. Even your namesake Peter, the one it is claimed Jesus loved, denied Him three times according to Luke 22, right? But your thinking was wrong. I'm not trying to tell you your business as a man or a Pastor. But people like you and me get up in the pulpit or our bimah; we're Yahweh's voice. When trust is betrayed it's betrayed twice. First the person who trusted Yahweh's words. Then the trust Yahweh put in us to speak them.'

Peter thought a long time. 'In that case, I'd better not tell you the rest because it gets worse,' he said, barely above a whisper.

'If – that's what you want,' Eli smiled kindly. He could see how torn up and conflicted Peter was. Even his hands resting on the table Eli noticed a small tremor. Peter searches Eli's face, really looks, wanting to believe he can be trusted. Peter looks down, he knows he's too traumatised to keep carrying his burdens alone.

'Alright,' he sighs the word. He looks down at his hands. And when he looks up he appears to have made up his mind. 'Because of me ... a life was lost. Didn't do my job. Didn't see the signs ...'

'Has this anything to do with the girl at church that day? Melanie?' Eli asked. Peter went silent, looking at his hands. Eli didn't want Peter to shut down and gently tried to encourage.

'Peter. You want absolution find God. You want a friend I'm here.'

'What if I told you,' Peter said, 'there's something unforgivable. I – I took a life. It will haunt me to my grave. God's final act of judgement on me was the church fire.'

It took a few moments for Eli to process what Peter said. He could feel his chest tighten and stomach tighten. The more Peter confesses, the worse the crises appears. But Eli needs to know more, his voice firm, but steady and encouraging. 'You're saying you're responsible for somebody losing their life?'

Peter takes a shuddering breath. 'The only way I can answer –'

'Isn't that a yes or no answer?'

Peter erupts. Slams his palm down on the table knocking over cups and bouncing cutlery. His hands shakes and sheens with a fine layer of sweat. He looks distraught, wide-eyed, furious but also frightened. 'The only way –' He stops, pulling himself back as customers and staff stop and stare. Peter takes another shuddering, almost panting breath then returns back to business. Peter leans forward in his seat, face taught, strained and pale. He runs a hand through his untidy hair shaking his head looking emotionally exhausted. He starts again, quieter, but the roiling tension remains. 'The only way I can answer is the way I can. The only way is to tell what led up to things. How evil piled one thing on top of the other beyond my control.'

Eli said softly. 'Take it easy, take your time.'

'Kids bought up in Christian families are supposed to set an example. Not worst but best. Especially respecting parents. Bible talks about *"an unruly and rebellious generation."* Make no mistake, they're two very smart cookies, I'm very, very proud ... but I can honestly say I don't understand my own children. I've tried to give them everything ... too much. Maybe Lee's right. Too full of myself and ministry to see it.'

Peter sits in brooding, almost guilty silence. 'Lee was right, the Lim's were big benefactors so we had to go to their daughter's birthday. Jacob and Mary wanted to stay longer and hang out. The Lim's would drop them home later. Of course before we left, I prayed for everybody's safety and care. Ironically, for some reason I only understood later I used 2 Timothy 3? *"But understand this that in the last days there will come times of difficulty.*

For people will be lovers of self, lovers of money, proud, arrogant, abusive, and disobedient to their parents ..."

'Leanne didn't say two words to me, and I was still upset over Melanie. Naturally, I kept all that under my hat. Actually, I was working up to tell her about my prostate business when a phone call sent everything flying into panic and chaos.'

'Lee answered the phone but the speaker button happened to be still on ...'

'Pastor Schembri residence. Mrs Schrembri speaking.'

'I'm George Brewis,' the voice came through. 'I used to go to your church. Look, don't want to frighten you, I live on the other side of Healesville. Your daughter, son and two other kids are in my lounge room.'

We looked at each other. 'They are?' Lee asked.

'Yeah. Look. They didn't want me to call, but there's been a car accident.'

'A car accident!' Leanne blurts out shocked. I was instantly on my feet.

'A car accident!' I repeated, flustered.

'Is anybody hurt? Do they need an ambulance? Can I speak to my daughter?' Trying not to let panic block her thinking but there was a quaver in her voice both of us could hardly breathe.

'They seem to be okay. Pretty shook up. I'll put your daughter on Okay.' Even though we could both hear out the speaker in her stress Leanne held the phone to her ear pinching the bridge of her nose with thumb and forefinger determined to maintain control. We heard some kerfuffle, and then could hear Brewis say: 'Here's your mother,' in the background, then Mary came on the phone, crying. 'Helaina was driving. She came off the road on a bend.'

'Helaina was driving? She can't drive, she's on P's –'

'What! Helaina was driving!' I said.

Leanne cuts me off with an angry sweep of her hand. 'Are you okay? Who else is with you?'

'Jacob and Patrick. I'm fine, so is Jacob. Think the others are. Helaina's walking; she just got a cut to her head. The man put something on. George, the man who phoned you, gave us a lift here.'

'What are you doing on the other side of Melbourne? Why didn't you stay by the car and wait for the police?'

'We haven't called the cops.'

'Why not?'

'Haven't.' There was a silence on the phone as Leanne frowns looking questioning at me. I already had my car keys twisting impatiently in my hands.

'It doesn't matter. Do you know where you are? Put George on.' Leanne tries to take a calming breath. 'Thank you and bless you so much for helping them.'

'No worries. Just did what I had to do. Luckily, I still had the church card in my wallet,' he said. 'They didn't want the cops called. Just as well I came along first and not the cops. Be charged for sure. Car's still there. Thought I better call you guys first. I'll give you my address …'

'Neither of us really understood what Brewis' meant, "Be charged for sure" but obviously bad,' Peter continued. 'We sat in silence thinking about a range of things that could mean. Lee was doing the same, then she said, "They'd been drinking. That's why they didn't stay with the car."'

'I could see her hands twisting anxiously, I knew what she was thinking, and I was praying for the same, alcohol was bad enough, but if drugs were involved again the church wouldn't help this time. Then, I thought what do I do? Report it? What if somebody already has? And if alcohol or drugs were involved – what then? Why? *Why* has God let the Devil do this? Just another Job dump?'

Eli could see the pain and conflict in Peters face. What he was going through seemed to be endless, just like Job.

'If they've broken the law again, I say nothing, what then? I could tell the look on her face she was thinking the same. Confession is not good for the soul. That's *bullshit!* This could finally break our family, and no matter what, I'd be blamed. If I say nothing I'm wrong, if I turn them in I'm wrong. And yesterday in my fight with Lee, she said I had to forgive – no throwing the first stone – but threw all the scriptures about judgement in my face. I was not *there* to take care of my own children was the very clear message. "*Therefore*" this happened. The accusing, invisible finger pointing. Now that it has, what kind of God's vicar am I going to be? One who believes in justice or selective justice? One rule for others but not my family?'

'Do I judge, counsel, and forgive other people's wrongdoings and sins but overlook the bad and, perhaps, illegal things in my own family? If I report it they'll never forgive me. And one day I'll still be judged by God? And what will it look like to others if drugs or grog are involved and the truth gets out? So, in addition to being a failed father, I have become a liar and hypocrite.'

'Do unto my own family differently than I'd do unto others. God's pinned a target on my faith, honesty, and conscience. And the devil takes pot shots whenever he likes, and I can do nothing. And what do I say to other people going through awful times? Pray? *My God!* I never stop praying, and still all this *shit* happens. A faith leaders life is supposed to be an inspiring, hope filled example of how things work with God on your side; not how you endlessly struggle, break your back and bash your head against a brick wall. What am I doing *wrong*, God? What? Please, please, answer me. What am I doing wrong? I lost count the number of times I prayed that.'

'What are you going to do if it is drugs?' Lee asked. That wasn't the question, *Will I turn in my own family?*' I felt sick and lost. 'I'm going to get them help. There's no more chances or excuses.' I could feel Lee's eyes burning into me because I had no idea what *help* meant.

Lee turned her head away and looked out the window. 'We all need help.'

'I felt our family was collapsing like a house of cards, Eli. If God doesn't help, who can? It must be *me*.'

Peter looks up into Eli's face who sees Peters eyes glisten in the lights.

'That's all I could think of praying, Eli, all the way there. What am *"I"* doing wrong?'

'Lee was out the car almost before I'd stopped. She'd hardly introduced herself before almost barging into George Brewis' house. He'd said he used to come to church but I didn't remember him. You know how you pray for the best but there's that little part of you that makes you ready to expect the worst? But that wasn't the case thank God. George had really looked out for them.'

'They were huddle around a table in the lounge room. Both Mary and Helaina, the Lim's eighteen year old daughter, were blotchy with fright and tears. Timothy, the Lim's son, and Jacob were sitting close together as if trying to be "brave" and give each other support. They all briefly looked at us then quickly away at each other as if passing on some message between them. You know how you immediately get that sinking guts feeling there was something illegal.'

Eli nodded and Peter continued. 'Lee comforted Mary and Jacob. Tim was supporting his sister who was shaking with nervous hiccupping. Lee didn't say anything for a moment. Just sat there frowning, I knew she was thinking about all the different hideous scenarios that could have led to this outcome.'

'Lee asked if Tim had called their parents. Helaina almost jumped out of her chair yelling not to call. That's when my heart really sank Eli, I knew something was up then. Lee said they're going to find out sooner or later, she can't keep a car accident a secret. Helaina burst into tears. They were physically okay apart from bad bruising and I knew what was coming. Lee told Helaina they can't keep it a secret, their parents will want to know where her eighteenth birthday gift has suddenly disappeared to. All of them were crying at this stage. Tim asked in his naive teenage hopefulness if we could put the car at our place. Unfortunately Eli, I lost it then, everything boiled over.'

'You *mean hide* it!' I was really angry, totally fed up, all the stress and anxiety over so many disasters were bubbling in my brain like a volcanic boiling mud pool, and frankly, I'd had enough. The earth was flat and I was totally and completely fed up with falling off the edge. Unfortunately I ripped into them all, wanting to know what happened, where the car was, is it drivable? I was shaking, I couldn't control my hands. We could see they were lying and covering.' Peter shakes his head. 'God Eli, they had a smash and I'm flipping out yelling at them, not what a "loving parent" is supposed to do, but Lee had already said I wasn't one so …'

'What happened then?' Eli asked.

'I asked if they'd been drinking. They all said they hadn't. Lee looked at me and we didn't believe them or else why leave the car. Poor Helaina was just a mass of red blotches and tears, but almost yelled that nobody had been drinking, and we could test her. Nobody was looking at Helaina, as if deliberately trying to avoid something. She said she hated alcohol, she was making all the right noises, but her eyes were trying to tell the others something, although they seemed to be deliberately avoiding her. She just lacked the certitude – that total conviction – that the accident was purely due to her inexperience behind the wheel. Helaina started crying again and Lee supported her but I could tell she was as pissed as I was. Neither of us were prize understanding parents that night, least of all me as a so-called comforting pastor. Lee reminded Helaina she's on "P's" and this could all be a horror story with them in hospital or worse the mortuary.'

Just then George Brewis stepped in and said all the corners are hair bend there. Apparently he was following not far behind their car and he said they were travelling way too fast for the road. Lee and I looked at each other and after a bit were ready to put it down to speed and lack of driving experience, especially bad roads, so I eventually said …

'It's only by God's grace and mercy worse didn't happen.' I heard myself say almost by reflex. Perhaps it was the shock of the accident, perhaps just rebellious anger full of tears and embarrassment, I don't know, but Mary blasted at me, "Yeah. Right. As if he cares, what about all the shit that's happened!"

'I'm just standing there, Eli, I don't know, sort of in shock, numb, insulted by my own daughter in front of everybody and a former church member. I tried to get my brain to hurry up with a response, but the force of her accusation paralysed me a moment.'

'I looked at Lee but she ignored me and asked George Brewis if the car was drivable? It was half buried in a ditch he said, a write off, but you can't see it easily from the road so probably nobody would report it. He had a towie mate that for cash would pull it out and take it to his yard on the quiet. He suggested we do that until we work out what we're going to do. I looked at Lee and she gave me a nod, but I had that dreadful gut feeling again something wasn't right, what weren't we being told.'

'I take it your feelings were right?' Eli said.

Peter nods in agreement. 'George Brewis asked if he could talk to me privately in his kitchen. I felt my stomach hit the floor. I could feel Lee's eyes drilling into my back like hot pokers. From memory, this is how it went …'

George leaned against his bench top folding his arms. 'Pastor, you didn't mind I bought them home?'

'George, I can't express our gratitude for your kindness. Whatever I can do to help you in return.'

'No need for that,' George said.

Peter sighs out his stress. 'The Lord was really looking after them sending you along.'

'Bit surprised seeing Mary and Jacob?' Brewis said.

'They're, ah, going through a … difficult stage right now. Lot of school stress, peer pressures, all that.' I really wanted to scream domestics are hell, our families falling apart, we're bankrupt, I'm sick and they have no respect for me or love of God anymore. I felt myself pulling my lips into a tight, angry, frustrated line I'm sure George noticed but was decent enough to ignore.

'Sorry Pastor, but I overheard them talking. They were *hotboxing* before the accident and blame Mary.'

'Hotboxing?' I asked.

George sighed, looking awkward, 'Well, smoking weed with the windows up so everyone gets a lungful at the same time.'

'Oh God!' I heard myself say, almost from somewhere else. 'So ended up in an accident that could have killed them.'

My mind was reeling. Another nightmare scenario. No wonder they didn't want the police there. And it appears Mary was the instigator of it all. When the Lim family finds out they'll blame me and leave the church for certain. Questions will be asked. And right now in the middle of our financial crises. Could it get much worse? Though we were initially ready to blame Helaina, being the oldest, they were saying it was Mary's fault. I felt like if I'd taking a step in any direction I'd be kicking my heart across George's highly polished parquetry floor. Now I recall Mary saying taking drugs was no big deal. Dear God, I heard myself pray, she's been bought up in a Christian home, where God, did I go wrong? Evil has my own daughter, and all my prayers haven't protected her. I felt a total failure and sick to my stomach. When and where will this nightmare end?

'Did they say where she might have got drugs?'

George shrugs. 'Kids get 'em Pastor.' George must have been reading my mind as he looked very sympathetic. 'Look, not my business, especially to a Pastor, and I guess it's harder for you and Lee being community examples, but stuff happens. Kids don't live in a vacuum. They know right and wrong, good and bad. *Their* choice, *their* bad, not yours, know what I mean? How many cops have done their own kids for speeding or drink driving? It's not as if they're turning into pot heads or something.'

If you only knew George, if you only knew, I said to myself. I felt my stupid heart clutch at the possibility that *this time* they she might actually wake up to the fact that if they carried on like this, they'd either blow her chances of getting grades and going to university by getting expelled or end up shunned by everyone as too much liability or worse, go to jail. 'That's very kind, George.' Feeling responsible and guilty for just about everything, it took every ounce of self-control to sound normal, but if I was the problem I had to know.

'Honestly, George. Tell me. Was it me the reason you left church? Something I said or did?'

George looked at me sympathetically. 'Honestly. No Pastor. Not you or the church. Just stopped believing. Try and do the right thing, live by the Bible; prayed, tithed, fasted, studied, more prayer, worked my guts out for my family. For what? Didn't ask for much until a big one comes along, and it hits the fan. Don't suppose you remember my train wreck of a divorce. My ex, right, wouldn't know a prayer if she fell over one, but walks away with my house, custody of the kids, business went bust. All I got out of it was a heart attack. What are you supposed to believe *in*? Have faith! Great. In *what*? Storing up treasures in heaven? What about down here when you need help? Do everything right and still end up with sweet F.A. Sorry, Pastor.'

'No. That's all right.' I answered.

'Mates going to footy Sundays – I'm at church, praying. Begging for help and nothing. Had to rebuild almost from scratch. Great example of God's mercy and favour? Don't get me wrong: I still believe. My belief just ran out of faith. Had enough.'

'Thank you for your honesty, George. And again, everything you did. I won't pretend I have the answers, George. In truth, I have very few. But too many lose faith and belief when God doesn't do what they want. But would we have more believers if He did everything people wanted? I don't think so. I don't know why He doesn't answer prayers or answers them in a different way than we want, especially in times of tragedy. There's a lot of things I don't know, or I'm not meant to know.'

WITHIN THE RESTAURANT FEWER CUSTOMERS remained but Eli's and Peter's table had grown in the number of bamboo covered pots and cups of kopi coffee.

'Wise words. Bet they didn't make one bit of difference.' Malaysian hostess in traditional uniform of colourful kemban, which included sarongs tied above the chest, attends their table clearing the empty pots and used cups. Eli smiles gratefully and Peter forces a small smile. She wipes the glass down, smiles pleasantly and leaves. Peter nods, leaning forward.

'Not one bit,' Peter answered. 'Never saw George again. Lim family and number of other big backers left. Massive hole in donations. For a while, I was just so angry with Lee and the kids. We had a huge row, and I told them I had cancer.'

'How did they take that?'

'How did they take it? Oh, generally supportive. No big rush to hugs, but they cared. Lee surprised me. She was quite upset.'

'How are you going with that?' Eli asked concerned.

'Had surgery and chemo. Treatment was humiliating, invasive and hideous. Ongoing. But as they say, not dead yet.'

'Let's keep it that way.' Eli said.

Peter sits back in his chair, shoulders slumped, looking defeated, fiddles aimlessly with a spoon.

'I'm so fed up with it all Eli – and it isn't "always darkest before the dawn" crap. I've *really* had it. Just one thing after another. Church, health, marriage, family, finances. I've read Job a dozen times trying to understand why God allowed it. Test his faith? So we're *all* Job's. I'm lost Eli. What's the point? What's it about, what's it *all mean*? Is there an answer?' Peter almost groaned. 'I hope you don't mind. Like I said, I find it easier talking to a Rabbi than I do other pastors.'

'Maybe they don't want to be your friend,' Eli said smiling warmly.

'A very patient friend, for which I'm very grateful. One of life's gifts.'

'There's an old Yiddish saying Peter, "Never complain about life. It's free."'

This forces Peter to almost smile. Then he becomes morose again. 'You know what I've learnt about faith in hard times, Eli? There's a world of difference between those who quote faith and belief scriptures when there's no threat to their belief, than those who have to live it when their lives are in crises and falling apart.'

'You're thinking about George?' Eli queried.

Peter nods, 'He just "stopped believing." Worst of it is, I can understand it.'

Eli still feels an intense disquiet for Peter, that all of the unburdening and confession is really just a cover to say goodbye. Everything Peter talks about seems about losing himself; his faith, his God. As if he can't see the point or meaning to anything anymore – like he's looking for a divine sign "exit." For a moment Eli is self-absorbed, but Peter says, 'Once a month, I'm one of a group of volunteers who attend a hospital in a non-denominational capacity. My turn tomorrow, as a matter of fact. Lee often pops in with fashion magazines for the nurses. Jacob and Mary meet her in the staff cafeteria then go shopping. Anyway, domestics aside, I was a bit taken aback to find a lot of patients held the same view as George. So one time I organised a get-together with those who quit their faith or confirmed atheists. Long story short, it was illuminating to say the least. They were convincing rather than convinced, and almost all totally unafraid of dying or afterlife judgement.'

'I spoke about that theological thoroughfare, the Road to Damascus, the freeway of faith, along which countless critics like to think is faith fantasy. Despite the gist of their argument that God is an invention and that Marx called religion the opiate of the people, suggesting that it dulled the sensibilities, I argued that, like many erstwhile infidels, there remains the real possibility, in the last seconds, they will recant, reminded of a slanderous prophecy familiar to atheists,' Peter said, *"In the terror of your days you'll see the error of your wicked ways. When the Angel of Death roots on the head of your deathbed like a dirty great vulture. You shall beg God's forgiveness."*

Peter shaking his head. 'After the laughter stopped, I tried to explain a bit more ...' Eli smirks, shaking his head. 'Why are you smiling?' Peter asks.

'So the so-called "doubting Thomas" "ex-Pastor" ministers about faith and belief in a hospital to "doubting Thomas" patients trying to save their immortal souls by faith and belief?'

Peter sighs and shrugs. 'What can I say? Anyway ...' Eli suppresses his small smile. 'Well I argued such pathetic pillow talk can go either way: Many former Christians are, themselves, death bed converts: converts to doubt in their disbelief, that their remains a sliver that there *is* something else, something more: converts to the realisation that their belief in their unbelief had been a deception. As for atheists, I said, fifty percent says I'm talking rubbish, fifty percent says there is judgment, heaven and hell. You deny God, He denies you. I said I know where the smart money would be on if it were me.' He shakes his head and face becomes serious. 'And then one asked if God gave them cancer?'

Eli asks, 'What did you say?'

'You say no of course.'

That doesn't sound too convincing to Eli, more a deflected answer. But before Eli could ask, Peter continues. 'He didn't believe in God's existence. If there is one, the man said, God is cruel as cancer had to come from somewhere. He also said man is a master of his own fate. Not God's. That God was man's creation to give answers that they are too afraid to give themselves.'

Peter looks across at Eli briefly then at his clasped hands. 'Somebody else said scripture has no real meaning. Words can be interrupted in so many ways that they cease to cause comfort or knowledge, but rather confusion and doubt.'

Peter is reflective, 'I don't think I succeeded very well.' Then he said almost deliberately to take the focus off himself. 'What happens in your Judaism Eli? You try to reignite faith spark in failed believers?'

Shaking his head. 'For one thing we don't door knock or crusade to strangers on the street,' Eli said. 'We don't convert anyone to Judaism. People usually come to us. Of course, Jews are very family orientated and most problems of faith are dealt within the family. If somebody claims to have "lost faith," a Rabbi or other nominated person would try to sort things out. But it's all usually very in-house.'

'People lose faith in Judaism just like Christianity. Faith and belief in faith can severely test people,' Eli reflected.

'Matron said almost the same,' Peter said. 'She said she lost her religious faith watching prominent Christians die, naming a few members of religious hierarchy whose last hours had been anything but serene and dignified. Whereupon her observations were endorsed by a surgeon I spoke to who'd been astonished by the agitation and anxiety of church people about to undergo surgery. Instead of looking forward to a botched operation, which might gain them early entry into paradise, if death means to see the face of God, to spend an eternity in some blissful state in His proximity, instead they were almost pitiful in their agitation.'

Eli looks at Peter quizzically. 'I wouldn't judge, Peter. Perhaps they just wanted to hang on to life – after all, as far as I know, it's the only life we've got.'

'Well, Eli, perhaps your right. But I'm not sure. Real faith. Real belief seems very illusive for the many in my experience. The matron made an interesting point. She said, if you really did or do believe, if you had faith as surely as, for example, you have measles, there'd be no need to constantly profess your profound certainty, let alone to go in for weekly recharging of spiritual batteries in kirk or church.'

'Hmmm. I don't know about that, Peter.'

Peter leans forward over the table as if in emphasis. 'During my life I've met countless people who wanted desperately to believe. They've prayed incessantly, wandered from cult to church and back again looking for "the one." They've changed convictions with the fashions, as if belief's were Frisbee's, hula-hoops and yo-yo's. As well as giving the matron map references to Damascus she said, they are forever telling her that faith is such a wonderful support in times of grief that without faith people could not endure tragedy, of which, she's seen too much. She said she agreed to a point but there are times when faith and religion seems to intensify anguish. Take the worst case of all: when parents are coping with the death of an infant or child. A little soul that's hardly had time to blink at life. She said Christianity may prop them up for a moment or two during a church service or at the graveside, but you knew the question in their minds. "God, why did you allow this to happen? How could you let my child die?" Her opinion was to accept the fact of death in all its simplicity and inevitability, without an iota of transcendental belief.'

Eli nods, reflectively, but his expression doesn't agree. 'I suppose you could see, in her position, with all the tragedies she must endlessly experience, the real temptation to become jaded and cynical.' Eli stops, letting the statement hang between them.

After a moment Peter asks.

'But?'

'But, I'm afraid I don't agree with you or her.'

Peter sits back, eyes narrow in a question. 'Well … that's no surprise.'

'Only my opinion, Peter, but the rhetoric of faith aches with uncertainty just by its nature. People talk of clinging to their faith, of the leap of faith. The force which is meant to be so powerful and substantial that it anchors life, and if you believe, after-life, remains for many feeble and unsure – except in the case of soaring conviction, willing to be put to the torch rather than renounce their faith, the true saints and martyr's, the true faith hero's. Such people are exceptions, the rest of us just have to go on believing what we'd do rather than knowing we could. I think when truly obtained, faith would be ineffable.'

Eli looks down a moment, reflective, troubled, undecided, as if making a decision. Then he looks up.

'I knew somebody like that.' Eli took a moment to gather himself, face dark and grim. Peter sat back, folding his fingers and waited. He could see the strain and pain in Eli's face.

Eli sighed very deeply. 'There was such a man of faith. A man I met in the death camp. I remember him clearly. Do you recall me telling you about the Rabbi risking his life to save the child?'

'When the poor little thing was getting numbers tattooed?' Peter nods.

'Yulen Turovsky. Rabbi Yulen Turovsky. Ukrainian Jew, one of the most remarkable faith hero's I ever met. He was unbreakable in his faith. Nazi guards targeted him every day because of it. Could have shot him, right there, any moment, any reason or no reason. But that didn't satisfy their bloodlust. What they wanted was to see him broken. To deny his faith. Every day he was brutalised in merciless hell. Somebody asked, "Why did he keep believing?" He said, "Believe, despite all the evidence to the contrary, despite all your constant doubts, reach out and try to have faith. The gravitational pull of reality is trying to drag you away so you must try harder and harder – you must pray for strength."

'In short, what he meant, if you have faith, pray for faith. Not on the grounds that you can't have too much of a good thing, but because we all know that, except for a fortunate, faithful few, faith can, and does, fail. That's why I don't judge people like your Matron, or even George ...' Eli fixes Peter with a firm look. 'Or, if you're wondering, you either my friend.'

Peter smiles at Eli's sincerity. 'You see, sometimes it doesn't withstand the battering ram of life. Sometimes, it's easier to talk about having, easier to say than believe. A scintilla of light of belief in faith, a scintilla surrounded by the echoing darkness of doubt and evil. It's tough. One of life's trials for believers. I failed. You failed. Not everybody wins.'

Eli shakes his head and sighs, deeply troubled.

'You wrote a book because you believed men had falsely, for their own selfish reasons, changed, distorted and deleted the original word of God. Although you were driven by what you believed true, your error was not to condemn the men, but to doubt God, calling yourself another Job. In that your faith failed. Then you felt a hypocrite teaching faith to others and felt unworthy by the title, "Pastor."'

'We are all just failed men, Peter. We are umbilically attached to titles that identify us, and of which we try to be worthy. But this man I met was different. There is a legend about him. That once he was ordered to deny the faith, and they tied up seven men, four Rabbi's and three Catholic priests and shot them, shot them before his eyes, and still he would not deny the faith. Is that story true? Yes. I have never met a single one who doubted it.'

'You see, I'm nothing special Peter. I know a few things that's all. Just a man with a title trying to live up to expectations. You say your kids let you down, Leanne? Life? That's nothing. I failed. And still haunted by it. Rabbi Yulen Turovsky not only saved that child, but my life by stopping me. He stopped me killing a man.'

Chapter 8

'That was a terrifying experience', Eli said shaking his head. 'I, a Rabbi … could have killed a man.'

'Yulen Turovsky?' Peter frowns, 'I don't know but it's as if I've heard that name somewhere. It sounds somehow familiar.' he said out loud too himself. 'Forgive me, Eli! I didn't mean to be rude, please go on.'

'When I lost my faith. I lost my way.' Eli continued, his voice burdened and quiet. 'I lost all judgement. I didn't care. All right or wrong. If Yahweh did not care about us? Why should I care about him? Even being a Rabbi didn't matter.'

Peter nods a little, but doesn't reply. This is Eli's time, even now, all those decades later, his memory wounds appear to remain raw. Eli has listened to Peter patiently – now, it was Eli's time.

'Word came, spread like wildfire, Nazi's were losing. The Americans and Russian's were racing each other to see who would be the first in Berlin. Guards were moving prisoners out, marching them West to other camps. Long lines of the living dead. We had no food. Most in rags, no shoes. Many shot where they fell, too weak to walk.'

I couldn't – 'Eli stops, takes a breath. 'I couldn't stand the cruelty, the evil insanity any more. And when a guard was horribly, ruthlessly beating this old man with his rifle butt, I couldn't take it anymore.'

'I … I fought the guard to save him. I wanted to kill him. I tried to kill him. Others joined in. Suddenly I felt myself pulled back and away. It was Turovsky.'

'But what if you had killed the guard?' Peter asked.

'I would be dead. Like the others who were immediately shot. Left to rot where they fell as a warning. There were many legends about Turovsky. His passive resistance. The Nazi guards called him *"Die Planke."* The plank. They meant it as an insult, meaning as thick as a plank, stupid. But some overheard guards saying he was unbreakable like a solid plank of wood. So they would dehumanise, beat him mercilessly. They could break his body which they did, but his faith and spirit? No.'

'Well, my faith tank is empty, Eli. All that's left of belief just vapours. To still believe, to inspire in hell like that? Amazing.' Peter gestures with his hands, palms open and up as if an appeal. 'If it's alright, could you please tell me a little more?'

For a long moment Eli looks away from Peter into the distance without really looking at anything. He pulls in a long breath, holds it a moment, and slowly exhales. Images roll in front of his eyes that cloud, flicker and sadden.

'I remember a day when it was pouring rain …'

'I had been in the Sorbidor death camp in Poland a long time. Over a year. Felt a lifetime.'

'An extravagance of rain,' Eli said. 'Rolls of thunder overhead. I was looking through the filth-smeared small window as the rain smacks, hisses, and puddles in the running mud outside the wood barracks. It was another selection. Even the sky wept.'

A man wearing a saturated cap, jacket ran past, splashing through what he couldn't avoid or weaving around the larger water puddles, throwing open our door and rushing inside. The room was full of men, wearing a uniform of filthy, thin and tattered blue striped "pyjamas." They all stared at the intruder, shaking rain off the arms of his coat and his hands, with mix of loathing, indifference or mind numbing fear.

'Kapo delivered our deaths.' Kapos, Eli explained, were inmates of Nazi camps who were appointed as guards to oversee other prisoners in various tasks. 'In our freezing hut,' Eli recounts, 'we waited our fate. I was there with Yulen. Some were shaking, trembling from cold but also aware of something bad, something hideous and impossible, haunts their minds.'

'New prisoners were coming, so many there was no room. What kapo bought were cards, with our numbers. We had no names. Just numbers. Whenever the cards came, we knew, it meant selection.' A moment of silence from Eli looking at his clasped hands on the table, haunting in his eyes. Then he takes a breath, holds it a moment, lets it out slowly, and then continues.

'The Nazi's God was Satan. First commandment of the devil is to kill. The kapo looked fed, with a coat – a *warm* coat.'

'He stopped at an emaciated, bald man with hard, angry eyes sitting on the bottom of a two tier bed bunk, wood framed made up of bare planks, with a threadbare blanket folded in one corner.

The man looks at the card, then up at the kapo holding it. The man doesn't move, so the card is dropped at his feet. 'Doesn't it disgust you? What you do? You're a Jew. You bring our death sentence.'

'I'm not the one killing you Schmidt. I only work for the devil,' he said. 'If I didn't somebody else would. We should try to maintain order. You can call me anything you want. What do I do all day? Do you know what I do? I take care of you. You are like my babies. I am like a mother for you.'

'Why?' Schmidt snarled.

'Why did I take a job like this? I got the chance. They asked me because I speak German, and because I have a brain. And if any of you were sufficiently smart, do the same.'

'I think you could have said no,' Idek, a sallow faced prisoner with a torn, threadbare blanket pulled tightly around his bony shoulders.

'I want to live … That is why I do this,' the kapo said. 'Want to live! Not like you scum already dead, dead as soon as you got here.'

'Not ashamed what you do?' Eli asked.

The kapo sneered, 'I have no answer for your God in His court you think Rabbi?' He crossed to Eli, looked him up and down, and then leaned in close. 'I do not care to know God. Because what I do, let me tell you what I do is nothing, nothing compared to what the Sonderkommando do! They push them into gas chambers and close the doors. I've seen it. I go through their piles of clothes, get their spoons and sell them to other Jews. We have cornered the camps entire spoon market. You think it's disgusting what I do but new ones coming today have no spoons for soup. So they'll starve. I sell them spoons. I do a service like a Rabbi.'

'So that is the way you think you will survive this,' Idek said.

'Maybe, maybe not. But I do as I'm told. And that increases my chances.' He then looks closely at Eli.

'Look, let me tell you about your God. Believer or no believer, when the door opens and the gas has done its job, they all look the same. I leave here alive, okay? One day the war will end. They might even lose. In which case, I will be out of here. All I have to do is stay alive until that day. If that means giving out cards and collecting spoons I give out cards and collect spoons. But I tell you this. When the gas chamber door's open, nobody is holding the Torah so in the end, what does it matter?'

He walked around our hut and gave each man his card with his number. 'When you get there. Strip off and wait to be called.'

'Strip off,' Eli said. 'Dear merciful God. We are freezing to death already.'

'Give your cards to the nice doctor,' the kapo continued. 'He's going to exam you. Free of charge. Don't say we don't look after you.' He pulled up the collar of his coat. 'The doctor will tell you right or left. Go where he points.'

He looks around at the faces. 'What are we doing here anyway? Have you asked yourselves? God's chosen. They say. What has the Jews done to deserve this? Ask your Rabbi's. You have two here. The Jews have a ... have a contract God, some kind of special arrangement. A pact? Am I right?' He said looking at Turovsky.

'In the desert, Moses led a covenant with God.' Yulen hit his arms with his hands trying to get some feeling back. 'He said the people obey God's law, and on the other hand, God said of all peoples, we would be his chosen a priestly nation. The psalmist sings "I agreed with the chosen one, I swear my servant David. I did sign your dynasty forever. Your throne will last from age to age."'

'What good has it done?' the kapo sneered. 'I can tell you – God doesn't come to Sorbidor. Only the devil. Probably half of you will die tomorrow. God or no God, pray all you want.'

The kapo opened the door and a wash of rain blew in and slammed it shut behind him.

AT THEIR TABLE IN THE restaurant Peter could see the depths of pain in Eli's face. Peter even felt guilt; he has been so consumed with himself, his trials pale compared to Eli's horrors. Eli gathers himself, 'They would cull us, like cattle,' he said. 'It was called selection. We knew around half of us will be selected for gas chamber within a couple of hours and most seem paralysed by fear, hunger and despair.'

'All their anger and fear turned against Torovsky and myself. If they couldn't reach, punish or beg God – we were Rabbi's, we were there. After kapo left, nobody said anything but everybody was thinking the same. I looked at Turovsky, he met my eyes. We were about to be selected to die, but he had a, I don't know, almost a peace in his face. It's hard to explain. I didn't see fear … almost an acceptance, a belief perhaps. Something was sustaining him I, and the others didn't have. I didn't understand it but in him, something. Well, you could feel the fear, the silence made it worse. Then a man called Idek said out loud what most of us were thinking about the lottery of his life.'

'So now we die. Right or left? Which is die? Does anybody know?' groaned Idek, turning to face the wall so nobody would see his tears.

'I think left is – is gas. Right is all right. I don't know. I just heard it. Do you know?' It was the French Jew Ricard who had asked. He now looks around desperately at the faces, but received no reply.

The prisoner Schmidt, was frail, but hunger made him angry, lashing out. 'God's curse on the Nazi's. I hope all their wives and children die in agony!'

All of us except Turovsky, almost jumped on the spot in fear looking around in panic.

'Shutup you fool! Are you mad!' growled Jacques in a low, forced, and strangled voice. 'You want to get us all killed. Anybody could be listening.'

'We're dead anyway!' Schmidt said.

'You might survive selection. But you won't survive a minute, or us, if somebody hears or kapo hears you,' Turovsky said quietly.

'Stupid fool. You think it matters any more,' Schmidt growled. 'Where is your God now Turovsky? And you Steinsaltz? He has abandoned his "chosen" people.'

'Hating Turovsky won't help us,' Ricard almost whispered, shaking with cold.

'Maybe hate and anger keeps him warm,' Idek muttered.

'Nothing. *Nothing*. Can help us especially *his* God who has forgotten us.' All his hatred was focused on Turovsky, who looked back at Schmidt calmly.

'Perhaps God must allow people to choose actions that lead to horrible results because human freedom of will is such an important virtue – a solution many consider the true one.'

'Bad Things have happened before. Read the Torah. Learn … read its history. We are Jews. We suffer. We suffer. It's God's will.' The elderly, deeply wrinkled and deathly pale, bearded Mordechai offered. 'Look … when we were released of bondage in Egypt, find land, freedom, what happened? We were taken captive again in Babylon. When we were released again and rebuild the temple, what happened? The Romans razed it. What happened on Massada … Spain … Russia, and now here?'

'The Torah. Yes.' Turovsky sighed. 'We have a few fragments between us.'

'In Ladontavick, my father was Rabbi.' Eli said with shuddering breath. Turovsky looks at him kindly. He reaches out and gently squeezes Eli's arm to give courage. 'They loved the Torah. On Shabbat, the windows of the shops were all closed. The Scriptures wrapped its wings of quiet about us, and the world simply vanished. Every man had his prayer book. On national holidays, festivals, workdays, the Torah was … the air was that breathed. I remember somebody wrote; in our poverty, it dressed and housed us. It was our palace and lived in its splendour.'

'So what went wrong?' said Ricard.

'Evil did not want our peace and joy, our worship, so bought the Nazi's,' Eli said.

'God! God! *God!* God doesn't exist. If he does, he's insane.' Schmidt said it with unbridled hate. 'After all that has happened to us, let others be his chosen people! A thousand million stars in our galaxy alone. If God loves Jews so much, why didn't he fill the universe with Jews instead of stars?'

'Schmidt is right!' the emaciated, and shaking white haired Mordechai said, with the threadbare blanket pulled tight about his thin shoulders.

'Of course I am!' Schmidt snarled. 'About what? He frowned.

Through shivers Mordechai answers. 'I heard a French scientist say once the existence of hundreds of millions of stars in the universe, each of which, perhaps, has its own solar system. Are we really expected to believe that, with all of that to tend to, God, if he's real, really pays minute attention to the events on this small ball of rock?'

'We all came here by train. Half the ones in my cattle carriage died. When they slid the door back, I fell out. I couldn't stand. I couldn't think. I couldn't breathe. The guard took off his belt and hit me with the metal buckle.' Ricard stopped trying to wrap his arms tighter around himself to get a little heat. 'On his belt it said "Gott Mit Uns", "God is with us". Who is to say He is not?'

Mordechai shakes his head. 'Maybe He's purifying us. Pruning.' He sighs, defeated. 'I don't know. How can anyone know …?'

'Maybe we are seeing it wrong and Mordechai is right. Imagine God is a surgeon,' Idek said, 'that what you mean? And he has to remove a gangrenous leg or an arm to cure the whole body. It's a violent act. It's painful. But it is also loving. How would it be if we were living through a time like this? Not a punishment, a purification.'

Schmidt turns on Idek angrily, like he could hit him, but knows that would mean instant execution for fighting, which is forbidden, such as loud voices, shouting or laughing. 'You fool. You complete *idiot* old fool!' he almost hisses. 'If He can do all things, why can He not purify His people without gassing them? How can He be all powerful and just? God can stop this. God can stop this evil. He can stop this! Abraham negotiated with God for Sodom. Jacob wrestled with the angel. The name, Israel, means "he who has struggled with God."'

'Tomorrow, perhaps you can ask him. We could be facing our creator,' Mordechai groaned. 'I know a little of the Torah. *Job*, chapter 22. Yes, Turovsky?'

'What?' Lieble said.

'The argument that God is indifferent is not unprecedented as it happens. It is written in Job. Am I right Rabbi?'

But Yulen did not answer as Ricard cut him off. 'I'm so cold,' Ricard shivering his blue hands jammed between his legs. 'God should be here being gassed, not us!'

'The Lord our God can hear you, even here. Ricard,' Turovsky said as a warning.

'If he listens to me,' Lieble grumbled, 'he does nothing about it.'

'Maybe that is what is happening here.' Turovsky said between white frozen and cracked lips. 'Maybe He is suffering with us!'

Idek shook his head. 'Where does all this goodness come from?'

'From the same one killing us?' came a broken, hoarse voice of Lieble, squatting, crunching into a corner, as if trying to pull the walls around him for a blanket. 'Even if I miss selection and the gas. The cold will kill me.'

'Who needs a God who suffers?' Schmidt clenched his fist at Turovsky. 'You Rabbi's know nothing! *Nothing!* We need a God who sends the angel of death to our enemies! Where is he? We ought to put God on trial. Charge Him with allowing genocide of our people. If I asked any of you here, not the Rabbi's or course,' he added with biting sarcasm sweeping his hand at us. 'The rest of us who've got any brains left, guilty or not? The question is whether God has broken his covenant with the Jewish people by allowing the Germans to commit genocide? Come on. Answer me. Is God guilty? I say God is guilty!'

Lieble climbs shakily to his feet, emaciated legs weak from hunger and cold. 'Why not? We are the ones who might die today. Why not put God on trial? Huh? Idek? Mordechai? Tell me. Is not God as a judge and us, His creatures are subject to His judgments without a voice? We *must* obey? Yes? What did we do wrong to be here? It is not always a happy ending for all lovers of righteousness is it? I wonder, what would be the end of a situation in which God is the accused in a trial instituted by His creatures if they had the chance. To judge the judge.'

Turovsky sighed deliberately and loud enough to make them all look, including me. He shakes his head repeatedly. 'Stupid,' he said. 'Stupid.' He looked around at everybody, his eyes finally coming to stop on mine. 'This how His creation meets the creator? Before you commit to such a stupid thing. You won't like it Schmidt, maybe all of you.' Turovsky looked around the room again, also at me. For some reason I looked away, almost guilty, I didn't understand. Perhaps he was seeing something in me I refused to see in myself. .

Then Turovsky continued, 'Although difficult to accept, God's true motives can be many, especially when it comes to the communities involved. God sometimes allows the wicked to continue their existence to test the attitude of society and bring to light the true character of each individual, toward repentance, or eternal damnation. Satan himself has not yet been destroyed by God for similar reasons.'

'You talk like a fool Turovsky. *That!* That is God's defence for abandoning us to murder?' Schmidt turned away. 'Satan lives in Berlin. They call him the "Fuhrer."' Mordechai said. 'You know what Fuhrer means in Latin? Caesar. The Nazi's learned their evil from the Romans. God didn't save our people or our Temple.'

'He let the Romans destroy both. I know the Torah a little. The record of God's deeds in the Torah against us are many. The true answer is that God is *not* good. I say *guilty.*'

'And what did the Romans want? That the Jews live like Romans and abandon the Torah.' Turovsky looks around the room. 'And where are the Romans now? Schmidt? Idek? Mordechai? Ricard? Lieble?' He looked at me, almost through me, searching something inside somehow. 'Eli?'

For several moments the only sound was hoarse, frozen breathing and the groans and shaking of limbs turning to ice.

'They are dust.' Turovsky waits for comment. 'And the Torah?'

'Still living,' I said. 'Still flowering, still illuminating the world.'

Although in agony with lips so split, Turovsky smiled at me, his remaining teeth stained and broken from beatings, but gratitude and affection in his eyes.

Schmidt almost spits in contempt. *'No answers Turovsky.'* Fury in his eyes and he focuses on Eli. 'Or you. You and your fancy Torah. What good is it now? You hide scraps, bits, and live in fear kapo find it. You pray with somebody watching. What God do you call that? All powerful! Not powerful enough to make His will our lives.'

'I do not know the mind of God, Schmidt,' Turovsky said. 'Do you think I ever imagined it would end like this? Yahweh doesn't make evil. Evil makes evil. To help men grow, God gave man free will. But man's will is evil will. Yes, there is evil in the world because God gave man free will, but man opted to use that will to make evil their God. It is very simple.'

'Simple?' Liebler asked.

'We are not puppets. We choose. We can always choose.'

'You think so?' A tall, emaciated bearded man slowly climbed down from one of the top beds. Deep dark lines under his eyes. His pallid skin pulled tight over high cheeks that makes him look even more skeletal. 'Free will? Free will, my ass. I will give you free will. My name is Ezra. I tell you about my children, and then tell me about free will.' He stops, leaning heavily against the bunk frame as if about to fall.

'I come from Hoengen. Near Aachen. And the Einsatzgruppen came. They broke the doors of the synagogue. They burned the Torah and the ark. And then we cowered inside. We thought we would burn there and then … If only it have done. I have three children. The oldest would be seven now …' He stops, a moment he couldn't speak. 'They're so beautiful. That does not … never mind. They put children in a truck. I ran after them and shouted, "Please give me my children! Give me my children." And this officer, put his hand up. It stopped. He said: "What are yours?" I thought he would give them back. I showed my three children. The eldest, was crying, and the other two … No, that's not all. He said, "Three cute kids. I tell you what you can do. Choose one. Pick one. Choose one and you can stay with him. "And the boys, listened. Spread their hands. Were so scared. They tried to get to me and said, "Please, my eljeme. Eljeme to me." Free will to choose. Which should I choose? The youngest? At most? The weakest? The fittest? To choose? To which I should choose? I cannot say. I do not want your free will. Or Yahweh's. I loved my children. You talk about free will. Where was then my will? What choice had I? That Nazi could choose, not me. Where was my free will? I ache from their loss … I am truly lost … there is nothing that can console me now. I am changed. So are they. My will is to go left in selection. I have come to believe that death is a fate better than life … then you will be reunited with lost loved ones.'

Slowly almost painfully, he bends and lies down on the bare boards of another bunk. He sighs. 'My free will is the war will end. Hitler will die. Our people and the Torah survive. My children are waiting.'

For a long time, there was silence in the hut. Heads were bowed, hearts and minds locked into themselves.

'I know one thing. I know this. This *I know*,' Turovsky said. 'The day of liberation is approaching each day. Each day closer. The war will end. And God will see to it. And with the aid of God, some of us we will see it. Listen to me. We know that … we cannot know the mind of God. God is too great. And all we can do is pray, have faith. When you arrived here, they took away your property, took away your names, shaved your head, and took your children … wives, mothers … even pulling gold fillings out your teeth. Everything was taken, stolen. No matter what happens today. Don't. *Don't* let them take your God from you too. Whether you think or believe He exists or not, don't let them take that away too. Do not let them steal your God. No matter how … how stupid and useless it may seem, the pact is His. Hold on to your faith. Faith … faith. Yahweh is with us.'

'In that moment. I can't remember loving or admiring a man more in my whole life than I did Yulen right then.' Eli said. 'But it was hard to see through the tears. We didn't know what to do or say, or how long we had. Word had come they had started in block 7. We were block 8.'

'So what do we do now?' Asked Schmidt. He seemed lost and humbled somehow, trying to reach out, wanting to be part of something Yulen possessed, and I doubted even I had. Right then … I had no faith.'

'I don't know what you will do. But I will pray. And I will pray loudly. And I don't care if they hear.' Yulen searched inside his clothes and removed several, torn and stained pages of the Torah. He began to recite in prayer. Out loud.'

⚜

IN THE RESTAURANT, TABLES ARE being cleaned by staff as only a few people remain. Two of those were, only hours before, perfect strangers, but now sip their kopi coffee as if bonded as lifelong friends, certainly no longer "book ends" but, in a sense, now reading from the same page. Peter's mood is reflective and sombre. He is no longer self-absorbed; his compassion almost reaches across the table to Eli, who sits for a moment in moody silence, thinking of Yulen, and all those tragic souls left behind.

'I didn't have his faith. Or his courage. I remember cringing inside we'd be heard. But one after the other, all drifted over to stand near him. The last was Ezra.' Eli breathes deeply trying to calm his pounding heart. 'And that is what we did,' Eli said. 'We all prayed.'

'Eli. Forgive me. I have no right to ask but … who survived that day?'

Eli sighs deeply. Peter looks at him, guilty. Instinctively, he gestures as in an apology. 'If too much –'

'No. No. No, my friend. We die, but evil does not age, does not die. It is as alive now in men's hearts as then. The more survivors speak, the more others will recognise the same evil.' For a few moments, Eli sipped his coffee, gathering his thoughts.

'They forced us to march from our hut to the medical block.

The so-called medical block was just a freezing, long concrete building with rooms. They herded us one end and ordered to strip. We were drenched, chilled to the bone, and shaking with cold and fear. Some were so afraid that their legs gave way, and we held them up. There were big purple bruises on these skeletons everywhere from beatings. I don't know how some were alive. Our feet were turning blue on the freezing floor.'

'Talking was forbidden; you could be beaten to death right there. But it didn't stop Yulen. He walked among us, whispering; "Don't give up on your God. Don't let them take your God away. Pray. Pray."

Amazed, Peter sighs, shaking his head. 'Even then.'

'Even then,' Eli said. 'We were naked, squeezed close to keep warm and somehow protected, as stupid as it sounds, as if hidden, they wouldn't see us. Fear does that. You can't think.'

'One after the other, the guard would hit you with his truncheon. That was the signal to run down to the doctor sitting at a table at the other end. I remember he was talking to an SS officer sitting on the edge of the desk. We had not seen water for a wash or shower for months. To stop prisoners panicking, when they arrived those selected to die would be told to go into a building to shower. It was a lie. It was actually a gas chamber. Survivors new the truth about so-called showers. Everybody had open sores and wounds, our skin crawled with lice. We couldn't smell each other, our sense of smell had died a long time before.'

'But I remember the doctor and SS officer holding like a rag or something, with something on it to block our stink. All the time they'd raise it to their nose and sniff. You ran down, gave your card, the doctor pencilled the number in a book, then looked you up and down, decided if you were fit to work, and in a moment, a second, pointed with the pencil left or right.'

'Some were frozen to the spot; they were shoved out a door by guards. Many screamed, cried, and begged. It made no difference. The pencil decided if you lived or died. Right or left. Just like that. It was hideous. Cruel beyond words. Our lives meant nothing. We weren't people, but problems. Myself, Yulen, God must have been with him, how broken he looked, Lieble went right. Idek, Schmidt, Ricard and Mordechai went left. They were never seen again. Ezra went to find his children.'

Eli looks at the table, shaking his head. There was nothing anyone could do. 'We were still freezing and naked, and you went out the door to the next table. I don't know how I was feeling – numb, sick, or grateful. I thanked God a hundred times in my mind. We were split up, put in different barracks, and compounds, assigned different work details. I went to a building where they made metal parts for tanks. I learned how to use a drill and metal lathe. We were allowed to wear civilian clothes, and the rations were a little better. The work was backbreaking, and many collapsed and died from exhaustion, so new ones came all the time. I prayed one of them would be Yulen, but it never happened. I only saw him once more when the camp was liberated. We went our separate ways. I have searched so many years. And prayed every day of them that I will be truly blessed and find him.'

Peter frowns, almost with a scowl; he wants desperately to say something, but something checks him and holds him back until he knows more. 'How did you get to the park? Did you drive? Have you a car?'

Eli shakes his head. 'I take a couple of trams. Who can find a place to park these days?'

'Ok. Then let me thank you a little by driving you home.'

Eli makes a gesture like sweeping through the air with his hand. 'Oh, you don't need to thank me at all. I've rather enjoyed arm-wrestling you all day. You buy our next meal.'

Peter stares at Eli for a long time. 'Do you think there will be a next one?'

Eli shrugs and smiles warmly. 'I'd like to think so.'

'Perhaps something kosher?' Peter said.

Eli claps his hands. 'That would be great and my pleasure.'

Leaning forwards over the table, Peter looks at Eli with a questioning frown. 'Just one thing. Your Rabbi friend. Yulen Turovsky. Jewish Ukrainian you said. Do you have any idea if the name *Turovsky* is very common?'

'Why do you ask?'

'Just wondering?' Peter said with a shrug, abstracted, but obviously thoughtful.

'Just wondering?'

'That number they put on his arm, the tattoo, I imagine it'd still be there. You don't know his number? '

'What's this about Peter? And don't say just wondering.'

Peter narrowed his eyes, leaning forward. 'Help me here, Eli.' Peter gestured appealingly.

Eli shrugs and sighs a little. 'It was a long time ago. And no I don't his number or if the name is common. Why do you need to know?'

Shaking his head, 'If I say anything now and I'm wrong, it'll be another thing I can't forgive myself for. Look. What are you doing tomorrow? Are you free?'

Eli almost squints, examining him, intrigued but cautious. 'I can be.'

'God works in mysterious ways to perform His wonders they

say. If I pick you up at, say, 10 a.m. Is that too early?'

'And go where?'

'I'm working at the hospital tomorrow. Will you come with me?'

'Yes. But you won't tell me why?'

'You've suffered enough Eli. I won't add to it by making a heart breaking mistake until I know more. You'll have to trust a Gentile.'

Eli smiles. 'I've trusted a few,' he said with kind humour.' Then his face changed to a look of real sincerity. 'But I think Peter-the-Pastor will be my first real Gentile friend.'

Peter looks across the table at him, genuinely moved, he felt very emotional. Then he thinks a moment. 'But be warned, you might meet my family.'

'Oh. I'm sure it'll be a pleasure.' Eli said, causing Peter to lean back in his chair raising an eyebrow with a small smirk.

Chapter 8

THE NEXT MORNING AT THE Peter Schembri house, Jacob looking neat in school uniform, back pack slung over a shoulder, is bumping shoulders and hips with his sister. Her signature and rebellious protest; tie askew, half undone and twisted to the side, as they collide to the car parked in the driveway. Pulling open the rear doors, they unsling their backpacks and toss them into the back seat. Leanne, wearing an upmarket fawn business suit, opens the passenger side door, throwing a displeased look at Peter over the car roof.

'A Rabbi? *Really*, Peter?' The "really," implying "what now?"

'An amazing man. Holocaust survivor.'

'Christianity to Judaism *now*?' Leanne rolls her eyes and sighs with sarcastic impatience as they climb in and buckle up.

'What? No way,' Jacob said alarmed. 'Jews don't eat pork. Pork is so cool.'

Mary's eyes narrow mischievously. She elbows him in the side. 'They used to call men pigs. Chauvinist pigs. Especially brothers.' Jacob glares at her trying to look bored. Not getting the reaction she wants she redirects her taunts. 'Mum-eeeey.' Her voice sang with amused satisfaction. 'Has Peter had the chop? Isn't circumcision part of the Jewish deal?'

Peter snaps a warning look at his daughter in the rear vision mirror and pulls out of the driveway turning into the road. She smirks leaning back in the seat. 'I'm not *becoming* anything. There's a special reason I can't share until I check something out.'

Her smile is pained. 'Every day is a class act with you, Peter. Did he read your book? What did he think?'

Peter stiffened and replied with forced dignity. 'A lot for me to think about. I don't know right now.' Peter says with a burdened sigh.

Leanne snorted softly, looking out her side window. 'He didn't like it.' Peter studies her for a moment and her mocking smile. 'Well, not alone is he. Not saved the church or us has it?'

'That's not helping, Leanne.' But he knew she was telling the truth. Nothing seemed to be working. What possibly could he get out of today? Another embarrassment? Even if it worked out – what then? Peter scolds himself. He should have waited, checked *first*. But he was committed now. In an hour or so he'd pick Eli up at his house.

'Nothing is helping right now, Peter.' Leanne said with enough of an edge to make it a warning. 'What did your Rabbi say about the fire?'

'Eli is not *my* Rabbi,' Peter said angry at the mocking tone. 'I told you last night. It reminded him of the Nazis burning his father's synagogue and killing all those innocent people. A war crime. Apparently it happened all over Poland. Something we couldn't even begin to comprehend.' Although tragic, for Leanne that all happened a long time ago. Her concerns are more urgent.

'Did you happen to mention we're about to lose *our* home

and our lives are about to be flushed down the toilet?' Her tone accusing. Peter looked at her as a warning she ignored.

'We talked about a lot of things,' keeping it low key trying to avoid a domestic in front of the kids.

'We'd better start talking about things happening to this family.' She said. 'It *won't* go on like this.'

Jacob and Mary exchange an anxious look. The relationship between their parents is worse than they thought. Mary is distressed and angry. She crosses her arms as if blocking out the growing tension in the car.

'Is this really the right time, Lee?' Peter's tone betraying his expanding frustration and sadness. He looks up into the revision mirror. The accusing and blaming eyes of his children are drilling into him.

Lee scowled. 'God isn't hearing you any more, Peter. You aren't in his good books.' She said scornfully. 'You think you're another *Job* you said last night. Bit melodramatic, isn't it?'

He is becoming annoyed and defensive. He seems to be isolated by his family as responsible and wearing *all* the blame. 'I don't seem to be able to help anyone at the moment. I'm counting on something happening today. If it does, miracles still happen, and perhaps … there's hope. Besides, I found it easier to talk to Eli than anybody else, especially stone-throwing, hypocritical, judgemental Christians. I believe we met for a reason.'

Lee ignored the barbs, fixing him with a mocking stare. 'Maybe you can move in together. Sounds like the perfect bromance.'

'You see. You are really awfully mean to me at times.' He gets no response. Lee keeps looking out the window.

'You're very witty today,' Peter adds.

'Thank you.'

'I didn't mean it as a compliment.'

'You mean, you don't approve of my doubts about some mysterious Rabbi with all the answers suddenly manifesting out of thin air with the Ten Commandments tucked under his arm or something?' Peter thought he detected an extra edge, as if something was really bothering her this time.

'I don't, Leanne, when you're being unreasonably judgemental.'

Her voice was a barely contained pent-up shrill, 'I'm unreasonably judgemental because all this makes me unreasonable. Besides. I thought you didn't believe anymore.' It was a baseless accusation but served the purpose to push Peter's buttons of already wounded insecurity.

'I *never* said that! I just –' He stops, stung and defensive. In frustration he slaps the steering wheel with his palm, his tone furious, overly defensive. He sighs, fighting to regain control but sounding truly lost. 'I'm … I'm confused.'

Her face actually puckered in rejection, as if she'd drunk sour lemon juice. 'Oh, by the way. While you were out last night, the police called.'

'What did they want? Is it about the church fire?'

'I don't know. They wouldn't say. They just said they wanted to talk to *you*.' She said with emphasis.

'It must be the fire. Perhaps they found what started it?'

'I don't know. It could be that.' Leanne keeps staring at him looking for any changes in Peters face.

'There's nothing I should know?'

Peter frowned. 'Of course not.'

'Is there, Peter?' Suspicion in her tone. As if holding something back.

The frown turning to incredulity. 'I told you no.'

'What about Sunday, the day of the Lim's birthday party?' Mary and Jacob exchange a guilty look, a disaster of their making both wanted to go away. 'I was there when you were praying remember. Something about a women you'd done something to.'

Peter's eyes shoot straight to the rear vision mirror to see Mary's eyes widen and mouth drop open in shock. Jacob just stares unblinking, he doesn't know how to react. Then blinks several times and looks at his sister whose eyes are still big and mouth open until it's then covered with the palms of her hands.

Peter is irritated and defensive, almost embarrassed Lee would even raise this in front of the children. He issues a firm warning. His fists grip the wheel so tight his knuckles show white.

'This is not the time or the place, Leanne.'

Who exhaled, a sound of irritated suspicion. 'Oh, but *it is* Peter. Whatever you've done affects *us*. As if it hasn't enough already.'

'I haven't *done* anything. And I want you to stop it. I mean it, Lee! Just stop it!'

'I think your prayer went something like: "What have I done to her? God, what have I done?" Is that right? I think that's what you said. That sounds like a prayer begging forgiveness because you screwed up. With a *women*. What did you do, Peter? Before some other catastrophe comes crashing down on our heads. Is that why the Police want to talk to you? Can you put your hand on a bible and swear before God nothing happened with a women? Will you do that Peter? We have a Bible in the glove box.'

'For God's sake Lee, I'm driving or haven't you noticed!' Peter fumes. 'It's not your business. Nobody's business except between me and God! You have no right!' He knows he can never swear on the Bible of innocence. Even his excuse of driving and the sanctity of the prayer is a lie. That has been eating at Lee all this time? He's trapped. Trapped between his family and God. On both accounts, he's guilty.

'If you've nothing to hide you've nothing to fear. If you can't be honest with your wife about her, what hope is there?'

Finally he erupts. 'Shut up. Shut. Up! For five minutes all of you. God! It's enough! Please! Enough!' Enough of pain. Enough tragedy. Enough lose. Enough everything. Peter's eyes start to reflect and sparkle as tears form.

For a long time they drive in tomb like silence, every passenger rigid with tension and confusion. The family has reached the edge of the domestic cliff. But Lee isn't intimidated by Peter for long. Her eyes fix on him defiantly.

'You're so chummy with the Rabbi I bet you told him.'

Almost weary, Peter shakes his head. 'Oh, for God's sake Lee.'

'I'll ask your bro.' All Peter can do for a moment is close his eyes, praying for all this to stop. He feels guilty because he is. Failed his God, himself and his family. That guilt batters him and flushes his face. The reaction Lee was looking for.

'It's over, Peter.'

A pitiful gasp from the back as Mary bursts into tears. She buries her face in her hands. Jacob's head hangs chin to chest, eyes glassy. Domestic distress and life's battering has reached overflow crises for the Schembri family.

Aden College almost took up the whole block of an old money neighbourhood. Upmarket vehicles jostled and dived in for parking spots as doors flung open offloading students lugging their oversized backpacks.

Peter zoomed as a vehicle pulled out near the decorative iron gates. Peter twists around, his mouth open to say farewell, but without a word, Jacob and Mary shove open the doors and climb,

Mary slamming her door shut. Leanne immediately goes to them. Peter couldn't hear what was being said from the footpath, but from the body language it was: *What the hell is going on Mum? This is sooo uncool* would be Mary's angry protest. Jacob stands staring tight-lipped, but Mary argues with her mother, hands and arms gesturing and waving, as Leanne tries to apparently pacify and calm. Lee was shaking her head again, and then they all looked at the car – at Peter. They were arguing about him as if he was singly at fault.

Mary suddenly whirls around, almost hitting her mother with her backpack, and the kids storm off past the ornate gates and disappear behind other students entering the college grounds. For a moment, Peter sees Lee hang her head and touch her fingers to her forehead, as if struck with a sudden migraine.

She crosses back to the car.

Peter pulls out from the kerb, and several moments pass before either of them speak.

'Are they alright?' It was innocent, but too much for Lee.

'They're not *all right*. No. We're not *all right*. Nothings *all right*.' Peter sighs quietly and decides to leave Lee's deliberate baiting; this isn't the time or place for more. For a short time they drive in burdened and tense silence. Peter extends his hand towards the CD player.

'Don't put on any of that crap Christian music, okay!' Peter retracts his hand as if he had burnt a finger. Again, they drive in silence. 'When are you seeing *your* Rabbi?'

Peter steals a look at her and her deliberately caustic emphasis on the "your." Whatever he tries to say, it'll probably be wrong, so he takes the middle ground. 'After I drop you off at the hospital, I will go over and pick him up.'

'I'll pass on that meeting, okay?' It wasn't a request. Peter doesn't comment, but Lee, staring out her window, misses the deep disappointment in his face. Maybe for the best. He stops himself. Perhaps God hasn't planned anything, and today will be a crushing disappointment for him and Eli. I should have checked it out first before asking Peter scolds himself. I should have gone in and checked after dropping Eli home last night. Oh God, Peter said in his head, please don't let this be another, another disaster. I'll have to tell Eli the truth no matter what, Peter tells himself. Maybe there are no miracles any more. I don't know what I know any more, he thinks, dejected and depressed. You can understand why people find it all too much and want out, Peter broods to himself. I mean what's the point, he asks himself, when is there enough?

Lee's strident steps to the hospital doors carrying her attaché case were the broad brush stroke of her mood after she shut the car door behind her without saying a word to Peter. He was parked in the five-minute patient drop-off bay, watching his wife walk away as if it were out of his life. In over thirty years of ministry, Pastor Peter Schrembri had lost count the number of times he'd counselled, prayed for, guided, and just been available for couples in marriage crises. Now he was at a loss for how to save his own. He didn't even know the right prayer, if there was one, or the words he needed for Lee or for himself. He sank low and heavily into the rich, custom leather of his seat, leaning his forehead on the wheel between his hands.

Peter swings his car around a corner and sees Eli waiting on the nature strip in a suburban, non-descript street outside an unremarkable house. Striking rows of sun flowers boarded the tiny front yard. There were also two cars parked in the driveway.

Eli climbs in and Peter pulls away. Eli glances over and sees Peter is again radiating stress and tension.

'Yesterday was quite a day,' Eli said. 'Amazing who you meet on park benches,' Eli attempting to lighten the mood. Peter doesn't respond and almost immediately, the same demanding anxiety for Peter's welfare makes an unwelcome return. Eli had felt more at ease saying goodbye after dropped home. He was feeling confident Peter's well-being was assured over night because of their agreement to meet today. Eli was actually looking forward to meeting Leanne, Jacob, and Mary if that happened. Perhaps it would help him understand what pains the heart of the Shrembri family, especially following the terrible destruction of the church – something, for some odd reason Eli couldn't shake or explain, that caused him growing unease of how exactly the fire happened.

In fact, if he were completely honest with himself, there were a number of things causing Eli to feel deep disquiet, including the business with the women Peter seems determined to avoid. But at what point, Eli asks himself, do help and support become intrusive and even threatening, considering they had almost just met? They've covered a lot of geography in each other's lives. But what happens if Peter is not the weak, confused, fragile, inward looking depressive Pastor, parent, and husband Eli has, perhaps, believed him to be? But the biggest and most troublesome and worrying are the two elephants in the room. He won't tell what happened with the blind girl, but most disturbing, "responsible" somehow for the tragic death of another women? The last sends a shaft through Eli, but right now all he can do is pray and hope for the best.

'How were things when you got home?' Eli inquired.

Peter sighs. 'Everybody was in bed. Couldn't sleep. Got up.' There was a long pause. 'Tried to pray.'

Eli nods to himself, pleased to hear that. In contrast, Peter's face is set, he has a small shake of his head, and his lips curl sullenly. 'I felt like I was talking to myself.'

'Of course I talk to myself,' Eli said. 'Sometimes I need expert advice.'

Sullen silence from Peter. Eli sees his jaw muscles flexing. 'Oh, loosen up, Peter. Clamp your jaws much tighter; you'll break your teeth.'

Caught off guard, Peter looks awkward for a moment. 'I'm sorry.' He glances at Eli. 'Since losing the church, I don't know where I am ... I feel like I'm ... drowning. Like I've swum out too far and suddenly I can't see the shore any more. Nothing but crashing waves and darkness pushing me out further and pulling me under.'

'You lost *the building*. Bricks, mortar and lots of fancy glass. Not your church.'

There was a small pause – Peter seemed a little surprised, then annoyed. 'It *was* my church. That building, *was* magnificent. People came from all over just sit and marvel at the glory. It is irreplaceable.'

'The only thing irreplaceable to me is faith. And it costs nothing. What did it mean to you? Your church?'

'A symbol,' Peter said with a long, reflective sigh. 'Power of God. Christian power.'

Eli frowns, 'Power is always dangerous. It attracts the worst and corrupts the best.'

'I never asked for power. Only to know the truth before I die. Death comes without apology. Know what I pray for all the time?'

Eli looks at him. 'Something God didn't give Job. A miraculous ladder to climb up out of all this mess.'

'Did you ever think you might not be meant to go up and out but through? You know what they say, when you're going through hell keep going.' Eli looks at Peter and his eyes narrow suspicious. 'Peter. I'd be very disappointed the only reason you bought me here was to talk to your family!'

'No! No,' despite his denial Eli suspects he isn't being truthful. He doesn't want or like to be put in this situation. Either way, if he refuses he may offend Peter. If he agrees Leanne may judge it as uninvited interference in private matters.

'I need *help* Eli.' He had a desperate tone, even a little fearful. Eli silently agreed Peter "needed help," not only with his relationships, but his whole life. Eli sensed a crises of some sort was coming like some sort of fearsome storm, and he was fearful for Peter's mental and emotional survival.

'It's not my place, Peter.'

Peter shot a look at Eli, despair and outrage on his face. 'Come on, Eli! For *God's sake!* I'm being crucified. Blamed for *everything*. This is *hell!* Almost bankrupt, church burnt down, losing my family, cancer crap, facing divorce but it isn't your *place!*'

'Peter –'

Bashing his fist on the steering wheel, Peter erupts. 'No, no, no no, *No-!* Enough! *Enough* of this shit. Got all the smart assed answers in the world when it suits you. I'm *circumcised!* Does that count? Couldn't you at least *pretend* I'm Jewish?'

Eli says nothing just looks at Peter whose hands are trembling on the wheel. Peter looks so distraught Eli thinks he might break right there and then.

Like a haunting echo from another time in the death camp,

Peter's emotional collapse tugs at Eli's memory of others who were lost and afraid and saw no hope.

"So what do we do?" Asked Schmidt.

"We pray." Yulen Turovsky said.

And that is what Eli did. He looked out his side window without seeing anything beyond it except Rabbi Turovsky's face reflected in the glass. How much had he aged? Is he still alive? Would they recognise each other now? Eli had lost count the number of prayers over the years that he'd meet Yulen again, one final time. Are there any miracles left he wondered?

PETER PULLS HIS MERC INTO a reserved parking spot marked "Pastoral Services" in the hospital staff car park. In silence they climb out, separated in more ways than one. While Peter gathers folders from the back seat, Eli has a sense – and gazes up at figure watching them.

The window was like a little movie screen, and there was Lee, framed within its walls, arms folded, peering down. Eli had no idea it was her, but with her fixed expression guessed who it was. A little moment of inner amusement: the movie screen transformed into the mouth of a cave with a threatening dragon challenging him. Eli turned his head to ask Peter, but when he looked back, Lee was gone.

'It's not a chapel, just a non-denominational prayer, meditation and timeout room and pastoral services office on the ground floor,' Peter said. His mood dark they head towards doors with a "Staff Only" sign. Just before entering, he stops.

'Do you mind if I buy cappuccinos I owe first?'

With a smile, Eli says 'You don't *owe* anything.'

'I think I do. The truth is before inviting you I should have done some research first. I have to check something out. It wasn't *just* to talk to Lee I invited you here,' he said deliberately. 'God works in mysterious ways. As they say.'

Eli smiles easily, with just a hint of cheekiness. 'As they say.'

'A very important patient record I need to check. Can't explain but don't want another screw-up.' Eli shrugs, *whatever you want.*'

Staff canteen is very good, but pastoral office is stacked with books. Even the Torah.' Peter raises an eyebrow as if to say, *'You'd like that.'*

Eli smiles 'Including yours?'

Peter sighs, 'Hospital board hasn't approved it.'

'I'm sure they will.' Eli smiles encouragingly. 'What say I do both, get a coffee and see you in the pastoral office later. Maybe you can show me around. Most interested to see what pastoral services do here.'

Peter shrugs and keys in a code on the security device activating doors that slide open. 'As needs – just be available really.' As Peter gestures for Eli to enter, where they are greeted by harried looking Asian nurse in green scrubs.

'Pastor Schrembri. Just the man.'

'Sister Lee. Good morning. I'd like you to meet my friend Rabbi Steinsaltz.'

As Eli and the nurse shake hands. 'Nice to meet you.'

'I haven't seen you before. I always know who's on duty. Do you work here now, Rabbi?'

'Oh no. I'm just here to keep Pastor Schrembri out of trouble and see what pastoral services get up to.' Eli says it with a smile.

'Well, that's fortuitous …' looking at Eli.

'How so?' Peter asked.

'You recall the patient in East 3C admitted a few days ago? His family came last night and again this morning. They're anything but happy, in fact at each other's throats. If the Rabbi doesn't mind he might be able to help.'

'Are they Jewish?' Eli asks.

'Their story is a bit complicated,' she said. 'The patient is critical, almost comatose and could go any moment. His Granddaughter says she's a Christian so would like a Christian service, but her brother said their Grandfather has Jewish roots. They're in your pastoral office.'

Peter frowns. 'You said east, 3C?' As a matter of fact that was the very patient I was going to look up in records this morning. I wasn't aware he had family?'

Lee smiles warmly with a shrug. 'The way they're at each other he hasn't. Nice meeting meet you, Rabbi.'

'You also, Sister.' As she leaves, Eli looks at Peter, 'The same patient you were going to check on?'

Peter doesn't appear to hear Eli. He kept staring at the floor with a burdened intensity as if he were the floor cleaning and polishing inspector looking for some missed or neglected spots or stains. Peter's shoulders slump and Eli's brow furrow's in care as Peter seems so distracted in his thoughts as if he'd lost all connection with the present and his responsibilities. A long moment passes. Eli is about to ask if something is wrong when Peter looks up, rubbing his temple.

'Headaches … every day.' Peter said, 'getting worse.'

Eli is surprised by this abrupt diversion. 'What's your doctor say?'

'Stress. What else do they say?' Eli waits, troubled. 'I was really hoping for more time,' Peter says, but his tone is so vague it's like he's thinking out loud, voicing inner turmoil. 'Explain to everybody how sorry I am for what's happened.'

Eli says nothing, his eyebrows pinched in serious concern. 'Today, if things work out, you know there's a God. If not, just another thing. Sometimes you just can't make everything right. No matter how much you want, some things just can't be fixed, and all you can do is wait for the curtain to fall.'

Eli feels a dreadful grab in his heart. 'Peter. Where's this coming from?'

'I have a dreadful feeling it's all coming to an end. Today,' Peter says, 'whatever happens, just another piece of the puzzle slotting into place.' For the first time Peter shifts his gaze to Eli as if realizing he is there. 'Sometimes you just run out of time, Eli.'

'Peter.' Eli said, 'You're frightening me.'

'Conscience.' He said as if summing everything up for himself. 'Conscience isn't a gift from God. But a sentence from Satan.' He sighs. 'Better see these people.'

In silence they walk the polished corridor, then Peter's mouth almost drops in surprise as he comes to an abrupt halt outside the lifts. His eyes skated back and forth, emotions cascading from disbelief to annoyance.

'What are you doing here?'

The eyes of Jacob and Mary met his coolly, then flick between Peter and Eli. 'Meeting Mum.' Mary said it defiantly.

Peter is furious. 'How did you get here?'

'Bus. You sound like a cop.' Mary tossing her mane that wasn't there, her clipped Mullet style made twitchy by the gesture.

'Does College know where you are? Am I going to get a call asking where you are? Why are you not there?' he demanded.

Eli stood awkwardly, growing alarmed how quickly Peter is winding himself up. Mary and Jacob stare defiantly. Peter guesses the college doesn't know.

'I don't need this! So you think its okay just to ditch class whenever you want?' Peter erupts. 'I'm paying a small fortune and your – don't you care? You're throwing your futures away. I won't have this. Am I making myself *clear?!*'

Visitors and staff look at the commotion, especially the loud man dressed like a Priest, sounding anything but "priestly," and a Jewish man looking seriously uncomfortable.

Peter pulls himself back, more for Eli's sake, and the audience now leaning heads together, talking. Peter sighs, trying to dispel some of his rage. 'My children. Mary and Jacob. That *should* be in college. This is Rabbi –'

Mary cuts in with a sweet smile. 'Rabbi Steinsaltz. Kinda guessed. The little hat gave it away. Hi.'

Eli warms to them almost immediately. They just seem like two very normal but disturbed, hugely unhappy and deeply troubled teenagers. 'Nice to meet you both.'

They locked eyes with their father and for a moment, no one spoke. Peter was barely holding it down. Jacob gives his sister a nudge. 'Well. Catch ya,' Jacob said. They turn to leave, and Peter snaps. His voice was again too loud. 'Where do you think you're going?'

'Canteen.' Mary replies.

'Like hell you are. You're going back now!'

Jacob and Mary meet his eyes defiantly. 'You are so uncool. No way. We're staying to meet Mum.'

They both look at Eli, and their faces soften, ignoring their father. 'Stay loose Rabbi. Maybe catch you later.' Eli has a little smile and nods. Mary and Jacob turn their backs, going down the corridor. 'Get back here!' Peter yells not caring who is listening.

Over her shoulder Mary calls back insolently, 'Whatcha gonna do, call the cops!'

Peter stares, embarrassed but helpless in the face of their defiance. Eli could see him struggling to find something to say, as they walk away lugging their backpacks. Peter looked at Eli awkwardly, shaking his head, 'See the way they talk to me. What I have to put up with. In Ephesians 6 it says, *"Children, obey your parents because you belong to the Lord, for this is the right thing to do. Honour your father and mother. This is the first commandment with a promise; if you honour your father and mother, things will go well for you, and you will have a long life on earth."* In Proverbs 29, it says, *"Discipline your child, and they will give you rest; give delight to your heart."* Disciplining any kid today you'll get arrested.'

'Ephesians 6 also says Peter, *"Fathers, do not provoke your children to anger by the way you treat them. Rather, bring them up with the discipline and instruction that comes from the Lord."* Peter, I know fear and worry too well. They're really, really deeply worried.'

Peter is barely controlled. 'We're all worried Rabbi. But this doesn't help anything.' He snaps. 'Things are bad enough without this. *Christ!* I feel I'm not only losing my church and my marriage, but also my children. How much worse can things get for God's sake? This is all so cruel and evil beyond belief.'

'You're attacking your children – *in public*. Do you understand how wrong that is? No wonder they're walking away. They're *afraid* of you Peter.'

'*Bullshit Eli –!* Like Lee, the only thing they're all afraid of losing is a spoilt, selfish lifestyle my church *paid for!'* Eli sees Peter's hands visibly trembling. Eli reaches out and puts a comforting hand on his shoulder. He searches Peter's face, looking deep into his eyes. He also feels afraid for Peter's mental and emotional life that's almost collapsing.

'Pastor, you can't keep this up. You need help. Peter. *Please.* I've seen too much of it not to know it and you're on the edge of a massive breakdown. You must find God again. You've never needed Yahweh more. Please.' Peter is looking at the floor. When he looks up into Eli's face, Peter looks deathly pale. He stares. And then, all at once, mysteriously, some sort of hostility, some level of tension, seems to leave him. His moods seem to pendulum between open hostility to almost emotional defeat almost in the same breath.

'God doesn't care. And you know something Rabbi Steinsaltz, I don't care either what happens anymore.'

Suddenly, with a groan, Peter puts a hand out on the wall to support himself. Fingers of his other hand go to his temple as if he's suddenly rocked by an intense, debilitating migraine. Eli is alarmed, and automatically reaches out.

'Peter!'

'It's nothing.' But his face in pain says otherwise.

'I'll get somebody.'

'I'm alright. Awful headaches. Just another Job bucket load, and why not.' Peter said bitterly. 'God told Satan to wreck Job's life, but not kill him. So I'm safe.'

'You're *not* Job! Stop saying that.'

'You think so?' Peter said cynically.

Eli watches Peter walk away toward a door signed *Pastoral Office,* with a terrible sense of dread and powerlessness. Eli sighs deeply, shakes his head and follows.

Eli sat on a two-seater lounge observing the middle-aged, blond woman, hair parted at the centre going down to her shoulders, with red eyes, dabbing at her face with tissues. She glares at the bald, heavy-set man sitting beside her, arms crossed, a scowl on his face says he has better things to do and other places to be.

Peter sat behind a plain desk with box of tissues, phone and a folder. 'Did your grandfather ever express his wishes about a funeral?' Peter asked.

'We weren't very close.' She glares at the man. 'Some even further.' He rolls his eyes, shakes his head and sighs.

'I see,' Peter said, non-committal. 'What about a will?'

'He didn't leave one as far as we know. Grandma Tilly passed a long time ago. Our mother was an only child and said the subject never came up with her. Now he's in some sort of coma or something.'

The man sighs again making his impatience felt. 'Look, my sister cares, I don't. She goes to church, I don't.' He raises his hands and gestures towards the women, palms up, as if to say: *What's it matter?* 'I mean Jennifer, be realistic. The last thing we all chew on is six feet of dirt. What does it matter who puts him there?'

'It matters to me, Geoffrey!' She said, glaring at him.

He sighs dismissively, leaning forwards in his seat. 'Look. Don't get me wrong, Padre –'

'Pastor' Eli corrected.

'Whatever. Let's just cut to the chase. I *should* be at work. He's always been kind of on the periphery, at a distance if you know what I mean. Never had a serious sit-down about anything.'

'We have a large family,' Jennifer said, 'and after Tilley passed, Mum looked after him, all of did one time or other.'

'Yeah. And what thanks did we get!?'

'He's been in and out of a number of nursing homes over the years. It's been, um, difficult.'

'He's just a pain in the backside. Nasty, bad-tempted old pain. Fights, argues, nothing ever good enough – families did their best. I'm not sorry it's over.'

'Plug it Geoffrey. He's *still* our granddad.'

'Tell me when you've seen him lift a finger to help anybody ever. Who's he ever cared about apart from him? And what was all that crying almost every day? All that "I want to go home stuff." I said he needed to see a shrink years ago. Still can't believe all the crap we went through over some stupid old book? Better off in the ground, if you ask me.'

'Well, no one is asking you.' She clicked her tongue in irritation. She stares at him for a moment with furious, wet eyes. Taking a small breath, she turns her attention to Peter, explaining. 'He had this old book with all this weird writing in it. He used to hang onto it, even while asleep. But he was almost blind, even with special glasses. So we took it off him and got others with large lettering, but he wasn't interested. That's when all the crying started.'

Peter gives the obligatory kindly Pastor smile and nod without understanding anything.

'Perhaps we could get back to funeral arrangements,' He runs a finger over a page in a blue folder open on the desk. 'You've been calling your Grandfather "He,"' Peter said pointedly. 'But his name is Harry Morgan. Do you know if Mr. Morgan went to church at any time? Or had any type of belief, faith or fellowship?'

'He wasn't a Christian, we know that,' she said.

'That's right,' Geoffrey adds.

Peter frowns, looking between them. 'You seem pretty certain?'

'Not once, when we were kids, never had a Christmas or Easter with us.' Peter picks up on the edge of bitter resentment in his tone.

Jennifer continues, 'Said he didn't believe in Jesus only God.'

'He had a series of, what do you call them, Jenn?'

'Strokes.'

'Yeah. He seemed to go off the beam then.' Geoffrey shrugs. 'Be mumbling away like he was praying or something. For *hours*.' He looks at his sister, who nods. 'Nobody could make head or tail out of it, so we thought, you know, it's the dementia.'

'There's not a lot in the nursing home files,' Peter says, 'about Mr Morgan's life before coming to Australia in 1946. It says here, "Possibly Jewish," with a question mark. Can you explain that?'

'Tilly told mum there was some sort Jewish way back,' explains Geoffrey. 'But he never wore one of those little hats like the Padre.' Looking at Eli and gesturing with his hand as he said it.

'Rabbi.' Peter corrected.

'Whatever,' Geoffrey shrugs.

'But the name Harry Morgan doesn't exactly sound Jewish?' Peter queries.

'Yeah, but that's just it, Harry isn't Harry.' Geoffrey said with almost a sigh as Eli and Peter exchange a look. 'Look. Jenn can explain it.'

Jennifer glances kindly but awkwardly at Eli, even a little embarrassed, but her Grandfathers funeral is priority. She takes a breath. 'Alright. I'm sure the Rabbi knows all about it. Lilly told mum there was a lot of hostility against Jews as refugees. Lilly's family was dead set against her marrying a Jew.' She flicks an apologetic look at Eli who smiles kindly. 'There was a lot of prejudice, she said.'

'To us he's Harry, Geoffrey said. 'According to Mum that's not his real name.'

'She said he had to hide he was a Jew, can you believe that?' she said. Geoffrey sighs impatiently. He makes his indifference known.

Peter picks up the explanation taking some of the awkwardness off Jennifer. 'I think I understand. I've read Jews had the hell of the Holocaust in Europe but sometimes ignorance and anti-semitism followed them as refugees.'

'Yes' she said. 'Apparently one day, everything went in a fire that could link him to being Jewish. Now he's dying in that bed poor thing.'

'But you don't know his real name?' Jennifer shakes her head glancing at Geoff who shrugs. However, a change has come over Eli. His mood dark, broodingly unhappy, face tense, something roiling in his mind. Suddenly, uninvited and unexpected, his tone critical, even accusing.

'That book ...!' Eli snaps.

Peter, caught off guard, stares, surprised by his harsh attitude. Jennifer and Geoffrey look at each other, confused.

'What about it?' Geoff asked.

'When you took it ... his world – fell apart you said?'

The siblings exchange a confused look. 'Wanting to "go home?" She shakes her head looking at her brother. 'We didn't understand,' she said. 'It was falling apart! Pages came out,' she adds trying to explain. 'Harry was clinically blind. Just mumbled away for hours holding it. We got stacks of large print in for him.'

The room swirls suddenly tense and unpleasant. Peter eyes pinch and he frowns at Eli's abrupt manner. Suddenly Eli is on his feet, he crosses the room and pulls a gold embossed and lettered book off a shelf. He turns back, spreading open the pages. 'Did it look something like this?'

Geoffrey frowns, 'Maybe. I dunno. Who knows?' He shrugs and Jennifer looks puzzled.

Peter doesn't like where this is going. He shoots Eli a warning. 'Eli!'

Eli snaps the book closed forcefully. 'If Mr. Morgan is Jewish,' Eli said, 'that *book!* ...' he voice has an accusing edge, 'falling to bits as it was, just might, *might* have been the Torah. Our Hebrew Bible. Something more precious than his *life!*'

Brother and sister look at each other alarmed, an annoyed Geoffrey is now on his feet, personally offended and protecting his sister. 'How the bloody hell would we be expected to know, *mate!*'

'*Rabbi!*' Peter cuts in. Peter's sharp tone breaks the mood, Eli blinks, and suddenly aware he is out of line. But Geoffrey is coiled. Jennifer tugs at her brother's sleeve urging him to sit. He shrugs off her hand.

'Mr Morgan's family are here to do what's best and respect his heritage says a lot, wouldn't you agree, Rabbi?' It wasn't a question but a warning. 'I would struggle to recognise a Hebrew Bible!' He then looks between the siblings. 'Would you know a Jewish Bible?'

'No way,' Geoffrey said. 'Not even one of ours. Don't give a *stuff*. Okay.' Peter knew that was a slap at all religious "authority" in the room.

'We just wanted to help with something he could read!' Jennifer snaps. After a few moments the tension dissipates, as Geoffrey reluctantly sits after another harder sleeve tug.

Trying to pacify the room, Peter is sensitive to Eli but feels his hostility misplaced and unfair. 'Rabbi Steinsaltz is sadly a Holocaust survivor,' Peter explains. 'He said Nazis destroyed all Jewish religious books they could find. Prisoners risked their lives to pray just with scraps of pages. If it was the Torah or something, and considering how attached and upset Mr Morgan was losing the book …'

'Our Harry?' Geoffrey and his sister are shocked. 'In a concentration camp?' she said.

'We don't know that for certain – so best not *overreact*.' Eli knew that was directed at him. Peter deliberately tries to take the heat of Eli who is now looking down, sad-faced and a little awkward; his emotions diffused, he wishes he could take the words back.

'The Rabbi has been searching for decades for one particular man who became very close, saved the Rabbi's life in fact. He's never stopped believing and praying he'd find his friend. I'm sure you can understand how soul tearing and difficult that would be?'

Peter looks at them appealing. 'I'm sure Rabbi didn't mean anything. Mr. Morgan had a wonderful and caring family. What do you say, Rabbi?'

'I'm very sorry.' Eli looks at them with sincerity, embarrassed. 'You did your best.'

'Damn right!' Geoffrey said. The siblings look at each other as if deciding to accept the apology. But Eli is still driven by a conflicted inner turmoil, and shakes his head.

'I don't believe it's the man I'm looking for as you describe him. He was the kindest, most gentle man; inspiring, not harming …' Eli falls silent, ache in his face: is his idol ruined if Yulen has also changed that much? Something he never even dared to consider, he sadly voices his turmoil, almost to himself. 'But … so many

I've counselled, the horror of the Shoah and time changed them completely ...'

Peter is staring at Eli with compassion. Eli takes a deep breath. For him, there is only one way to know the painful truth. He looks apologetically into the faces of Geoffrey and sister. 'That doesn't excuse my behaviour ... but ... there's something that might help us understand more about your Grandfathers life.'

Again the siblings look at each other, but this time, confused. They all watch as Eli removes his jacket dropping it on the lounge. Unbuttons his shirt at the wrist and pulls up his sleeve.

'Does he have one of these?'

His exposed forearm reveals a tattoo of faded, barely discernible numbers. For a moment, nobody speaks. Peter looks at the marks, then raises his eyes to find Eli looking at him. All the countless words spoken and written about the Holocaust are, in a sense, still words. But it was suddenly there, suddenly visible, suddenly real, suddenly terrible, the indelible wound.

'Oh wow.' Jennifer said quietly.

Geoffrey nodded. 'Yeah. He does. Yeah.'

'Just make them out. Real faded, but numbers,' Jennifer said, pointing at her arm.

Eli rolled down his sleeves and dressed as she continued. 'That mean's – Oh God! We had no idea!' She looks for confirmation from her brother. 'Just a tattoo we thought, you know.'

For the impatient and indifferent Geoffrey, the revelation brings a new respect for Harry. 'Wow. Didn't figure that. No wonder he clammed up. Poor old Harry! Bit of a mind slap, heh?'

Peter is quiet, leaning back in the chair, disturbed and thoughtful. Eli slips into his jacket and sits on the sofa. 'Please. With your permission, could I meet Mr. Morgan?'

Jennifer looks at her brother who shrugs. 'Please. It would mean so much,' Eli said.

Her attitude towards Eli has changed completely. 'I mean, okay. But it's like no one is there. But if you want to. I'm in a bit of a shock. Who would've thought?'

'I have a suggestion. How about you go wait with Harry and we'll be along shortly? Okay?' Peter stands and walks around his desk as Jenn and her brother also stand. Peter extends his hand touching her upper arm as those in ministry often do putting people at ease. Peter crosses and opens the door for them. 'I'll discuss with Rabbi Steinsaltz how best to proceed then we'll talk it over with you. How does that sound?'

'No worries,' Geoffrey nodding.

The siblings look at Eli and he gives them a grateful smile. 'I know Mr. Morgan's room. See you in a few minutes.' Peter ushers them out and closes the door.

He goes back and perches on the edge of the desk, folding his arms. 'What was that?'

'I said I was sorry. I meant it.' Eli folds his own arms, each side locking themselves in. He really doesn't want to go over this ground again. But Peter is like a dog with a bone, gnawing that Eli embarrassed him in front people he was counselling.

'They did just about everything they could for their Grandfather and you make them feel crap over some book you don't even know what it was! What's wrong with you?!'

Eli is nodding, accepting the judgement. 'There's no excuse. I'm just – a little tired.' He rubs his hands over his face, speaking of great weariness. Peter, on edge and strung out, takes it as criticism.

'If helping out is too much, there's the door.'

'You want that?' Eli snapped.

'Do you?' the angry reply. Both men stare at each other for a long time. But it's Eli who takes a difficult, conciliatory breath.

'We're both pretty wrung out. Let's drop it.' With deliberate purpose, he stands and collects the Torah off the desk. 'Now I'd like to see Mr. Morgan.'

But Peter doesn't move. Lowers his head, as if deep in thought. Then looks up, 'You're hoping its Yulen Turovsky, aren't you?'

'A long, long time of prayer if Yulen's alive bring me to him. Maybe meeting you … Yahweh answered.'

Peter stares at him, 'That's *absurd!* Concentration camp in Poland decades ago to a hospital I'm involved with by some fantasy miracle? You can't seriously believe that.'

'Didn't your Jesus say, *"Oh ye of little faith."* Or is that just another wrong translation?' Peter's eyes narrow and face sets into a hostile stare. Eli meets his eyes. 'I agree, it would have to be a miracle. But why not? In Hebrews, 11.1: *"Now faith is being sure of what we hope for and certain of what we do not see."* Our elders in the past were approved because they showed faith.'

Peter's defiant stare remains. For Eli, the gloves are coming off.

'For a "doubting Thomas" Pastor, miracles ended in the Old Testament. I happen to believe they never ended,' Eli said. 'Standing here surviving the Shoah is a miracle. I happen to believe God has not yet said the last word on His miracles.'

'Yeah. Right. Where was mine?' Peter fumed, face flushed angrily. 'Where's the miracle saving my church, saving my marriage?'

'I don't know why you lost your church. But I do know that you don't have to lose your marriage or family. But much of that *"miracle,"* is up to you. The problems you have, *you* have to fix. Yahweh won't do it for you. Why should He? What do you want – miracles on demand? Would you or anybody else believe in Him anymore if they did? In my experience people claim to want to know the truth then reject it because it's not the truth they wanted. Not everything you face can be fixed, but nothing can be fixed until it's faced.'

Peter isn't in the mood to be lectured, and Eli rejects Peter's self-serving depressively destructive selfishness. Since they first met, in a room dedicated to pastoral care and counselling, real fractures appear between them that go to the core of faith and friendship.

'You're in a faith crisis and drowning in doubts and fears, looking for a ladder to climb out and turn your back on it all. But the thing really turning your guts to jelly, *if,* by some miracle, Yulen Turovesky is in that bed, all your God hating, *bible bashing is wrong!* Now. Can we go?'

Peter still doesn't move, folding his arms. He appears to deliberately hesitate, as if delaying being proven wrong – a moment of truth for him. Peter would be the first to concede Eli is right; he doesn't know what to believe any more, and the possibility the man in that room may force him to look beyond himself makes him feel increasingly uncomfortable. He stares at Eli, his eyes hooded.

'What if it isn't Yulen Turovsky in that bed?' Peter persists.

'I will pray for the man who is. It's my duty.' Peter gives him a sideways look, then looks away.

'Your *duty,*' Peter sneers.

'You remember duty, don't you, *Pastor?* Old-fashioned, boring, out-of-favour duty. Used to be very fashionable once, like good manners, fairy floss, and clean air. Duty to your family. Duty to your church. Duty to yourself. Duty to the Holy Word!'

Before Peter can reply, Eli has crossed the room and opens the door and looks at Peter. 'I don't know where Mr. Morgan is but I'll find him.' The challenge makes it very clear Eli's drawn a line in the sand.

Chapter 9

THE ELEVATOR OPENED AND STAFF wearing green scrubs moved out with Eli and Peter following behind into the Intensive Care ward. The sense of lives on the line and medical battle to pull them back from the brink saturated the atmosphere and Eli felt it immediately, tensing his stomach. Wrapped in their own thoughts, this time they appeared like bookends again facing in opposite directions. They carry the tools of their identity; one a Bible, the other the Torah. Both are aware that in a few minutes they will face a common destiny and faiths tested that may challenge and separate them irrevocably.

Peter excused himself, going to a desk where he spoke to a nurse with a stethoscope slung about her neck. She obviously knew him, smiling a greeting and after a few minutes, looked past Peter to Eli.

She nodded several times as Peter spoke, he then turned and nodded at Eli. For a man who had threatened to search the hospital, suddenly his legs felt leaden, stomach floating with a sense of unreality.

Could all his prayers and hopes come true today? He squeezes the Torah, takes a long, shuddering breath, tries to steady his pounding heart, and resolves to put one foot in front of the other, crossing to Peter.

The sister nodded pleasantly at Eli, and he smiled back following Peter as he lead the way along the polished passageway, with curtained off rooms on both sides. They walked a short distance, then stopped at a room.

Eli had no idea if it would be Turovsky. He could only hope. He could hardly feel his feet or hear his steps but he remembers in the death camp what Yulen Turovsky told him: *"The Hebrew term for courage, ometz or ometz lev, literally means "strength" or "heart-strength." As you know Eli, Ometz is a core Jewish middah, a spiritual and ethical trait with which each of us is innately endowed as human beings formed in the divine image. Even those who consider themselves fearful or anxious can access the quality of ometz lev in any given moment. Now, this moment, when you go into that place for selection, you must have ometz lev. They can kill us, but not our faith. Because of that faith, we will one day win. Remember this always,"* Yulen whispered, *"Kol haolam kulo gesher tzar me'od, vehaikar lo lefached klal. (The whole world is a very narrow bridge, and the main thing is not to fear at all)."*

The two passages from the Torah, Eli repeated over and over during selection, and in innumerable times of horrors before and after, the first Isaiah 46:4, *"Even to your old age and grey hairs I am the One. I am the One who will sustain you. I have made you and I will carry you; I will sustain you and I will rescue you."* The other was Proverbs 24:16, *"The righteous fall down seven times and get up."*

As he walked his legs were rubber, but he would not fall, because he prayed like a continual loop, and refused to bow to weakness, doubt or surrender. He prayed so hard, he was unaware

Peter had already stopped at the door of a room, Eli taking another step, turning back after he realised.

Peter looks deeply into Eli's eyes, and they stare at each other a long time. Peter says eventually, 'For *you*. With all my heart I pray he's here.'

'If he is,' Eli said, 'God bought us *all* here.' Eli reaches out with a strong grip on Peter's upper arm, squeezing firmly. 'He didn't quit on Job. He won't on you. He doesn't on anybody.'

Peter looks down, unable to hold Eli's intense gaze. But doubts, even fear, still cloud Peters face.

Eli surveyed the room. The empty, neatly made bed on the left and the curtained-off enclosure on the right. Apart from hospital background noise, there were no other sounds. He swallows, breathing, becomes shallow and feels clammy and a little sweaty. He takes a calming breath, but that doesn't help. He goes to the curtained-off bed.

The curtains are opened a little to admit Eli, followed by Peter, then closed up again. Inside the contained space, Geoffrey is in one corner, arms folded, a distressed Jennifer seated, hovering near the man. Above his stiffly starched, stripped pyjamas, his eyes are sunk into his pallidly exhausted face. Slack-mouthed and empty of expression, his liver-spot hands are folded together on the turned-over sheet in front of him, almost in an attitude of mournful prayer.

Jennifer is red-eyed and flustered with stress. Tentatively, she puts her hand on the top of his. She glances at Eli and Peter at the foot of the bed, then leans toward Harry.

'Are you in pain? Do you understand what I'm saying? *Harry?* See! Nothing. Do you want some water? I think he's gone. I'm not sure he's still with us. Should I get the doctor?'

With a huge sigh, Geoffrey shakes his head. 'Oh, for God's sake, sis, give it a rest. Of course he's not gone, or they'd be in here doing something. He's just … not *here*. Like I shouldn't be.'

Peter glances at Harry but then focuses entirely on Eli, who is intently looking from the foot of the bed. His brow deeply furrowed, and his eyes were pinched in intense concentration. He's just not sure about the man in the bed.

'Sis. Nothing they can do any more. Like, you know, curtain call.'

She flares up, 'God, you're cruel and heartless. He's our *Pop*, Geoffrey!'

'Would you mind if I came closer?'

Geoffrey shrugs. 'Sit over there, Rabbi.'

Jennifer indicating a chair opposite. 'Do you think I should call the doctor, Rabbi?'

Eli moves around the bed and pulls a chair towards the bed opposite her, but he hasn't taken his eyes off the man. He sits, leaning forwards, his face almost rigid in concentration. Then, like a sudden lifting of memory fog, something, like chilled fingers, grabbed his heart and stomach at the same time. He feels ice run down his spine. For a moment, his head swims; he feels lightheaded and presses heavily on the bed to keep his balance on the chair to stop falling. Eli's jaw drops; he blinks, and forgets to breathe. And then, all at once, he tries to speak with a suddenly dry throat.

'*No.*' is all Eli can say. 'No. *No.*' almost a gasp, as if impossible to believe. The siblings look at each other. Eli's face is suddenly pale. He has little breaths, and in barely a whisper. '… All these years … so much … so long … Elohim Tov,' he struggled to say. 'Baruch Hashem.' *(God is Good. Blessed be God).*

Jennifer gives Eli a long searching look, while Geoffrey focuses on Peter. 'Don't tell me he knows old Harry? You're kidding me? What the heck's going on?'

Peter face is a statement, an amalgam of confusion, joy for his friend, but almost bewilderment for himself. For, right there, in front of his eyes, lies an apparent miracle as Eli had challenged him to consider.

Before, Peter's doubts and insecurity, gave him both sanctity of a choice in what and when to believe; but this was an indelible testimony his rational mind couldn't challenge, dismiss or doubt. He could not argue it away with science, facts or theology. Here was substance made flesh, against all rational odds, and it challenged and shook him right down to the core of his being. There was no mythical ladder for him to climb through or over the reality. For moments his mind went numb, and he had to remember to take a breath.

Jennifer, wide-eyed, sits back not knowing what to think. Eli takes the feeble, tissue-thin, blue-veined hand in his own as if holding a sacred parchment.

Suddenly, there are heartbreaking sobs. Eli leans forwards, gently laying his forehead on the old man's chest. As Eli openly begins to weep, Geoffrey and his sister are caught off guard and are soon embarrassed by Eli's unrestrained crying. Peter is also caught, uncertain if he should move around to comfort Eli.

'S – Sorry –' Eli said, choking with grief. His tears caused Jennifer to cry, looking between Harry and Eli.

Geoffrey looks hugely embarrassed and doesn't know where to look as both Eli and his sister weep over the man in the bed. Choking with grief, Eli stiffly shakes his head, as if unbelieving.

The tears splash on his cheeks as defenceless as a child. It's as if all those decades of horrible memories had finally found their release. Eli lifts his arm pressing the jacket sleeve into his face. Weeping openly now, brokenly.

Then, in a series of struggling but diminishing chokes in his throat, Eli regains a form of self-control. So does Jennifer, who jabs at her eyes with tissues.

'This is Yulen Turovsky,' he barely chokes out. 'A Ukrainian Jew ... and Rabbi.'

Geoffrey is fixed, staring, recovering from the shock, all he can think of is *'What?'* Geoffrey and his red and wet eyed sister staring at each other, trying to make sense of it all.

Eli, for the moment, is incapable of anything except holding Yulen's fragile, stringy hand between his own. An awkward moment as everybody struggles to find their personal composure.

'Your Grandfather,' said Peter, 'saved the Rabbi's life. He defied the Nazi's. He's a hero. They called him *Die Planke*, the plank, because they couldn't break him.'

Geoffrey blinks and swallows, greatly over-impressed, shakes his head, 'Him, lying there? Fancy that, eh? A hero!' he says this with a new found, but incredulous family identity and respect. 'What a turn-up!' Suddenly, for Geoffrey, "Harry" has come in from the cold.

Geoffrey looks at Yulen with new, disproportionate awe. 'You wouldn't think it, would you? You hear that, Sis? You'd never think it. Not in a million years. We all used to think he was just a cranky old –'

If she could, and if there were a vase of flowers nearby, she'd give it to her brother square in the face. 'Shut up your big stupid mouth for God's sake!'

'The Nazis could kill him, us, at any time.' Eli forced himself to say. 'For nothing. But they wanted first to kill his faith. But we knew he would die first. That's why they hated and hurt him so much.'

Peter takes a huge breath. He has no idea how to manage this moment, not as Pastor or "believer." It is too raw, heady, unrepentant, shredding his buffer of scholarly theology, and Eli's words torment him; *a miracle made flesh.*

Eli has regained his composure. He strokes Yulen's forehead tenderly. 'This man. This beautiful soul. Sent me a gift. Sunflower seeds and dirt.'

'Dirt and seeds?' frowns Geoffrey. 'What sort of gift is that?'

'The most wonderful in the world.' Eli replied. 'After our camp was liberated, we were walking and he picked up a handful of earth. "The earth is sacred because it is all we have to stand on," he said. "And to which we all return. The seeds are sacred because the Lord locked life inside them. One day, flowers will grow here again. I would like Sunflowers. They look up at the sun. We look up in hope with them." We went our separate ways. Somehow … he found out where I was.'

Peter thinks back to when he picked Eli up at his house seeing the sunflowers in his front yard, at the time, at that time, too blind to anything except his own problems to take notice. Geoffrey sort of smiles making an awkward apology.

Peter becomes aware of Eli looking him. His expression reads, *where is your faith now?* Even though the moment has such import, it is broken as Eli sees Peter's face suddenly twist in pain, and massages his temples. Peter is almost completely distracted by a crushing headache. Eli frowns worried, but most focus is on Yulen and tenderly strokes his pale, deeply wrinkled, and spot-marked forehead.

A total change has come over Geoffrey. Suddenly so angry and protective. *"Die Planke."* Boy oh boy I'll never forget for that.

The words were not wasted. They came to roost in an old, wounded, but heroic heart that would not deny faith. Yulen's indomitable spirit that would not surrender or bow to tyranny. A name to mock him, but identified his unbroken resilience; like an echo from hell, he's called back from past pain. Suddenly his mouth gaps in a huge breath and his eyes spring open, staring up at the ceiling as if in great shock. For a moment, they were all stunned and staring.

In a barely heard croak, he says, '… *Die Planke* …'

Jennifer, overcome with joy and relief, leaning in, words tumbling out in a rush. '*Pop!* It's me. Harry, it's Jenn, Oh, thank God, thank God, I thought – Harry, can you hear me? Do you understand? Jenn, with Geoffrey.' Is all she managed before her eyes flooded and her face was drenched with jubilant tears. 'There's a priest, and Rabbi here! Somebody you know –'

His milky eyes try to focus, but it's obvious he's almost blind, barely whispering, 'Rabbi?' he wheezes.

Eli leans in very close. 'Yulen. My good heart,' his voice breaking. 'Eli Steinsaltz.'

Yulen gasps for breath, almost as if in shock. 'No … How … how …' His frail and trembling arm reaches out as searching fingers find Eli's face. He gasps for air. Then Eli takes the friable, pale hand and lays it on the Torah. Yulen's fingers trace the embossed, raised letters תּוֹרָה, like reading braille.

'Oh, Oh, Eli. *Elohim hitsil otanu,*' he says in a whisper.

Eli looks around briefly. 'He said, "God saved us."' Eli's throat was thick. At this, tears flood Yulen's eyes and stream down his withered, deeply wrinkled, and lined cheeks. It's too much for Eli, as his heart breaks and his own tears find their way out, as do Jennifer's. Even Geoffrey deliberately rubs a hand over his forehead, covering his eyes.

Jennifer leans forwards, holding his arm. 'Oh God Yulen. We didn't know.' It's like an asking forgiveness and an apology rolled into one. 'We didn't – We're so, so *sorry*...'

With barely the strength left to raise his hand, Yulen gestures for Eli to come close and puts his ear to Yulen's mouth. Eli listens, then sits back.

'He finds it easier in Hebrew. He knows who you are. He knows your whole family. He is so sorry for the times he was such a burden and a problem. He knows everything that happened and everything that was said.'

'Oh God!' Jennifer said. She shoots a piercing, almost accusing, and angry look at her brother, who doesn't meet her eyes.

'He understands why you took his Torah. He forgives you. You didn't know but had a true heart.' Jennifer gently squeezes Yulen's arm in gratitude. 'He loves you all, very, very much and so wishes he had time over again to be part of your family. He thanks you from the bottom of his heart for all you did. There is nothing but love in his heart for you all. His heart is light and not burdened. He wants you to feel the same. No regrets. No pain.'

Eli sees him indicate and lowers his ear near Yulen's mouth, then straightens. 'If you want to remember him –'

'Of course we do!' She says stressed, cutting in. Then leans into Yulen. We'll never forget you! Never!'

Eli continues. 'And to honour him, learn about the Shoah. Teach others what you know.'

'We will. I promise. Won't we, Geoff?'

Geoffrey's face sets, and he nods several times. 'On my word, mate'.

Yulen seems satisfied; he sinks back into the pillow with shallow, difficult breaths. 'He also asks ... to speak to me alone.' Eli looks at Peter, who has almost been a shadow, standing back against the curtains, saying nothing. Eli can't read his face completely, but his expression seems wooden, almost lifeless, his eyes dark, almost sunken. But he takes his cue from Eli.

'I think its best,' Peter says, 'we go to my office and let them have their time.'

Jennifer is worried, unsure, but trusts Eli. 'I'll be right back, pop.' She kisses his forehead. Jennifer joins her brother as they give Yulen a last look before parting the curtains and leaving.

Peter pauses, staring at Eli for a moment. His face seems to say; *you were right all along. But it's too late for me.* And with that, a sense of aching defeat, *everything* is just too late. Time has run out. Eli is hugely disturbed. It was almost Peter's farewell. But Eli must stay with Yulen as he speaks.

'Eli.'

'Yes.'

'Is it you?'

'I'm here.' Eli strokes his pale, trembling hand.

Tears spill from Yulen's eyes again and roll over the many wrinkles. 'I did not want them to see me die.'

Eli nods his understanding.

'Thank Yahweh for your mercy,' he croaks. '*O-h-h-* how I prayed ...'

Eli tries to swallow, his throat thick and choked. 'Elohim tov, dearest Yulen. God is good.'

'Sunflowers?' he whizzes.

'They bloom in my garden looking at the sun.'

He nods a little. 'Then it is enough –'

Yulen gasping for air that cause shooting pains, followed by a helpless series of shuddering gasps. He seems to refocus, looking deeply into Eli's wet eyes.

All Eli can do now is offer a shuddering whisper, 'Are you in pain? I'll get the doctor.'

'The dying is easy Eli … It is the living that defeats us. Eli …' who leans in closer. Yulen swallows with difficulty. His hand searches on the bed to find Eli's. What strength is left holds Eli's hand. 'There was a spirit here. Lost, broken, defeated … I felt it. You must save it. …'

Eli knew the "spirit" was Peter, and somehow Yulen knew. 'Yes.' Eli's voice breaks.

Then very faint, almost like a valedictory croak. 'My most dearly loved brother, always remember … if this is the last sound made by the last living man, it must be shouted loud and clear. *Life is a gift from God.* Shalom Aleichem my dear Eli. It is time … now I have found you … it is time … God knew …'

Eli can barely see as tears flood down his face. 'God knew.'

Yulen is no longer trying to breathe. He makes the peculiar noises of a man on the edge of death. Eli has heard it before – too many times before – and he knows it's the end. Yulen has a bubble on his lips, and a small, odd gurgle comes from his mouth. Eli weeps openly, leaning forwards to kiss his forehead. But Eli can hardly see through the flood of tears.

'Aleichem shalom Rabbi Yulen Turovsky.'

With eyes almost blinded with tears, Eli recites the Viduy Prayers, the Hebrew last rights.

"I acknowledge before You, Adonai, my God and God of my

ancestors, that my recovery and my death are in Your hands. May it be Your will to heal me completely. And if I die, may my passing be an atonement for all the sins that I have committed, and grant me my portion in Gan Eden, and allow me to merit the World to Come, which has been reserved for the righteous… Barukh ata Adonai Eloheinu, melekh ha'olam, hagomel lahayavim tovot, sheg'molani kol tov. (Blessed are You, LORD our God, King of the Universe, Who bestows good things upon the unworthy and has bestowed upon me every goodness.)"

There was so much more to the prayers. But for Eli, it was all he could manage, his throat chocked as tears flooded his face. He lays his forehead on Yulen's chest, as it goes still.

Eli looks as thoroughly miserable as miserable can be. Lost in his own melancholy, his feet shuffled along with no life in his steps. Staff and visitors pass; he wouldn't know. He had closure, in a sense, but left with a tormenting space filled with horrid memories that, when he tends his garden, will always be there, past nightmares and today's memories.

Peter wasn't in the pastoral office. Jennifer and Geoffrey said he'd excused himself earlier, telling them he'd leave arrangements to Eli. He feels icy fingers grab at his stomach, as an absolute fear boarding on growing panic surges through him. This is bad, dreadfully bad. Eli arranged for the PA system to put out urgent calls for Peter as he searched every floor, every room he was permitted to enter. He was puffing a little and a light sheen of sweat glistened on his forehead as there was only the meditation room was left to check.

A small room with rows of bench seats on both sides and aisle between them. Subdued lighting, ambience is sombre and still. Only one person, a women is present. Eli turns to leave, but is somehow challenged. His concern for Peter is now roiling anxiety, is desperate to search again but some sense holds him. Again he looks at the solitary figure with head bent, at the front.

He doesn't understand the why, but decides to go down and takes a seat opposite the person on the other side of the aisle. For a long time they sit in silence, staring ahead at a plain blue curtain covering the wall. Eventually, the women speaks without looking around.

'I bet your Rabbi Steinsaltz.'

'I bet your Leanne Schrembri.'

'Peter sent you ... to "talk" to me?' Lee exhaled, a sound of suspicion and deep irritation, still looking ahead.

By contrast Eli's voice is kind, fighting his roiling stress and urgency over Peter. 'Oh – I don't presume to give advice to women. They very seldom take it anyway.'

The tiniest hint of a smile pulls at her cheeks. 'You are very discreet.'

'A necessary virtue,' Eli replied. 'As a matter of fact, I was really hoping to find Peter here,' his voice made edgy with anxiety.

They look at each other for the first time. She studies his face. Really studies it. His grey eyes sparkle under thick, white bushes of eyebrows. 'You won't find him here, Rabbi.' She looks back at the curtain. 'His ego couldn't squeeze in this small room.' She drops her eyes to the floor and, after a few moments, looks up again. 'I suppose you think that's catty?'

Although his anxiety for Peter on the edge of panic, his

experience senses somebody in distress and real need. He can't be everywhere, and right now he's here. Eli smiles kindly. 'I also don't presume to judge. Albert Einstein said, whoever undertakes to set himself up as a judge in the field of truth and knowledge is shipwrecked by the laughter of God.'

With Eli's gentle attitude, Leanne seems to deflate, her shoulders slumping, as her protective wall of hostility seems to leave her. Eli sees who she is – just a hurting, wounded woman who is lost, desperately lonely, and confused. He sees her bottom lip tremble as her eyes look at the floor without seeing anything.

'So, you're the man with answerers. Peter is very lucky to have such a solicitous friend.'

'You give me too much credit. Whatever else I may be, I'm a realist about my age and what I know. I am an old and simple man living with too many mistakes I'd like to forget.'

Again, she has been silent for a long time. 'We were happy once.' She says suddenly, obviously wanting to talk. Eli doesn't feel like a stranger exuding the sort of compassion and care that opens the way.

'We started small ... few people for worship. He wasn't satisfied. Peter had grandiose plans he was some on sort of divine mission about Bible *truth,* and theological hierarchy, whatever that is, was trying to silence him. Problem was, I kind of went along with it. It was like he always had to prove himself. The bigger the church, the more so-called "truth" in the message.'

Eli looks at her kindly. He hears the ache and deep regret in her voice.

'He was always at church or meetings, dinner with the Mayor or some well off nobody. Past three years he's been late or missed Mary's and Jacob's birthdays. One time he went on

TV at Christmas to be part of a charity phone-in event. Charity had Christmas, we didn't. Now we don't even bother. We lost our family. And I let it happen. Promoting the church, bums on seats became everything. Truth is … we all got greedy – me, the kids. Eventually, the message was all about money and how to get more of it. The more we had, the less of our lives we owned. What do say to that, Rabbi?'

'Eli. Please. I'm an old-fashioned man. I believe in God, life, love, and the pursuit of happiness. Ambitions like hunger, it obeys no law but its own appetite. Success is not a bad thing. But you have to know the rules of the game. You shouldn't underestimate how much you might lose to receive. Success is very greedy for itself.'

Suddenly she shows an unexpected spasm of emotion and her voice degenerates into a near, embarrassed and barely held-in sob. So she clears her throat.

'Why is my marriage like this?' Eli's brow furrows deeply, looking at her with great compassion.

'Is it so wrong for us to enjoy some of life's luxuries? Is it so wrong that countless charities need us? Families have food, clothes, and school books because of the church. Must Pastors lives only know poverty? Is it so wrong that we can enjoy nice things ourselves? Is it because of this that we have separate lives and beds? And the answer to why my marriage is like this is … just that my marriage is like this. You know, sometimes I'd give anything to be that woman. The one in the lounge room again. Singing. Making a meal for those who came to join us. But we seem to be given our roles. I'm this sort of wife. They cast me. That's his wife. And what does the man in the hat say to all that?'

Eli smiles. 'The man in the hat would probably have to put it to a rabbinical council ... and study the ramifications. But the man wearing the hat would have noticed that in all you've said, you never mentioned the word "love."'

'Do you mean I don't love him? – Or I do?'

'Oh, I cannot say that. Nobody can. There is only one area to search. And if love is mislaid, where did you see it last? And if you can't remember, maybe there was no love in the first place.'

'Oh, there *was!*' Her feelings are raw as Eli nods.

'Then it is mislaid.' He said it reassuringly. 'And you must set about to find it again.'

'How do you move forward when so much has happened?'

'Sometimes,' Eli said, 'you have to take a step back to move forward. C.S Lewis said "You can't go back and change the beginning, but you can start where you are and change the ending." Most things can be healed in time if time is used the right way.'

Her voice was thin and tired. 'Life is so insecure and so full of doubts isn't it? How can peace ever happen?'

'There's no guarantees. One has to abandon altogether the search for security; and to reach out to risk the living with both arms. One has to court doubt and darkness at the cost of knowing. Each of us Leanne, can only walk the path he sees at his own feet. Each of us is subject to the consequences of his own opinions and options. The only guarantee in life, is that you have to live it. Your only choice, is how.'

Her voice is suddenly thick, full of suppressed emotion ready to break through the surface in a storm of misgivings, doubts and confusion. 'Are you married?'

'No.'

'It's no bed of roses being married to a Pastor. Its endless service; service to God, service to your husband, your family, your church, community, it never stops.'

'Giving. Giving.' she sighs. 'As the wife of God's vicar, people think you have a seat closer to God's ear. How wrong they are. I pray, and pray, for the kids, our marriage, the church … And my reward? A pile of ashes. Nobody knows if prayer will work do they?'

'It's the eternal quandary Leanne, Eli said. 'No matter your words it is still Yahweh's grace that weighs. If prayer fails I am in a greater darkness yet; not knowing whether I have presumed too much or believed too little.'

Leanne laugh's a little. 'So the wise man *doesn't* know?'

Eli chuckles. 'Well. *This* man doesn't know.'

'And what wise words have you learnt as you got older?'

Eli waves his hands as if gesturing; *who knows?* 'Oh not many, except the older I get, the earlier it gets late.'

Leanne tries to smile and appreciates his gentle humour to support her, but her grief runs deep. She slumps with a little pained groan, looking very exhausted. She sniffs, fighting tears, and her voice almost breaks. 'Why is life so hard, Eli?'

He tips his head a little to the side as if considering. 'When I hear somebody saying, life is hard,' he says kindly, 'I am always tempted to ask, compared to what?'

It's not the answer she wanted and fixes him with a stern, almost unfriendly look. Eli meets her eyes, and his mouth peels back into a family-sized smile. Lee is immediately disarmed, her smile in reply coming from nowhere, as she looks down shaking her head. She is grateful for his successful attempt to lift her mood, but her heart is still weighed down and her long sigh betrays that.

'So what do I do with my marriage?'

Eli sits back in the seat. For a moment he looks at the ceiling. He then clasps his hands as if in prayer.

"If I speak in the tongues of men or of angels but do not have love, I am only a resounding gong or a clanging cymbal. If I have the gift of prophecy and can fathom all mysteries and all knowledge, and if I have a faith that can move mountains but do not have love, I am nothing. If I give all I possess to the poor and give over my body to hardship so that I may boast but do not have love, I gain nothing."

Leanne looks at him and picks up the next verse. *"Love is patient; love is kind. It does not envy, it does not boast, and it is not proud. It does not dishonour others; it is not self-seeking; it is not easily angered; and it keeps no record of wrongs. Love does not delight in evil but rejoices in the truth. It always protects, always trusts, always hopes, and always perseveres."*

Together, they recite the third verse.

"Love never fails. But where there are prophecies, they will cease; where there are tongues, they will be stilled; where there is knowledge, it will pass away. We know in part and we prophecy in part, but when completeness comes, what is in part disappears. When I was a child, I talked like a child, I thought like a child, and I reasoned like a child. When I became a man, I put the ways of childhood behind me. For now, we see only a reflection as in a mirror; then we shall see face to face. Now I know in part; then I shall know fully, even as I am fully known."

Eli looks at her encouragingly and stops letting Leanne continue and answer her own question.

"And now these three remain: faith, hope, and love. But the greatest of these is love." She looks at him admiringly. 'You are a man with answers after all.' Leanne says warmly.

He smiles. 'Only Some. Perhaps. God allows me to know and say some things. But not too much. That is why I always pray, Abba, Father, put one hand around my shoulder and the other over my mouth.' He smiles and nods to himself. 'In that way I mostly stay out of trouble. I tell people that is why Yahweh made that little cleft under our nose.'

'Do tell,' she asks.

'Well, because Yahweh knew we would always struggle with a dangerous and rebellious tongue, to help save His creation, He made a cleft, under the nose, above the mouth. It is a place to rest your forefinger in that cleft for two reasons; it shuts the mouth and imprisons the tongue. Perhaps also He gave us two ears and one mouth so we listen twice as much.'

Leanne can't help but smile. 'Where do you get all this stuff?'

Eli laughs. 'Oh, I pick a bit up here and there.' Eli falls silent, deeply burdened and distressed. 'Leanne ...' he stops. She looks at him chewing his lip in troubled inner turmoil. 'You're a nice person, so are your children.' Leanne looks awkward, a little ashamed, he reads the look. 'You've all made mistakes that are damaging your lives. If you want to you can fix that.'

Eli turns fully in the seat to face her. 'You hardly know me. You have no reason to trust me. But sometimes, Yahweh leaves us with no choice but to act for the good. Peter's heart is breaking. And I'm very, very worried about him. His life is nailed to a cross of guilt he carries and he's losing everything.'

Suddenly Lee's eyes are swimming in tears. What she knew and tried to keep secret is exposed by the kind and insightful man that sees to the heart and the collapse of their lives. Tears spill down her face, of guilt, of bitter regret, fear and loss.

'What is it? Leanne? What is destroying this good man?'

She struggles so hard to pull herself back she forgets to breathe until there is a small, shuddering gasp. She looks in Eli's eyes, sniffs back more tears, and then looks away. Leanne says heavily. 'Something very, very bad and awful did happen. And I must take some of the blame.'

Jacob and Mary stand at the door watching Eli and Leanne in deep conversation. They exchange a look and go down the aisle. Eli and Lee sit back as they approach. Jacob and Mary stare at Eli accusingly reacting to Lee's red eyes and tension.

'What's going down, Mum?' Mary said without shifting her gaze from Eli.

'It's alright. Rabbi Steinsaltz and I were just talking. But more important, what are you doing here?'

They exchange a look, shrug and sigh. 'Today's so uncool,' Mary said.

Leanne looks between them and their depressed faces. Eli watches sympathetically. 'We'll talk about it later. Have you seen your father?'

'Sure,' Jacob replied. 'Couple of hours ago in the canteen.'

'He hasn't answered his P.A. calls,' Lee said.

'He's gone. Thought you knew!'

Eli is immediately on his feet. 'You mean left the hospital?' Jacob nods. For some odd reason Eli feel icy fingers suddenly grab his stomach and twist. He has a horrible sense of foreboding, a dread.

'He just said give money to the Rabbi and car keys to you.' Mary passes the keys to her mother and Jacob fifty dollars to Eli. Jacob continues, 'Oh, he also said to tell the Rabbi. "God bless you. Thank you for everything. Enjoy the Cappuccinos."' Lee and Eli exchange a look; this whole situation is becoming especially strange and serious. Lee looks between the kids, frowning and very edgy.

'Did he say anything else? Jacob?'

'Not much. I mean, what's the big deal, he's always going off on his crusades or something, Saint Peter of the perpetually pained. We're so over it!' Jacob looks at his sister who scowls like she's bitten into a sour lemon and nods. Eli flicks a hooded, disappointed look at them, then focuses back on Lee and her rapidly rising stress.

'Answer me!' Lee snaps. 'What did he say?'

The siblings exchange a puzzled look 'Yeah. Bit weird ...' Jacob says as Mary shrugs and frowns, looking at Jacob.

Lee barks with an unmistakable warning. *'Mary!'*

But Jacob speaks up, confused and growing alarmed by the tension coming off the adults. 'He said ... he loved us. What's going on, Mum?'

'Anything else. Come on! I don't want to have to drag it out of you, for Heaven's sake. Work with me here,' her face flushes.

'"Too late the hero." Something too weird like that,' Mary answered.

'Too late the hero? He said that?' Lee confused, looks at Eli. 'Do you know what that means?'

'From memory, I think it's a name of a movie. About a peace loving man in a war who sacrificed himself for the good of others.'

Mary added. 'Yeah. And to tell the Rabbi, James 1:6.'

'James, 1:6? Are you sure?' Eli asks, Mary nods. *"But let him ask in faith, with no doubting, for the one who doubts is like a wave of the sea that is driven and tossed by the wind."* Eli explains.

'Whatever. He was really out of it. Not like Peter at all. Really weird. You know.'

Lee's anxiety spills. 'No I don't! Weird, how? Mary! Stop being stupid. It's important we find out where your father is and why he left the hospital without telling me. I want a straight answers! Now!'

She tilted her head defiantly, looking at Jacob, the held down stress of the siblings reaches boiling point.

'Weird. *Weird*. Okay. I dunno. *Weird like your marriage.* Weird like our house. Weird like everything. Weird!' She glares at her mother, her eyes hooded and disdainful. If it was meant to make Eli feel awkward, and Lee embarrassed, it failed. But all Eli sees is two stress driven teenagers, lives in turmoil and with the decay of their parents' marriage at the core.

'Oh.' Mary said with forced indifference, the facade crumbling. 'He also said he had a headache.' They grab their bags and she looks at Jacob. 'We're going!'

Lee is immediately on her feet. 'You're not! Wait for me in the Pastoral office. I'm not having anybody else disappear until I know what's going on!'

'Oh wow. Far out. We're not kids,' Jacob argues. But Lee's not wearing their insolence.

'Then stop acting like it,' she orders. 'I have some business and I'll be right back. Got it!' She forces a deep, calming breath and looks at Eli.

Mouths open, big eyed, fuming. Both glare their protest at Eli. 'That's so *uncool!*' snaps Mary. Eli sits, deeply disturbed.

The lonely, forlorn figure of Peter rubbing his temple, slumped forwards on the seat where only yesterday, a total stranger intersected with his life, bonding over God, faith, love, and the meaning of it all.

He looks but doesn't see the indifferent bustle of the intersection. His wounded soul only sees "through a glass, darkly," as described in the letter by the disciple Paul in 1 Corinthians 13. Paul meant that nobody really knows God until you meet Him face to face, the image is at once vivid and memorable: our mortal vision of God is like when we try to see through an obscure piece of glass, will be clouded and imperfect.

Days ago, across the road, stood a glass temple, not clouded or imperfect, a tangible vision of glory in belief. Now, like all his hopes and dreams, ruined lumps of congealed ash that once reflected majesty and splendour. After investigations have concluded, machines will clank through to clear the ruins leaving nothing but memories.

In the story of Job, God allowed Satan the Devil, to inflict horrible tragedies on him to test Job's faith. The Devil could do anything, except kill Job. Peter remembers the words; we are not punished for our sins, but *by* them. Even his torturous, eye-clenching, headache part of that.

In the book of Kings, Peter reflects that tribes and peoples have always worshipped foreign Gods. Even the so-called wise King Solomon built shrines for Ashtoreth, where children were sacrificed. But today's god is Mammon, so Peter speculates upmarket units will tower where once his "Crystal Palace" stood.

From the seat, Peter picks up a copy of the Bible and a copy of his own book. He holds one in each hand as if weighing them, judging their worth.

'You wrote one. I wrote one.' He looks across the intersection at the devastated church's remains. 'I don't understand why I failed. I did everything to make sure we succeeded. What am I supposed to learn from this; you're a vengeful God that demands everything gives nothing? All I ever wanted was to know the truth ... and be well off. How do we help the poor being poor ourselves? I tried Jesus. I really did. But I never really knew what you wanted.'

He replaces both books on the seat. 'Why did you choose me?' His voice breaks, thick in his throat. 'I am no good for you ... not for anybody. Better off without me ... they wouldn't even miss me.'

Peter struggles to his feet as if burdened by an invisible but massively heavy load. The wind blows his pile of white hair into a twisted mess. He doesn't care. He turns in a complete circle, searching the sky.

'There is no "meaning to life"' Peter mutters to himself. 'The meaning of life is no meaning, only suffering. Endless ... so what's the point? There's no hope!' His words sound convincing in his own ears.

'*Yeshua*. Where have you gone? Why can't I find you? Show me the way! I'm lost!' But no answer from heaven, only the incessant din of the intersection. 'No answer? No shining example of faith or hope.' he says. He remembers the words he said to Eli, "*How can I be trusted to trust God?*"

Peters looks to the sky again. 'Is that what you want? You want me to come home? What you've been trying to show me but the Devil blinded me to truth. Losing my church wasn't punishment but setting me *free*? It was a sign. God making a way where there is no way ...'

It is so clear the elated Peter thinks to himself. The burden on family and church is gone by removing himself. It's the only answer that makes any sense. He grips his fingers together in prayer so tight his knuckles turn white. Bowing his head, he prays, 'Oh, praise you God for showing me my ladder at last!' He then looks up with glowing adoration to the darkening, overcast sky and mouths the words, 'Thank you.'

With surging purpose, confident that he finally understands the collapse of his life and faith, without a backwards glance, he leaves the books and goes down the steps to the footpath.

He is no longer "Job," a victim of circumstance or merciless heavenly tests. The veil of self-doubt and fear has been lifted, some sort of spirit has finally shown him the way.

IN THE HOSPITAL PASTORAL ROOM, Jacob and Mary are making their displeasure a performance they are not indulging in the canteen. They slouch in glum silence, big theatrical sighs. Eli sitting on the sofa watching them with mounting impatience. Peter missing and at high risk consuming his thinking, especially after the cryptic messages he said to his children. Mary behind the desk and Jacob in one of the chairs.

'Enough of this.' The siblings, caught off guard, look at each other. 'If you've got anything else on your chest except your chins get it off.'

'You're so uncool!' said Mary defiantly.

'It's the price of being adult,' Eli snaps, no nonsense. The urgency of Peter missing tormenting him, the Eli has no time for bad attitudes. 'Why are you making hell for your parents?'

'*Us!*' Jacob almost jumps in his chair. 'What've *we* done? What about *them!*'

This sparked the rise out of Mary. 'Yeah. Right. Blame *us! They* fight all the time. He's never home, when he is they fight more. They're always picking on us …'

As Jacob continued 'We heard what they said.'

'Especially Peter. About how lazy we are,' Mary's voice a mix of anger and hurt.

Jacob pulls his lips tight, then snaps in reply. 'How it's a waste sending us to college.'

'How we'll never amount to anything.' Mary's voice when it came was small, reticent, and wounded.

But Jacob had found his anger. 'Just throwing good money after bad.'

Eli pressed his thumb and forefinger into his eyes. He looked down with a small head shake, then looked up with a sigh. 'Parents sometimes say the things they shouldn't, kids sometimes say things to parents they shouldn't. But I know they love you.'

'Sure! Then why are they getting divorced?'

Eli responds to the bitter pain in her voice. 'I don't think they are. Hurting people hurt people and say things they don't mean. Your parents have made bad decisions and *are* in a crises, but you-don't-help!' He deliberately spaced the words for emphasis. His unblinking stare skates back and forth between Mary and Jacob. They gawped wide-eyed, not expecting to be in the spotlight. 'You know one of the biggest problems with teenagers?' It wasn't a question. 'They want to be treated respectfully at the same time acting like idiots. When adults call them out for acting like idiots, teenagers cry they're being disrespected.'

Jacob opens his mouth to protest, but Eli cuts him off.

'I'm talking! Being a teenager and going through stuff is a hard ask. But too many think they're too smart for their own good and are nothing but self-entitled brats. I've told quite a few if they think it's easy then feed, clothe, educate, and house yourselves. Many tried and were lucky to end up owning a sleeping bag. You two aren't innocent bystanders. You're old enough to take responsibility. It's obvious their marriage is struggling. If you know your parents are in crisis, why are you being so selfish as to pour fuel on the fire? If you think getting arrested, killed, or seriously injured in a car doing drugs is cool, think again! Regardless of what you think, they love you very much, despite what is said. You want to ruin your lives, go ahead. Peter and your mother are worried sick about you. That says love. You have so much going for you. Remember this. Decisions you make now – not Peter or Leanne, you – will, not might, *will*, affect the rest of your lives.'

Eli was in his power voice. When he focused, he had a tremendous amount of inner energy that just seemed to narrow to a point towards whatever or whoever he was focused on. Right then that point was all about Jacob and Mary.

'It's all about discovery in life. We all go through discovery but at times some do not survive or know how to survive. I think kids that grow up in religious families have an extra difficult time interfacing with society. You know, Jacob and Mary, true innocence is experiencing evil, knowing the difference and choosing innocence – being buffered from life does not make one strong when life bangs you around. God doesn't take care of everything; *you* must take the initiative to bail yourselves out of situations and have the smarts to do it. There are two sorts of people in this world; those who learn only by bad experience, and those who learn from everything.'

Eli stops, letting his words find their mark. They don't meet his eyes as he looks at them.

'You probably think I should mind my own business. But I hate to see the pain in this family. And it's a good family. I happen to like this family. It hurts me to see you all hurting. I believe a great evil is trying to destroy this family.'

This shakes them both, they look at each other wary then focus on Eli. 'But why?' Mary asked.

Eli took a moment before reply. 'Evil doesn't need a reason. Evil is as evil does, and all my experience tells me it's true. Something very evil is happening: kill, steal, destroy, the devils playbook! You can't see it, but that evil exits and it is as real as this room.'

He waited, leaving the room quiet for Mary and Jacob to consider and ponder what he said, confirming or denying his words essential justice. He had more urgent things to attend to: finding Peter. And for a reason he couldn't explain, Eli had a nagging, haunting sense time had run out.

'I have to go.' Getting to his feet.

'You looking for Peter?' Mary asked quietly.

'I'm looking for a *good man, your father!*' he said. 'And I pray I'm right where he might be.'

THE WAVES SEEMED DARK AND unfriendly to Peter, sitting isolated clothed in his gloom and depression. Not because it was dusk, but their usual ceaseless churning and methodical life, the ordered confidence that as one wave rolled in to spill and spend itself as the next asserted and followed, had blessed him with a sense of certainty and completion, peace and rest. The waters never lied or betrayed, never deceived or denied, always available to those who sought its solace. Angels have their harmony, but only the waves, for Peter, caressed him with melodic ease. But today, rhythmic percussion of waves denied caressing peace of mind where he could became lost and their foaming fingers seemed only to dig deep and painfully into his roiling soul.

They seemed foreign, even annoying, too loud, never stopped, never rested. His disturbed spirit took offence that he is not welcome here today.

'So?' Peter sighs. 'After all that has happened. All the hell I've gone through, even a moment's rest denied me. I'll rest soon. For eternity. They say there's hell on earth …' Peter looks up at the grey-streaked and clouded sky.

'You. God. Created hell for …'

'Fallen angels.' Peter jumps in the seat. 'But people on earth enjoyed evil more than good and so hell became a place of punishment and damnation for us all. That's what you Christian's believe. The Jewish faith is not so certain,' Eli said. 'Gehinnom, is a Jewish Hell. Only truly righteous souls ascend directly to the Garden of Eden, say the sages. The average person descends to a place of punishment and-or purification, generally referred to as Gehinnom. The name is taken from a valley called, *Gei Hinnom*, just south of Jerusalem, once used for child sacrifice by the pagan nations of Canaan, recorded in second Kings. Some view Gehinnom as a place of torture and punishment, fire and brimstone. Others imagine it less harshly, as a place where one reviews the actions of their life and repents for past misdeeds. Not all Rabbi's agree on Gehinnom.'

'What do you think?'

Eli shrugs. 'I don't know. So best behave.'

'How long have you been there?'

'Long enough,' Eli said, staring at the waves.

'How did you know where I was?'

'Scripture you told your daughter. *"But let him ask in faith, with no doubting, for the one who doubts is like a wave of the sea that is driven and tossed by the wind."*'

When Eli turned his head to look at Peter, he was stunned. Even in the encroaching dusk he looked aged, drawn, and dark with anxiety and despair. If Eli did not know him, Eli would struggle to recognise him in a crowd or passing on the sidewalk.

'I remember, a group of us waiting to go in the building for selection. A man, Catholic priest, Father Garbelli Amporth, was trying to comfort another man. He said, *"And do not fear those who kill the body but cannot kill the soul. Rather fear him who can destroy both soul and body in hell."* I asked if he believed in hell. He said one time during an exorcism, a real demon told him that hell is real. Heaven is real. The fire of hell is real, the demon said, but despite it being fire, it is not similar to our fire; it is not combustion. More the fire of conscience, fire of remorse, fire of guilt, and the fire of pain. The pain you caused others, you experience yourself – but it's increased a hundred fold, over and over; there's no escape, no relief, no end.'

'Was he honest? Honest with himself?' Peter asked.

'He was facing a death sentence. He could not afford to be otherwise.' Eli sits back in the seat heavily, eyes glazed in memory. 'As a Priest, he said something else I've never forgotten. He said it solved nothing by waving the commandments like a bludgeon at people's heads. There was no point in shouting damnation at a man who was already walking himself to hell on his own two feet. You had to pray for the Grace of God and then go probing for the fear that might condition him to repentance or the love that might draw him towards it. He was a beautiful man. Beautiful soul that left us that day.'

The bookends sit in silence until Peter speaks. 'He's better off … get out of this rotten, soul and hopes destroying world.' His tone ripped with bitterness and anger. They are silent again.

'God made you a smart man,' Peter said eventually. 'I don't know what he made me.' He shows an unexpected spasm of emotion, and for a moment, his voice is thick and degenerates into a near sob. So he clears his throat. Eli looks down. He is torn seeing his friend hurting like this.

'Right from the seminary. I've always wondered. How do you know, Eli? How does a man ever know if his actions are for himself or for God?'

For a long time Eli is silent. Words march through his mind. He has no idea which ones are the right ones. In the end, his answer is the one he has had to face too often. 'You don't know,' he said finally. 'You have a duty to act. But you have no right to expect approval or even a successful outcome.'

Peter looks at him. 'So in the end, we are alone?'

'Yes. Physically. Spiritually. No. People say *I am alone*. That is never true. You are in the company of God, or the devil. Never alone. Today I saw a hero die. There have been many like him. They all had one thing in common: they refused to surrender to circumstance. When you lose hope, you can die still breathing before they even put you in the ground. For those in ministry, it is often much more difficult. For some, it is impossible. It is a job where you must constantly think of others more than yourself. I have known many men of different faiths. Perhaps you are the last. Each of them, in turn, came to where you stand now. The moment of solitude. I have to tell you that there is no remedy for it. It will be with you until the day you die. And the longer you live, the lonelier you will become. You will use this man and that man for the work of the church. But when the work is done or the man has proved unequal to it, you will let him go and find another. Like it or not, you are condemned to a solitary pilgrimage from the day you gave your life to God to day of your death. Every believer eventually faces the Calvary of their faith. And you, Peter, have just begun to climb.'

Peter seems to shrink in the seat, leaning forwards with his elbows on his knees. Eli looks at Peter with deep compassion as he appears even more self-destructive and brittle, full of apparent self-loathing.

'You are changed,' Eli said.

'I do not feel changed,' Peter replied, sitting back.

'There was pride in you once. More, an arrogance, as if you carried the truth in a private purse and no one could dispute it with you. You even wrote a book more about your fears than your faith. Commanding the world to listen to *your* truth as you believed because only you knew it.'

'It failed. Like my church. Like my hopes and dreams. When I hated you, and I did, when you challenged me, it was because of that. I have learned who I am. A low man who sits too high for his gifts.' He nods several times to himself. 'I have decided to leave ministry.'

'Probably best. You can drown all your sorrows and join Gary,' Eli said flatly.

Peter flares. Almost stunned and almost yells. 'I thought you cared! But you only care about yourself and you're fucking Torah!'

Hurting people hurt people. Eli is unmoved, he is cajoling, but firm, his power voice.

'I do care. Very much. But not on *your* terms. Stop looking for someone to blame. The only person to blame if you quit is yourself.'

This isn't the reply Peter wanted. His fury deflates to exhausted hopelessness and despair. 'What's wrong with you? How can you say that? Why can't you understand how bad I feel?' Shakes his looking drawn and broken. 'Gary died because I failed to do enough … my … disgrace with Melanie …'

'Gary killed Gary,' Eli said. 'It was just a matter of time. The hard line in the sand is the hard truth some people refuse to be helped or saved. It's *their* choice. *Their* decision! Yahweh gives everybody a chance to change their ways and see the light. Did you ever try to explain to your wife about Melanie?'

Peter sits back in the seat with a loud, weary sigh and shakes his head. 'Oh yes. She ordered me to stop Melanie coming to church, and if any dirty, grubby little fantasy ever happen again we'd divorce. I couldn't bring myself to stop her, so Leanne accused me of having an affair, with a *blind* young women. See no evil she said. Can you believe that? Sometimes it's better just to shut up. Confession isn't good for the soul, it's a noose to hang yourself.'

For a few moments Eli reflects, watching the waves. 'What happened with Melody?' he asked.

Peter jerks his dead around and stares at him alarmed. 'How do you know about her!?' Then he nods to himself with a small sneer. 'Leanne. Of course.' The memories flood down and he lets out a shuddering breath. He leans forward, head between his hands as if trying to crush away horror. 'Oh dear God. Never forgive myself. Neither has God. He destroyed my church. Divine punishment.'

Eli shakes his head. 'God doesn't destroy churches. The devil does.' Grief is etched in Peter's face. 'Our actions give him permission. Who was Melody?'

'Didn't Lee tell you? What can I say? She was a nineteen year old drug addict. Heart breaking. She was the sweetest person you could ever meet off drugs. I baptised her, she almost became part of our family, came for prayer, meals. She also supplied the drugs.'

Eli nods with respectful listening but says nothing.

'Prayed, counselled, loved, guided, paid for all sorts of dependence services. Anyway … one evening … Leanne went ballistic, calling me a liar, we were finished, divorced. She took a call and a girl said it was *Melanie*. She was desperate, needed me, was just around the corner in a motel, come quickly. Things went crazy. If I went Lee said, stay because we were finished.'

Peters head hangs and shoulder slump. 'I don't know Eli, just how screwed up can things get. First thing I thought how far has drugs gone through the church? Well, you would, wouldn't you? Now beautiful, sweet blind Melanie? She sounded odd, Lee said, slurring her words, of course you think drugs, grog or both. The way it turned out I couldn't be more wrong … and that's when the whole unforgiving horror starts.'

Peter looks at Eli to see if he can read any judgement in his face, but Eli just stares ahead watching the waves.

'She called again. Begged me to come, thought she'd injected too much. I said call an ambulance, said she was too scared and needed somebody of God. I should have done my duty. She was a soul in distress, I was a priest. But I was weak and gutless. The terror in her voice haunts to this day. She had nobody else to help … nobody to care … unless I came to the motel she'd overdose because it proves there is no God. Like a coward I waited until Leanne went to bed, snuck out and walked to the motel ... oh God forgive me ...' A sob breaks Peter, his cheeks glisten and he can hardly breathe. Eli had the strangest, most inexplicable sense that this was Peter's moment, the crescendo of his personal crises. Something would shatter. For Eli, observing him was soul-tearing, like watching a man approach a precipice and continuing, deliberately, to slowly lean out, knowing he would lose his balance and fall, destroying himself.

Eli puts out a hand and gives his shoulder a firm, encouraging squeeze.

VENETIAN BLINDS PULLED DOWN AND broken, a room of utter destruction, as if a wounded animal had gone berserk. Chairs, tables, bedsheets spewed all over. There's a lump lying beside the bed. Peter, holding a bible, stands at the open door. He slowly survey's the room, cautiously enters before going to the side of the bed. For a moment he's frozen in horror. A body lay face down and twisted, knotted, and contorted, a suggestion of some soft pubescent texture in the limp, white skin. The arms flopped, dead, and a ribbon of dried blood from a vein – the body arched, coiled in some inexpressible state of dumb, endless, shock, pain, panic.

Peter kneels, lifting and rolling the body over. The eyes, bloated, distended eyeballs of utter horror, staring straight into Peters. The eyes seem to dwarf the face, which is cold, pale, drenched in sweat, tears, and smears of blood. The syringe, blood dipped, broken nearby.

Peter stares transfixed, and then overwhelming grief and anger rushing in like a wave breaks over him. A wet faced, broken Peter, lifts the body like it were fractured glass, and folds it into himself. One hand holds the back of her head as lovingly presses her face against his chest, toward his heart. 'God,' he gasps, 'how could you let this happen?'

He will never forget. It will haunt him, he tells himself. Haunt him always. If only, if only he hadn't been such a coward, if only, if only …

'I've *never* recover from this memory.' He told himself, over, over and over. From this image, this horrible, tragic loss … It wasn't Melanie, Lee, for some reason, anger or whatever, heard the wrong name. It was Melody.

THE ONLY SIGN ELI HAS heard is when he closes his eyes, and his face is matched by the crashing and thudding waves and spray. But in the natural order, the surge dissipates and Eli gathers himself. But Peter falls apart, his face awash with tears tearing from the very core of his being. He is truly broken, Eli lets him cry. In a series of struggling, but diminishing chokes in his throat, he struggles to find remnants of control.

'I'm so sorry, so sorry.'

'My father used to say how you do anything is how you do everything,' Eli said. 'Called it the first and last rule of life. We make our circumstances. But consequences are made for us. There are consequences for inactions just like actions. And yet we are here at this moment.'

'I failed.'

'God, family and yourself. So did Leanne. You think it's all accident or coincidence? A great evil helped every step of the way. Hell is all over your lives.'

'Hell? What is hell? I don't even know it if it even exists. I don't know what to believe any more.'

'If you still doubt after all this Peter, I'm sure evil will accommodate you with some horror experience you'll never forget. That's what the Devil does.'

Peter looks at him with alarm and confusion. He wonders if Eli is talking about the Holocaust or Peter's tragedies. 'It won't change anything. It doesn't matter what I believe.'

'Wrong! It matters the world what you believe. You might even say your unbelief started this. Can't you see how evil set you all up? *"Kill, steal, destroy"* Satan's playbook. He caused strife in your family to steal your peace. He pulled Melody and Melanie into your lives. Look how close their names are? He destroyed your marriage so Leanne's jealousy made her hear only Melanie's name when it wasn't, knowing your guilt would drive you to go to the motel where he killed that sad young women. And what did he win? Look at you sitting here now.'

'Look at the ruin of your family. You were all used, even Jacob and Mary. Evil is as evil does.'

Peter looks at him with a scowl. His tone was brittle with frustration. 'You might be right. It won't bring anybody back. And don't tell me to forgive myself. I tried.' For a long time they sit in silence lost in thought as the dusk wraps them in darkness and waves break, and foam swirls and spread glistening the sand. Peter continues rubbing his temple with fingertips.

'It has been an honour my friend,' Peter said eventually, his voice sounding as if it was coming from another place, dejected and burdened.

Eli looks at him with a terrible sense of profound dread. Like Peter is saying a very sad goodbye. Foreboding clutches Eli's stomach as he forces a smile of encouragement.

'The honour has been mine. But Peter … Peter, you must, *must* forgive yourself! If you don't – *Satan wins*. Destroying yourself, he *wins*. It's part of *his* victory. Don't you see? *The devil wins*. All of this could have been anybody. It could have been me.'

He sighs. 'Yes. But it wasn't. Now you think about why that is, and perhaps one of us will have benefited from this conversation. Yahweh bless you Eli.'

Chapter 10

'Strange.' Peter rubs a hand over his face looking around. 'Don't you think it's strange? And cold. Suddenly, so very cold. Do you think that? Nobodies around. Never empty like this. Not a bird – a seagull. Nothing.'

The beach brooded under a bruised sky, a sudden wind whipped up. That wind cut into the warm and unprepared flesh of Peter's face and he frowned.

'Look at the water. It's almost black, like oil. Hardly any foam in the waves.' A smell, heavy and cloying, sweeps from the ocean. 'What's that stink?' Peter looks at Eli as his face almost lost in shadows. 'The ocean doesn't stink like that! Like rotten sewerage or something!' But Eli is looking directly ahead, face fixed, ignoring him.

'It's so quiet,' Peter said softly, deeply troubled. Something is wrong, he thought, almost frightened. Something's dreadfully wrong. 'Suddenly all strange don't you think?'

There is no reply. He looks around and stares at Eli, who has moved away right to the end of the bench seat, almost exactly the way they sat as bookends on the seat in the park when they first met. 'What are you doing here?' He looked at him, bewildered. 'What are we doing here?'

Eli looked around at him. He thought the look on his face was one of gentle abstraction, perhaps mixed with minor annoyance. But in just a flash, a jumbled moment in the encroaching darkness, the face changed and was not Eli's but his own. He believed, in his mind, that the face was the expression of a man who was methodically unplugging himself from reality, one cord at a time. The face of a man who was heading out of the blue and into the black. Just a flash, then it was Eli's face again.

Peter jumped a little with shock. His eyes were wide and frightened, riveted on Eli, almost afraid to look away, as if the more Peter stared at Eli's face, the more anchored to reality Peter became. But Peter just saw Eli staring ahead, as if ignoring him. Peter thought Eli looked almost haunted. Then he watched Eli smile. It was the kind of smile Peter had never seen before. It was wise, cynical, and sad all at the same time. And his face was mournful.

Almost as if reading his thoughts, Eli looked around at him. Not at him, almost *through* him in a sense. Peter smiled weakly, but Eli didn't smile back. Then Eli seemed to withdraw into his own thoughts. An expression of great sadness and grief on his face that alarmed and puzzled Peter.

"*Forgive yourself!*" Yes. Easier said than done. 'Has anybody really ever done it successfully,' he asks himself out load. 'And how do you know if you have done it?' Peter continues talking out loud to himself. 'What measure do you know you have done it? Isn't not remembering just a cowards forgetting? Aren't second chances just the refuge for a life that failed, and bad memories just the price paid for what you can't fix?'

He bites down on his lip and puts his hands together, palm

to palm, tight, as if to keep himself from flying apart. Peter feels there is some part of him that actually wonders if he shouldn't just walk into that ocean and disappear.

Panic slipped its hood over Peter's mind. 'We lie best when we lie to ourselves,' he muttered. 'You really believe there's heaven and hell. The devil is real?'

There was just enough light to see Eli's smile: *Think what you like*, that smile said. *Think what you like, and I'll think what I like.*

Feeling in a state of absolute despair and confusion, Peter mutters, 'Oh my God.' He did not know what else to say. But did he believe the words or just toss them out like bad lettuce, *"Dear God," "Oh my God,"* or *"I swear to God"* people say by reflex without believing a moment God even exists. But when life goes bad things go wrong people believe straight away because God gets blamed. That's when Satan smiles.

'I love my family so much ...'

Suddenly Peter is on his feet, holding the sides of his head as if it were a bowling ball about to slip and fall off his shoulders. In panicked strides, almost stumbling, he ploughs through the sand towards the water.

'Peter! *Peter!* What are you doing!?' Eli shouts.

I don't know what I'm doing. *I don't!* Peter screams in his throbbing head. He isn't Job, he knows he doesn't have Job's faith or courage. Just feels his heart is torn, and mind broken; he can't manage, can't control, and can't deny – nobody can help. And worse – the greatest horror – he's completely alone; God isn't listening, isn't helping. If this is his Calvary, Peter tells himself, he can't do it; he can't climb, he just wants it all to stop. If hell exists, it can't be any worse than this.

Peter suddenly realises he's soaked, bashed by waves and

rocked, staggering, regaining footing, smashed again, eyes blind, burned and stinging, choking, mouth full of a foul, oily taste. He squints repeatedly, wiping his eyes with a drenched sleeve only making it worst, trying to look up where he thinks the sky is, *'God has giving up on me! I am alone,'* he tries to scream, half choking, gulping and coughing.

The water felt chilled, he shivered, and it was up to his waist. It had the same pungent, nauseous stink; it was noxious, and even in the consuming darkness, it looked unnaturally thick, as if he could plunge in his hand and be covered by a malevolent oily slick. But the roll of waves that hit and tossed him were real enough, and he fought, rocked and jarred to keep standing, his shoes sinking into the clinging, shifting sand and slipping away underfoot.

Problem was, Peter could not even remember entering the water.

'You're never alone. Never. Believe it!' He thought he heard Eli call. Peter's stinging eyes searched the thick darkness and finally found him. Loyal Eli had followed him into the water and was fighting to stay upright, buffeted by the waves that exploded and erupted over him in spills of flying foam.

'Hell or heaven. Believe it real or not. That's your only choice. Your choice can deny it all you want but that doesn't make it any less real!' Eli yelled.

A wave crashed into him toppling Peter, staggering and thrashing, his arms whipping and grabbing at nothing to recover balance. He choked and coughed violently swallowing water, frantically wiping his face to try to see. His eyes stung and were blurred.

'Go back! Go away! Leave me.' Peter screamed, his hair sodden and sticking to his saturated face like a mix of filthy brine, sticky

foam, and salty tears. The smashing of waves seemed to grow more furious.

'You can't escape!' he heard a voice call. Peter thought it was Eli but, for some inexplicable reason, it sounded different, almost right beside him.

'Don't be stupid, Peter. I can't help you; if you go deeper. *I can't help you!*' Peter thought he heard Eli yell.

Another wave whacked Peter like a gigantic fist, ripping him off his feet and causing him to thrash and flounder in the dark, bitterly saline, murky water. He desperately pulled in a lungful of air drenched with foul-smelling brine.

Then a greater horror as he frantically, desperately wiped his drenched sleeves over his eyes in a futile attempt to clear them – Eli was gone. He wasn't anywhere. He must be under, under …

Insanely panicked, he pushes forwards to where he thought he saw Eli last. *'No-o! Oh God, No-o-o-!* Peter screamed thrashing and grabbing, feeling under the oily, thick waves that seem to be becoming more resistant and solidified by the minute. He lashes the waves, beating them, arms frantically searching, plunging, sweeping, and trying to feel anything.

'God! God! Not Eli –! He's my only *friend!*' He screams at the sky, but his voice is just a faint, meaningless blip in the commanding smash of waves exploding over his back as he bends, thrashing at the black, churning, oily foam-ripped waters. '*E-e-e-l-i-i … Where are you?!*'

'I'm here, Peter,' came a quiet voice. Peter spins around in shock, his eyes bulging and his mouth hanging.

'Wha-*What?*'

'So are Leanne, Jacob, and Mary … and … I brought her here to you.' Eli was standing facing Peter, a small distance away. He was completely dry. In his arms appeared to be a slumped body, covered in a white linen shroud. He held it easily; it appeared light in his arms. One arm underneath the shoulders, the under lifting from the knees, the head resting against his chest.

Eli looks up from the body in deep grief. 'I have held too many like this.' He shakes his head, almost wearily. 'This is where she would have wanted to be buried.'

Peter stared, haunted, he had no idea where "here" was. Eerie and evocative – it seems to exist beyond all the usual barriers we use to anchor ourselves. Instinctively, he touches his clothes; he is dry, like his throat. He tries to speak in a hoarse whisper. 'Wha – Who –!'

Eli frowned in disgust. 'Your sister Melody.' Eli looks down at the small frame held in his arms. 'So I had to carry your dead conscience here for you.' He looks at Peter in disgust.

'No!' Peter gasps, looking between the body and Eli's accusing face. 'No. No. It *can't* be.'

'She was such a beautiful soul, you said, struggling with so much so young, redeemed by God, almost another daughter. You anointed her with oil, the sign of the cross, after her baptism, another soul saved, you remember saying that? What good did it do? Poor child. Poor, poor helpless child. So weak. So needing your help. So you let her die. Killed by you!'

'Oh God, no.' Peter gasped in horror and guilt.

'Yes. First you blamed God for her death, but you should have blamed yourself.'

'Eli. I beg you. Why are you tormenting me like this?'

'Did she have to die before you cared about her? Are you more concerned with her body than her life?'

'No. Please.' Peter gasped.

'You were willing to let her go to her death alone.' Instinctively, Peter reaches out, as if by touching the body it would show how sorry he was. But his hand is stopped halfway in mid-air by; 'Why should you help her now that she doesn't need you?'

'How could I have helped her? I tried to get there,' his tone pinched by the ache in his voice. '*I tried!*' he yells. 'She made her own death. I prayed, fasted, begged God. What good did it do? I *tried* to do what God wanted,' he challenged Eli's cynical expression and frown.

'What God *wanted*, Peter? Why should you believe it?' Eli asked. 'You've done everything you can to separate yourself from Him. When the light shone, you wouldn't accept it. When the dark came, you denied it. When the spirit of God beckoned, you refused it. When God says your life is kept for some purpose, why should you believe it? To make a gag for your conscience, is that it? You believe it because it suits you. Or maybe if Melody stood before you now, you would say you believed. You would repent and love God. It would be easy. But what strength would your belief have then? What would it matter?'

'For God's sake, why are you torturing me?' Fury and crushing sorrow in his voice. 'I thought you were *my friend*? I don't even know where we are or what's happening.'

Eli sniggers, his face twists to a cruel leer. 'Ha! You don't *believe* in hell or the devil you told me.'

Leanne's voice, high pitched and angry cuts through into his mind. 'Don't listen! Peter. It isn't Eli. Something is talking through him. Peter, look at us. *Peter!*'

Almost in a daze, he looks to the side to find Leanne, Jacob, Mary and Eli, standing together. *'Eli'* Peter blurts out.

'Peter. I'm here.'

His eyes fill, chest shudders. 'Horrible, awful things you said no real *friend* would?'

'It wasn't me. I'm here for you, Peter.'

Peter stares shocked, panicked eyes wide, mouth open, jerks his head back to where a moment ago he saw Eli holding Melody. But nobody is there. Peter turns back and looks across at Leanne, standing with Mary and Jacob in school uniform. Their faces frozen in fear. 'Mum. *Mum*, what are we doing here?' Mary asks, her voice shaking.

'All of us. All of us are here.' Peter says muddled.

'Where's *here?*' Jacob cries frightened. The four of them standing in the semi-dark. They were standing against a murky, rough wall that Peter couldn't identify, like a cave or part of a tunnel. Part of something that went over their heads and around them, trapping them.

(... Hello Peter ...)

A voice said. He jumped as if the words had been said right beside his ear. The voice was cold, alien, but somehow hypnotic and believable ...

'Who said that?'

They all look at each other, puzzled, frightened. 'Who said what, Peter?'

'My name. Somebody said my name.'

Leanne is wide eyed and growing frightened. 'Nobody said anything.'

Peter shakes his head vigorously as if fighting his mind to

come out of a dream, a deliberate, desperate effort to struggle his way out, to wake up, panicked, and then a voice was talking to him again, a soothing voice, believable and seductive right in his ear ...

(... *You have a nice family. A good friend. Pity ...*)

'Peter. *Please.* What's going on?' An edge of real terror in Lee's voice.

He looked at her blankly, trying desperately to make his mind work. There was a bad taste in his mouth; it trailed back along his tongue and down his throat like the taste of melted aspirin.

(... *So now you know how fear tastes. Time you found out, considering all you've written. It's a taste you're going to have to get used to ... You're a real know-it-all know nothing ... a walking encyclopaedia of dogma, you called yourself ... how small your big ego ... what's it all worth now? ....*) Peter was horrified. The voice knew it all, every word, intent, truth or lie, the voice "reads," nothing is private, personal or hidden, nothing –

'For God's sake Peter!' Sounding desperate and haunted. He could hear her clearly, hear Leanne, but another voice commanded his thoughts and mind completely. Peter panics and turns in a complete circle, yelling. 'Who is that? Who is talking?'

His hands flew to his cheeks and clutched them. His eyes widened, widened, widened. He felt his body growing cold. Now the voice sounded choked and ancient ... and still it crawled with corrupted glee.

(... *You refused to even remember her name, first Gary, then Melanie and Melody, but Peter, we're here for you, we can take away all your guilt and pain, we can bring peace, we can give you rest, rest-in-peace, they all say that don't they, but rest in peace is what's earned when you're here, not after, Melody, Jacob and Mary, all the same, all here ...)* He wanted peace, Peter said it many times, and a *tormenting* spirit is offering the very thing he wanted: forgiveness, but at a price.

'This isn't happening. *Get out of my head.*' They are stare at him in shock thinking he is having a complete breakdown. Problem is, Peter thinks he is having one also. Nothing is making sense except a dark, hideous sense of dread and fear.

'I command you not to touch them. I rebuke you Satan. I rebuke you in the name of Jesus Christ.'

For several moments there was silence. Then a scoffing snigger.

(... Do you now. Why should we listen to you? You don't believe you even believe. We read your book, we see everything, we listen to everything, we know everything, there's no secret people try to hide we don't know ... Your book did our work for us, you little devil ...) Peter clamps his hands over his ears in a futile desperate attempt to shut out the voices mocking, tormenting snigger, horrified in the realisation his book on theological "truth" delighted evil.

Leanne desperate tries to pull some threads of sanity together. 'Peter. *Answer me.* Who are you talking to?'

'I – I don't know,' his voice unsteady.

Peter is abruptly slammed back to the moment by Mary, her voice rising into a pitch of growing panic. 'How are we going to out of here? I'm *scared*, Mum.' She looks around quickly. 'Does anybody hear water?' Mary almost yells.

'So *what* do we do now?' Jacob asked. Peter heard the frightened tremor in his voice and knew the question was aimed directly at him.

(... What do you do now Mr family man?) The hideous mocking in his head, made worse by Lee's increasing bewildered and accusing desperation.

'What the *hell* is this, Peter? Where are we? Why have you trapped us in here? This is all *your* fault.' Leanne was losing control, her voice loud, she was glaring at Peter wanting answers. Unfortunately, he was only hearing other answers.

(... We can't give you eternal life, but we can touch you, and you will live a long, long life – and we can make you one of the gods of the earth if you let me lead you ... an even bigger church than you ever could imagine ...) Peter's tormented memory goes back to Eli and himself at the beach when he said "It was my church. That building, was magnificent. People came from all over just sit and marvel at the glory. It is irreplaceable." ... "A symbol," Peter had replied when Eli asked what it meant to him, "Power of God. Christian power." Where was that power now? Where was God? Eli had said of the ruin, "The only thing irreplaceable" was his faith. Peter felt shame he used the size of the church as the sole measure of his ministry.

'Why are you frightening us?' Leanne wet her lips with her tongue. *'Peter!'* She was looking at him with a furious accusation. Mary and Jacob had been looking around. Terror stirred inside them, rising quickly to panic. But Peter was consumed with himself, his flood of uncertainty, doubts and guilt.

'Is it hell? Have all my wrongs even condemned my family? God forgive me.'

(... Oh. I was waiting for that, they all say that, when it's too late, all beg too late ... feeling fear ... guilty about all the harm you did, all the evil words, selfish thoughts, foul actions, do you want me to remind you, name them, it's a long list, where to start?)

As if he had no power or will of over his thoughts, suddenly Eli is talking in Peter's head, uninvited, unwanted: 'A man, Catholic priest, Father Garbelli Amporth, I asked if he believed in hell. He said one time during an exorcism, a real demon told him the fire of hell is real, the demon said, but despite it being fire, it is not similar to our fire; it is not combustion, more the fire of conscience, fire of remorse, fire of guilt, and the fire of pain, the pain you caused others, you experience yourself – but it's increased a hundred fold, over and over; there's no escape, no relief, no end …'

'Who's talking? *Who is that?*' Peter yells.

'*We're* talking to you. There's no one else!' Leanne was staring at him as if he was losing his mind that the breakdown she'd feared in him had finally imploded.

'No! *No. No. There is.* I can hear it. Can't you hear it?'

'Perhaps,' Eli said, '… only you're *meant* to hear it?'

Peter holds the sides of his head, hands over his ears, 'Am I going crazy? God, is that it?' He then shakes his head over and over. 'What's happening? *Eli! Answer me.* Is this *judgement?* Stop it. *Stop.*'

(… *Come to me, come to me, and you can have everything you've ever wanted – money, fame, power and most of all Peter, forgiveness – I can give you all these* …)

'That water sounds … *close* …' a trembling and horrified Mary said loudly.

'Losing Eli in the waves,' Peter rambles to himself out loud struggling to make sense of anything, 'water all around us … What's going on?'

(… *It's what you wanted, we heard you, we hear everything, water and waves were your peace, so we're giving you more of your wants, even if it drowns your family … They don't love you … you gave them everything … all they did was laugh behind your back and think what a fool for paying* …)

Peter shakes his head that the "voice" seemed to know

everything about his life, every word said or hidden, every thought and emotion, nothing was secret ... but his most piercing pain, with the crumbling of his family, the mocking, tormenting words might be true. He forces it away trying to assert and believe in himself.

Peter looked around at them, his heart beating faster, seeming to pump in his throat as much as in his chest. 'I'll get us out. I'll get us all out. I *promise*.'

(... *Blame him, judge him ... do it ... you've mocked him before ...*)

Leanne shrieked, everybody jumped on the spot, as she put her hands over her ears as if it seemed that some sort of voice; seductive, captivating, alluring, but alien and evil, had spoken aloud, not only right beside her ear, but strangely inside her head at the same time. She erupted and was yelling at Peter; only *he* was culpable, guilty. '*Out of where!* Something's *horrible* is happening ... do something, for Christ's sake, won't you *do* something *right for once? You're* making this evil. You. *You!*'

Leanne then pressed her hands against her mouth as if surprised and shocked by her words. The sound of the water continued to swell until it seemed to surround them, a scary, reverberating stereo effect in the growing dark. A chill raced through Lee, and she crisscrossed her arms across her chest. She shivered and saw goose bumps ripple their way up her flesh.

Peter felt awful, responsible but lost, he wanted desperately to *do* something, but he didn't know what – if he was deliberately tormenting and punishing his family, he didn't know how to stop it. Then the voice, beside his ear, inside his head ...

(... *We can give you your wife back – if, if you want her, we can do it – she'll remember nothing as the five of you remember nothing, we can give you any woman you want, you want a new family who really loves you and obeys you; we can do it ...)*

Panicked, Leanne felt a sense of evil power growing around her, seeming to enfold her and certainly trying to split her off from the others and make her alone. Nervously, she reached out on either side of herself and clasped Eli's hand and Mary's on the other side, who then reached for Jacob's. It seemed to her that she had to reach too far, and she called out nervously, 'Hang onto hands! It's like we're moving away from each other! Pulled away! Stay close!'

They could still hear the dim thunder of water as if in multiple drains around them, but the booming acoustics of all of these tunnels were so crazed that it was impossible to tell if the water sounds were coming from ahead or behind, left or right, above or below. The light seemed to get darker, encompassing them as their fears and terror increased.

'Peter! *D-A-A-D, help us.*' Mary felt the tears sting her eyes and her cheeks; she could feel the lump of a sob in the back of her throat. No anger, at least not yet; only a sick sense of loss and abandonment and growing horror. But she knew she loved her father. Then, suddenly, water was following in from cracks and crevices, holes allowing it to spill down the walls. Mary screamed. And Lee's hysterical scream followed. Her lips, pressed so tightly together they had almost disappeared, were purple with shock.

The water foamed about Peter's ankles, then it was up to their shins. The thunder of the water had deepened to a steady bass roar. Where they stood, wherever it was, it started to shake steadily as it filled. Then it swamped their knees.

'I'm scared, Jacob,' Mary whispered. As if she said it aloud, *something* else would hear it.

'I-I-I am, too!' He stuttered.

'Mum!' She screamed again, beginning to weep now. 'We're going to die. I don't want to drown, Mum.'

'Peter! *Do* Something.' It was Leanne, a desperate pleading in her voice. But her voice seemed to be coming from somewhere else. They all looked at him, their eyes hurting and afraid. No one said anything – except the voice …

(… *A child blind from birth doesn't even know they're blind until someone tells them, even then they can only guess what blindness is; only the formerly sighted have a real grip on the thing, we are all around, people see us all the time by what we do and still don't see us …*)

'It's up to you Peter,' Eli said quietly. 'It's time to climb.'

He tried to untangle their voices and get a sense of what they were saying – anything to shake off that scary paralysis of the spirit. With a scream building in him, building up and up and up, the voice said the one thing he desperately wanted to hear.

(… *I can save you …*)

'Are you like God?' Peter asked.

(… *People do what they do; follow me, like a God, make me a God, I promise the world, I own it, the battle begins and ends in the mind and heart Peter, everything that belongs to me is in the mind; hate, blame … Gary blamed God for making him a drunk, Melody blamed God for not saving her from drugs, you blamed God for money and lost church, Eli blamed God for not saving them when faith failed, Leanne blamed God for not saving your church or marriage, you all blame God, we wait for that, then your mine …*)

'But who are you?'

(… *I have many names Peter, you've always wanted to know the* truth, I am the truth ... only I can set you free Peter, who I set free is free indeed ... It doesn't really matter who I am ...)

Then Peter realised the voice wasn't coming from either his own head or from besides his ear; it was coming from everywhere, from the centre and outside all at once.

(... I am the way, the truth and the light, nobody comes to peace except through me, whatever you want, I can give it to you, if you believe in lovely white tunnel of light for your soul, I'll do it, I am going to see that everything your ever wanted turns out, and I know everything you've ever wanted ...)

Foam spread across the water, broke apart, became meaningless again, and at that moment there was a loud splash on his right. Peter snapped his head around, shrinking back a little, and for a moment they believed they saw something in the shadows slither into the water. Then it was gone.

'Help!' Jacob screamed. 'I *can't* do this! Help! Somebody help us! Peter. *Dad!* Get us out.'

'It stinks', yells Mary. 'What's that awful smell I'm choking?' Mary's voice cracked between screaming and choking, 'Dad! Please! We've got to get out of here, *please*.'

(... Oh, don't worry about them Peter, your family isn't a family, but enemies, you are unloved, unwanted, I'll let you see me punish them if you want, see them all take punishment, they've crossed your path once too often – so listen, Peter, listen very carefully, follow the light, follow me to peace ...)

That rotting death and decay smell from the beach wafted out at them; the smell of the past became the present, horribly alive and obscenely vital, like clawed fingers clutching at them.

Leanne screamed at Peter hysterically, *'You're hurting our children! Stop It. Stop -!'*

Her hands flew to her cheeks and clutched them. Her eyes widened, widened, widened. She felt her body growing cold. Now the voice sounded choked and ancient ... and sniggered with corrupted glee.

(... *Blame him hate him blame him ...*)

It was like a vaulted dome overhead picked up her voice, throwing it back combining with echoes that were like the laughter of banshees, invisibly flying and flapping all around them.

Peter could not remember ever feeling this tired. He could easily just give up, surrender, and float away; the struggle was too great, he was guilty, abandoned, helpless, and hopeless –

'Can I never be forgiven?'

(... *never, you're never forgiven ... I never lie, trust me ... people always want to be forgiven but it's too late ...*)

Peter looked at Eli, then his family. He tried to speak but could not; his stress was simply too great. He settled for shaking his head, all he could manage. He could feel his heartbeat slamming in his head now, driving white spots of light across his field of vision. Then he was suddenly filled with an overwhelming conviction there was only one thing left to say ... He closed his eyes a moment, looked up into the pitch darkness.

'God! I am sorry.'

(... *Stop that, why do you say that, that won't help you, stupid fool; you still insist you see hope, stop it, you are never forgiven, it's too late, too late ...*)

The voice uttered a fruity little giggle that dropped in pitch until it sounded like a clogged drain bubbling thickly, like the water spilling in getting deeper, now nearly up to their waists.

'Even if I am never forgiven, Father ... I am truly sorry.'

(... *That won't change anything, it's too late ...*)

'I *know* who you are!' Peter gasped.

(... *You only think you do, what we let you believe ... but nobody is ever prepared for the reality, there is nothing after you die is what they say, they believe I don't exist, they believe there are no life consequences, that's my power, I am their demise ...*)

The last word became a long, low, fading noise that ended like a hiss in that sick, clogged, bubbly sound way that was so much like hissing laughter. Now the voice sounded choked and ancient, and still it crawled with corrupted glee.

(... *Do what you want, no consequence, that's what people think, but there are laws, like gravity, like all living things, they must abide by the laws of the shape they inhabit, like living and consequences, no one escapes ... it doesn't matter where you are, and it doesn't matter who you are, it doesn't matter how rich or poor you were, everything has a consequence ... no one escapes ...*)

Peter fought against himself to accept it was real; that in fact he was in the middle of a breakdown, a total mental collapse, or could he even be dying? Worse, he was insane, that everything was his imagination, all an illusion of his sick mind?

(... *This is no illusion you fool – this is my eternity, and you are lost in it, never to find your way back; we kill, we steal souls, we destroy lives. Why am I telling you this? We don't fear you. Atheists and nonbelievers always come here, they have no choice. Christians believe baptism, reading the Bible and going to church, they escape. They couldn't be more wrong. Besides, you tell anybody about this who in the whole world will believe your story? We don't exist remember ... we pulled the greatest trick on the world ever that hell doesn't exist, and the fools do it all for us ... you've found truth you wanted Peter the priest ...*)

The air had grown rancid and poisonous. The dark was stuffed with sounds, all of them magnified and echoing. They all could hear something splashing along near them, sometimes muttering something. They looked at each other, thinking it was one of them speaking. There was gurgling and strange clanking groans. Once, there was a ripple, like a small wave, that washed at them powerfully enough to rock them all back on their heels.

Suddenly Leanne was moving. The water is now swirling around their chests. Violently, she ploughed her way through the watery muck, making waves and eddies, over to Peter. Her hands grabbed him by his jacket, putting her face so close their noses were almost touching, and yelled in his face.

'*No more!* You're going to find yourself. *Do you understand me, Peter?* We all went wrong. We all fell short of God. Now, we need you. We need you to find Him!' She was crying now. 'So you stand up for us! You stand up for us like never before, or none of us are going to get out of here! God forgives. But *we* have to ask for it.'

Peter had no words, he could just stare into her angry face and wet eyes. 'God loves you! Do you understand? *And by God so do we.* Fight for us. You *are* Pastor Peter Shrembri. Don't let the evil lie to you. *Believe* in yourself.'

Then, as if one mind, everybody was moving, including Eli, going to him, forcefully bashing, wading their way against the slime that revolted them, dry reaching, stomach acid came up into their throats, burning, making each choke and cough, stomachs roiled against the stench and the filth that seemed alive. They all had to struggle and fight to reach the husband, the father, the friend, and the evil thick waters became more solid and resistant with every frantically struggling step.

They drew together, clutching each other. Whatever terrible thing was wrong here, whatever horrors there were, and they would face it together. They were with him, for each other, and for that little while, as the shadows were joining hands and now the darkness was almost complete, it surely would have picked them off one by one, drawn by the quality of their minds just as a lion might be drawn to one particular waterhole by the scent of zebra. But together, by instinct without words, they had discovered a powerful secret: that belief has a second edge. If there are ten thousand medieval peasants who create vampires by believing them real, there may be one, probably a child, who will imagine the stake necessary to kill it. But a stake is only stupid wood; the mind is the mallet which drives it home. That was the battleground.

Eli began praying, words from the Torah, his holy book; a Jew prayed for Gentiles and himself against a common, incomprehensible evil.

"*Grant, O God that we lie down in peace, and raise us up, our Guardian, to life renewed. Spread over us the shelter of Your peace. Guide us with Your good counsel; for Your Name's sake, be our help. Shield and shelter us beneath the shadow of Your wings. Defend us against enemies, illness, war, famine and sorrow. Distance us from wrongdoing. For You, God, watch over us and deliver us. For You, God, are gracious and merciful. Guard our going and coming, to life and to peace evermore.*"

Eli seemed to expand, grow in strength as his loud prayers came back like booming echoes. "*Lord, may all who know You be filled with Your Spirit, equipped by Your Word, and take courage in hard times. May we band together in the unity of the Spirit, and shine as lights to encourage one another, and draw unbelievers to you!*"

Eli looked around at them all, nobody would fail, nobody would be lost, and nobody would falter.

'Abba, we cry out and say "NO!" to the work of the enemy! May his plans be thwarted and may he be trapped in his own wicked schemes.' Eli sung his ancient prayer *in Hebrew*. But strangely, Peter understood all Eli said.

Peter closed his eyes. 'Jesus! *Yeshua!*' he cried in a thick, low voice. A black fear stole over his heart and closed his throat. Peter found himself afraid to speak, but knew he must.

'I believe. I *believe* your hearing me. It is written, *"When two or more of you are gathered in my name there will I be."* You are here now with us. In the bible it says your disciple Peter failed you. The one you loved denied you three times. Yet … *you forgave him. Forgive me, who denied you more,'* he yelled.

(… Stop that why do you say that? That won't help you, stupid fool, it's too late! …)

Peter forced himself to continue, 'Remember me just this once. I *deserve* my punishment …'

(… Stop it …)

But Peter didn't stop, his voice passionate, pleading, '… but my family, my friend, have done nothing wrong. Save *them*. I ask nothing. I give myself to you. Take *me* for them …'

(… Stop it! stop it! I demand, I command, that you stop it! …)

Suddenly they all sensed the voice that had consumed them, owned their minds and even their souls, the voice faded, faded, faded …

But the strangest thing, if it were even possible for anything to become more strange, suddenly they froze and stared at each other, wide eyed, as each one felt, rather that heard, simultaneously, the voice scream in their minds, a scream of frustrated petulant rage … but it was also a scream of fear and pain. The voice was not used to not having its own way; such a thing rarely happened; people wanted it, followed it willing, worshipped it in obedience ... but now defied and denied by a family's bonded love; a brave Shoah survivor's faith, and a repentant vicar. Then it was gone. The power of evil went with it.

But they were still *here*, about to drown in this hellish, flowing muck. Nothing changed. Nothing had changed at all. They all looked at each other, wondering why, or if, Peters confessional prayer had failed.

But Peter sensed them drawing closer to whatever passed for the real world, although he believed he would never think of it as exactly "real" again; he would see it as a clever canvas on which the ever changing scenes of life were sketched, to be filled in and made real by the lives who owned them.

He refused to believe Yeshua would fail his faith, or their lives. Everything at *His* time, especially miracles and answers. Words weren't enough. There had to be faith in the belief of believing, even as a mustard seed during the waiting.

'*Mum!* Mary screamed at the top of her voice. The walls channelled her shout and sent it back at them all like an echo. Leanne looked frozen at her daughter, thinking what more now. But Mary was pointing, thrashing about in the swill.

'*Behind Dad*. Over there. What's that?'

Jacob jerked his head around. A look of utter joy covered his face. 'It looks like a ... we're saved!' He yelled. Everybody stared, almost transfixed at the ladder, it looked dull, stained, rusted metal, that went up high, but the top was hidden. Jacob was hysterical.

'We can get out. *We can get out!* Oh, man. Oh God, *Dad-d-d!*' Waves, ripples and splashes of water sprayed as they all surged and waded toward it.

Peter doesn't wait, grabbing his daughter and pushing her against the ladder. 'Climb. Go. Get out. *Go* now. Jacob. Help your Mother and Mary. Mary. You first. Don't argue. Quickly. Push them up.'

In an urgent but soaked rush, Jacob his hand under his sister's backside, shoving her up, as she carefully puts one hand after the other on the rungs, and one sodden sneaker and climbs. Their clothes hang soaked and heavy, climbing is an exhausting effort.

'Where's it go?' Fear in Mary's voice as she calls down.

'Out' Peter yells confidently.

Peter pushes his son, grabbing his hand and slapping it on the wet wrung. Jacob looks at his father in panic, will there be enough time. He opens his mouth, but Peter is forcing him to climb, almost doubling up on top of his sister's legs. His sopping clothes weigh down and Peter reaches under him and shoves with such force Jacob almost misses and step and slips, then fights to recover.

'Lee. Go. *Go!*'

She grabs the rail and one of the steps. 'Peter? I ... I'm ...' they search each other's eyes. Her colour was almost back now, but in hectic patches that flared along her cheekbones. She looked both tremendously grateful and scared to death. But her heart was so saddened and breaking. He face was drenched but the fresh runs of tears ran tracks through the muck on her face.

Peter finishes her sentence for them both. 'So, so, Sorry. I love you Leanne,' he says, voice breaking. 'My wife. And mother of my children. We both know that love was not what brought us together. But you've endured me. You've suffered my words, and my neglect. I am sure that there are times when you've hated me. But you stayed with me, and for all that, with all my heart, I am so grateful to you. I'll love you forever my beloved. I'll be right there. Go. Climb. Quickly.'

'I love you too my dearest, so very, very much. Please hurry. *Please!*' He nods, and indicates she should climb now. She breaks free of the ever deepening sludge growing thicker and darker. Peter looked at her for a moment, as she climbed. Then he became aware that her face was losing definition, becoming not a face but a pale shape in the deep shadows.

He shakes his head to bring himself back. 'Now you Eli. Go. I'll be there.' Eli grips one of the rails but doesn't move.

'You made your ladder of faith and belief, my dear friend. I knew you would.' In Eli's face the most profound sadness and knowing. 'You won't make it out. Unless you go now.' Dragging his hands out the coagulating sludge, Peter reaches out putting his muck covered hands on Eli's cheeks, tenderly holding his face.

'Go Eli. You're a beautiful man. Proudly Jewish. Proudly Rabbi. More a brother. You were sent by Yahweh. Thank you for being there. I know where I'm going. I'm not afraid. No more doubts. Eli'.

Eli releases the ladder, turns, and the men wrap their arms around each other, squeezing tightly, chests shuddering, arms and hands shaking. Peter has his eyes squeezed tightly closed. The men embrace and hold tightly a long time.

When Peter opens his eyes, he's alone, Eli is no longer there. Vanished in the embrace. Neither is the ladder, just the ever rising stinking sludge and muck now up to his shoulders.

Peter raises his head and closes his eyes. He raises his sopping arms, spreading them up and wide.

'God. Yeshua. I give myself up … into your keeping. It is … Peter.'

AND THEN HE KNEW HE heard a voice, a voice so soft and strange, a voice that came from everywhere, a voice that called his name: *'Peter.'* But this voice was gentle and rich with love.

And at the same time waves of shock rode through him, lifting him dizzily up and up, outside of himself. The muscles in his stomach and legs and crotch all went loose and numb, and he thought in a detached way: this must be how it happens, when people die, you lose yourself, everything, all the senses we usually use to anchor ourselves to the world. The vertigo, that sense of being in a place that was really no place,

Far away. Unimportant. He could feel everything running out of him along with his life's blood … all the rage, all the pain, all the fear, all the confusion and hurt, and all the doubts. He supposed he was dying but he felt … ah, God, he felt so lucid, so clear, like a window-pane which has been washed clean and now let's in all the gloriously frightening light of some unsuspected dawning; the light, oh God, that perfect rational light that clears the horizon somewhere in the world every second.

Becoming clearer and clearer, emptying out, all of the impurities flowing out of him so he could become clear, so that the light could flow through, and if he had had time enough he could have preached on this, he could have sermonized: but there was something else he had to say first, but he didn't know what it was; he was learning, he was knowing … is it possible you learn more after death than when living?

Time passed-Peter had no idea just how much. He felt a swirl of talk and emotion somewhere far away. He could make out nothing exactly, but sensed the tones of things in colours and hues.

Peter was half-aware of what was happening; he felt it somehow, saw it somehow, but as if through a glass darkly. Peter felt himself lifted and dropped, swirled and pulled, as if he were shooting a fast throat of rapids in an inner tube. He could feel the light moving eagerly over his face … and the light was alive, the light was thinking.

There was a tunnel, perhaps it wasn't there, but one invented in his mind because that's the conditioning that people are instructed to believe right from children, after death, a tunnel of light, nobody knows, but you're still expected to believe it. But one thing was true, there was a light, blinding, and impossible to look at and he felt thrust, drawn toward it and he had no power over it, it glowed, radiated and moved, smiled and beamed. The light was alive.

Around him, all around, Peter felt he was in greater darkness than he had ever known, but he wasn't part of it. You could own the world, have all the power and influence ever known, but here the light owned you completely, whatever you were, here, wherever here was, you were nothing.

'Peter. Peter. Can you hear me?' There, that voice again, somewhere far, far off, but real, so real …

He was moving faster he believed, rushing on into the light. Light that flared around him. He tried to raise his arms out and above his head. He turned his face up, and suddenly he felt power rush through him.

Peter felt something begin to grow in his chest, something hot and choking and as painful as fiery nettles. And his head began to throb, if he could focus, he perhaps could ease it; he was dimly thankful for that blinding light, glad, if anybody else was around, others couldn't see this agony.

He heard a sound escape him-a wavering moan. There was a second; a third.

'Peter. Peter!' that voice, from where?

'Please!' he cried. 'Please, I'm sorry! I never meant for anything b-b-b-bad to huh-huh-happen!'

Perhaps there was something else to say, but he could not say it. He was squeezing his eyes closed, he felt he was sobbing then, lying on his back, everything, his whole life was flashing in front of his eyes at a dizzying speed. There was no guilt or praise, but a review that at times made him feel cringingly ashamed and at others ecstatically happy and hugely grateful.

And suddenly Peter snaps his eyes open and desperately tries to focus, blinking rapidly. Slowly, very slowly, dimness and blurring fades. His eyes water immediately and he feels soft tissues gently patting on his face and drying his eyes. He tries to move his head but sudden pain makes him grimace.

'Don't try to move, darling. It's me, Leanne.'

He blinks until his eyes focus and sees Lee looking haggard, worn, dark lines under her eyes look like bruises from a fight, she's without any makeup. She's sitting beside him tightly holding one of his hands between hers. He feels a presence on the other side, somebody holding his other hand. He blinks again and finally focuses on Eli – with a long, neatly trimmed beard.

'Welcome back,' Eli says with a family sized smile. 'You had us pretty worried there. But I just knew Abba would deliver you back to us.'

Peter tries to swallow, but his throat feels dry, raw and scaped. Leanne leans closer. 'Don't try to talk yet. You had your breathing tube taken out only a few hours ago.'

But he's determined to grab the moment with both hands and croaks, 'H – ho – how –'

Eli smiles again leaning close. 'How long you been here? Three weeks.'

'Head … hurts,' he says as a shaking, broken whisper. He slides his eyes across to Lee as she speaks.

Peter begins to sob, uncontrollably, openly, swamped and overcome. Lee looks up at Eli, 'I'll get the doctor.'

Eli nods, 'He'll be all right. He's just coming out of it.'

Peter fiddles irritably with a tangled beard while sucking on a straw in a container held by Lee. Pillows are stacked and supporting him to sit up. 'It suits you,' Eli says with a smirk. 'Makes you look distinguished.'

'I don't like it, makes Dad look old.' Mary in college uniform, sits on one side of the bed.

'Dad is old.' Jacob smirks sitting opposite her on the bed.

Peter gives a pretend scowl. 'Watch yourself,' he says in a raspy croak. The relief on all was almost palatable, but each looks fatigued with signs of strain masking their faces. Peter makes small movements with his heavily bandaged head, and the various medical drips taped to his hands annoy him. Peter drops his eyes, and becomes deeply serious and burdened.

'Something happened. Something I can't explain. Something … I can't find the words … as God is my witness, if they are the last words I ever speak, what I saw and heard is true.'

'We know most already,' Eli said.

Leanne smiles kindly, leaning in. 'You've been very vocal, darling.'

'You're the talk of the ward.' Eli grins and winks at Leanne.

'Wow. Sooo uncool. But we all love you,' smirked Mary.

'What do you remember,' Eli asks.

'You and me, talking … at the beach …'

'What else?'

'It was late. Dark. Cold. Suddenly it became deathly quiet. I had … Oh, this, this awful, awful headache. I remember saying thank you to you, and standing to go somewhere. After that …'

'You had a bleed on the brain, Peter. You stood up, then fell, cracking your head on the footpath. You almost died with a fractured skull.'

'But praise God, Eli was there, and praise the Lord, got help in time.' Leanne biting her lip in a fight to keep her emotions in check.'

'In fact you did die on the operating table. The surgeon's had to bring you back twice.' Eli said. 'You had no heartbeat or brain activity for over ten minutes. They fought to get you back. The second time they were convinced you'd gone but suddenly your heart started again.'

'One of the nurses who was there said it was a miracle,' Lee said.

Peter is silent, frowning, his face full of confusion as he tries desperately to pull so much together. But he will never forget. Never. He looks at Eli.

'The church?'

Everybody stiffens, the part they were waiting for but didn't want. Eyes look at each other, then focus back on Peter.

'Gone.' Eli said simply.

For a time Peter is silent. His expression impossible to read, his face a mask covering any turmoil or pain that roils his soul. His eyes move around the silent faces, one after the other. He comes back to consciousness with a changed heart and for the first time in life looks at his tragedy from a different perspective … as the glass darkly melted away …

'Only glass, bricks and mortar. It doesn't matter.'

The relief is almost palpable, as Mary says, 'Oh, Dad!' as she folds into him, followed by hugs from Jacob and Leanne.

Peter, although weak, squeezes Eli's hand with all his strength. With a croaky, emotionally thick voice he says, 'I wanted to know the truth. I have it. I wanted to be a rich man. I own it.' He looks around at them all bent over pouring out their love to him.

'I have the love and forgiveness of my God Yeshua. I have the love and forgiveness of my wife, my son, and my daughter. I have the love of my dearest friend. I am, indeed, a very rich man.'

Chins begin to quiver, and bottom lips are gently bitten in futile attempts to stem the spill of tears as they swell and tumble wetting all faces including Eli's.

Eli holds Peters hand tightly in both of his.

'Shalom Aleichem, Pastor Peter Schrembri.' And Peter's fingers squeeze Eli's and Leanne's hands tightly.

'Aleichem shalom, Rabbi Eli Steinsatz.'

Postscript

"Pastor Peter Schembri" recovered from his severe medical injuries and indeed become a "rich man" in more ways than one. Investigations concluded the church fire occurred as a result of an incorrectly installed gas operated hot water service. The church was well alight before emergency services arrived and couldn't be saved. The bank did own the land, but following a successful class action, Peter received a substantial sum. The church was never rebuilt, and the land did become a block of apartments. Peter went on to become a successful author of faith books and travelled extensively with his wife, detailing his experiences.

However, his accounts of his "vision" was rejected and written off by medical and mental health authorities as the result of "traumatic brain injury," although there was no medical explanation offered for the clarity of his memories and their amazing detail. He subjected himself to lie detector tests, and also underwent regressive hypnosis where expert researchers stated categorically it was almost impossible for subjects to fake or manufacture memories or experiences while the subject is in a deep trance state. His accounts didn't vary. Science offered no explanation of how, even in a hypnotic trace, he could detail and recount what he heard, saw and smelt. Further, critics have never been able to explain how a Christian Pastor heard and understood prayers in Hebrew with no training.

Regretfully, but unsurprisingly, the most hostile rejections came from religious organisations and clergy, who labelled him a charlatan, subjecting him to slander and absurd accusations of masquerading as a man of God to deceive the faithful, which this author has always found to be a hideous contradiction in terms. Undeterred he continued to crusade and evangelise recounting his experiences that evil and deliverance, Heaven and Hell is very real, up to the time of his death.

His last book (now long out of print) published was called, "*A Pastor Repents*" in which he disowned his book "*The Bible: The World's Most Dangerous Book.*"

"Peter" peacefully passed to his reward in 1985 surrounded by family – and a friend.

"RABBI ELI STEINSALTZ" maintained rabbinical duties and was a fierce supporter of "Peter" and his family. Following his "brothers" death, taking with him soil and sunflower seeds, he sold up and moved to Israel where this writer lost all contact. However information was received that he went to Abba in 1987.

"MARY" went to university where she qualified in Veterinary science and eventually became the manager of a highly successful Equine Hospital that dealt in the care of extremely valuable race horses. The last the author knew she lived in Dubai and highly successful.

"JACOB" became an international pilot flying for a major airline.

"YULEN TUROVSKY, JENNIFER and GEOFFREY and FATHER GARBELLI AMPORTH" are real people. However they are sketches based on what I was told. As far as this author knew "Jennifer and Geoffrey" did honour their grandfather's memory by studying the Shoah and visiting the Yad Vashem Holocaust Museum in Israel several times.

"SISTER LEE" was the authors Charge Sister on the floor at the Jewish hospital. She was very generous and kind and more times than the author can count permitted her office to talk with "Peter and Eli" that became the basis of this true story.

ALEICHEM SHALOM (unto you Peace)

www.ingramcontent.com/pod-product-compliance
Lightning Source LLC
Chambersburg PA
CBHW030545080526
44585CB00012B/269